The Popular Mood of America, 1860–1890

The Popular Mood of America, 1860–1890

Lewis O. Saum

University of Nebraska Press, Lincoln and London

Copyright © 1990 by
the University of Nebraska Press
All rights reserved
Manufactured in the United States
of America
The paper in this book meets the
minimum requirements
of American National Standard for
Information Sciences –
Permanence of Paper for Printed
Library Materials,
ANSI Z39.48-1984.
Library of Congress Cataloging-
in-Publication Data
Saum, Lewis O.
The popular mood of America,
1860–1890
/ Lewis O. Saum.
p. cm. Includes
bibliographical references.
ISBN 0-8032-4210-7 (alk. paper)
1. United States –
Civilization – 1865-1918.
2. United States – History –
Civil War, 1861-1865 –
Social aspects. 3. Public opinion –
United States –
History – 19th century.
I. Title.
E169.1.S268   1990   973.8 – dc20
89-70493 CIP

To the memory of my mother,
Martha Elsie Hunter Saum,

and to the memory of
Professor Lewis E. Atherton

Contents

Acknowledgments

The research for this book began a few years ago at the Huntington Library in San Marino, California. I returned there on other occasions, both to continue work on this project and to work on others. During some of my stays the Huntington Library extended me support in the form of research grants. For those, I am grateful and indebted.

When I left the University of Washington in the late summer of 1982 to begin a year's sabbatical leave, my friend Wilton B. Fowler was about to assume the chairmanship of the department. It pleased me to inform people that I had timed my absence in that way to allow him a fair and successful start. It now behooves me to acknowledge, in all seriousness, the fine job he has done for this department and the importance to me of his friendship and support. That support can be put in terms that all academicians will understand by noting, for example, his happy facility for providing research assistance. He has served the department well, and he has served me well, as leader and as friend. I thank him.

I also thank Judy Raftery, a good, gracious, perceptive and encouraging friend. Many others have treated me well, and I hope that I showed my appreciation. None of those who aided and encouraged me—either specified or unspecified here—bear any responsibility for waywardness of omission or commission in what follows. That must be fully ascribed to him whose name appears on the title page.

Introduction

While researching and writing a book on the outlook and attitudes of ordinary people in the pre–Civil War generation, as reflected in their own written remains, it often occurred to me that any further endeavors in that line would be left to others. Such research consumes a good deal of time. The logic of the situation, some incumbent obligation, however, moved me to take up the task again. Many have expressed curiosity, as well as some generalizations, as to the effect of the war and its concomitants on the thinking of common people, and a fair amount has been conjectured about the degree to which Darwinian evolutionary notions might have insinuated themselves into general beliefs. The former, it now seems to me, had a profound influence. The latter went unregistered in any explicit way in the sources covered in this study. Charles Darwin's name never confronted me, nor did any clearly recognizable gist of *Origin of Species* or *Descent of Man*. Of something that we style Social Darwinism, there is almost nothing to say. One nonchalant employment of the expression "Root Hog or die" struck me as more likely a distillate of folk wisdom or a semiconscious borrowing of the title of a popular Tony Pastor song of the 1860s than a reflection of a now discredited political economy.[1]

Letters, diaries, and commonplace jottings of unelevated people of the period 1860 to 1890 provided the basic sources for what follows. They derive from all areas of the nation. The introduction and an appendix of my book on prewar moods discuss various matters regarding the locating and certifying of such sources. By and large, the procedure that obtained there obtains here. Lengthy repetition does not seem in order, as those interested in such things can have resort to that book. Of course, available records by which one can more fully identify people changed somewhat. For example, the 1880 census dropped the practice of recording value of possessions, a significant but not calamitous loss for me. The 1890 census is gone, and that is another loss. The Soundex project, though often mystifying, makes the 1880 census almost as manageable as did the more pedestrian index for much of the 1850 census. Far more tellingly, military service and the designating and recording it involved stands not only as a dramatic change in the devices of identification but also as a dramatic change in the ways of a people and as an immense adumbration of change. Still, the kinds of sources and the ways in which they were more fully identified remain basically the same as in the preceding volume.[2]

There was, it seemed to me, much to be said for giving primary attention to essentially the same kind of people who claimed my attention before. The overwhelming majority of Americans in the prewar generation lived on farms and in villages. That was changing, of course; but Americans of the next thirty years lived, in ample predominance, in the same settings. The year 1890 would find them thirty years and almost as many percentage points from ceasing to be an essentially rural people. Many individuals used in this study were making an acquaintance or accommodation with nonrural ways. But an amplitude of other topics to pursue kept me from focusing systematically on the reactions, for example, of a twelve- or thirteen-year-old boy coming to grips with San Jose after an early childhood in the isolation of far northern California. San Jose in 1882 held the boy in awe, and he could write in dread to his father that unless his dog Nig had a collar and tag he would be taken to the "Poung" to be killed and rendered into gloves and chicken feed. The boy's dispiriting welcome at school proved almost as traumatizing as the fate with which Nig flirted—"they laugh at my clothes and call me old country." The writings of Milo Baker and many others like him in urban or proto-urban settings appear in this study, but a sustained effort to get a distillate of the attitudinal effect of urbanization will await another study, perhaps by another author. Too many other things demanded attention, by the common people of whom I wrote and, thus, by me.[3]

It proved fairly simple to move forward in this collection to determine that, whatever became of Nig, young Milo Baker did well in school, and, considering his setting, he did well in life. Nevertheless, the thought of moving into the twentieth century in full-scale research of people such as Milo Baker leaves me quite unmoved. Reasons abound, but studying this fuller modernity would require different methods, including oral history. Also, even in doing the present research an unsettling shock or two of recognition came my way. In one case the correspondence of a Civil War soldier and his wife petered out into near silence in the postwar years, with pension matters being about all that remained of the collection. Suddenly, the turn from one document to the next not only bridged a fair number of years but also brought those people and their descendants into the general area where I was born and raised. That soldier and his semiliterate wife were, apparently, the great-grandparents of a person I knew in my youth. In another case, some people with an unusual family name surfaced in a collection deriving from an Indiana setting. It so happens that from that general area and bearing that same resonant family name came the ancestors of a person once far more involved in my life than the descendant of the Illinois soldier. The historian's willingness to hear these people out did not desert me, but any curiosity about precise genealogical connections certainly did. These people and I shall become, to paraphrase Ambrose Bierce, better strangers.[4]

Another and vastly more important matter of what some will consider neglect bears mention at the outset. As in my study of prewar writings, my focus remains on people who represented the overwhelming majority of the population—humble but literate white Protestant Christians. My conviction, as stated in my previous work, remains the same; studies of the views of recent immigrants, racial and religious minorities, have tremendous importance. But the linguistic, cultural, and religious training necessary to study even one of those multifarious elements, not to mention identifying and retrieving sources to sustain such study, would beggar the powers of those having far greater attainment than I.

When, for example, the Gitchel-Larsen Family Papers at the Nebraska State Historical Society cease being entirely the English-language record of families such as the Gitchels and the Baileys and come to contain written remains of Scandinavian Larsens, is one to suspend study until Danish has been mastered? To put it in such terms may render the matter absurd and impertinent, but the thought of dealing in any other than a slapdash and highly derivative way with the panoply and polyglot of recent immigrants and other minorities in the years from 1860 to 1890 is both breathtaking and awe-inspiring.

In the horrors of yellow fever in Memphis in 1878 black man Henry Williams had occasion to write a bit about the setting of illness and death, and some of what he wrote proved pertinent to this study, not so much because of his color as because what he said fits a larger cultural pattern. Some four years later in Waco, Texas, Mittie Wiley wrote a couple of yet extant letters to a man in whom she had some interest. She appeared in the 1882 Waco directory as "col'd, cook Lazarus Lewine," her employer, Lazarus Lewine, being one of four members of that family operating a dry-goods and clothing establishment. Those letters, written on "Lewine Bros." stationery, have a primitive quality equal to many penned by white hands, and this Waco situation is tantalizingly fraught with cultural and racial resonances, especially so because the color of the man to whom Mittie Wiley wrote is not clear. Surely, other material from the likes of Henry Williams and Mittie Wiley remains, but finding and synthesizing a sufficient amount will require the efforts of younger and more energetic persons than I. And, after all, the most common Americans—unelevated, white, Protestant, and English-speaking—have some claim to our attention. The study of the staggering array of other elements I must leave, as I did before, to others, with respect, humility, and envy.[5]

Along with the heightened regard for alien and minority aspects of our culture, there has been in recent years a determined effort to differentiate the spirit of women's writings from that of men's. In my examination of prewar sources, I paid little attention to that theme because it seemed inappropriate. Quarrels and resentments abounded, and perhaps thus ever. But by and large, those humble men and women shared a worldview. That continues to be the case in the later period, but, as I suggest in Chapter 5, we can see emerging, even in these unelevated people, the incipience of twentieth-century notions. No great amount should be made of this, however fashionable it might be, and it surprises this reader of a good many manuscript collections, not to mention printed sources, to be told that "few manuscripts by women" have been preserved by traditional methods of collection. If, as that animated account has it, "private writings of all women, regardless of their station in life, have effectively been ob-scured," the obscurity rapidly recedes. For example, the manuscript letters of a mill-working woman which I used in the Vermont Histori-cal Society years ago for my prewar study have less obscurity now in an edited volume. Into an essay titled "Gold Rush Widow" another author wove generous excerpts from a woman's letters in the Samuel Nichols Collection at the Huntington Library, another collection on which I relied in doing that previous book. The lengthy diaries and letters of a New York woman who had gone to Georgia—again sources I used in their manuscript obscurity in the University of Geor-gia Libraries long ago—now occupy an edited volume by themselves.[6]

The mild surprise at being told that private writings of women are in short supply gives way to stronger reaction on being informed by the same scholar that the letters of a couple of men, ancillary figures to the women under consideration, betray homosexual involve-ment. That, too, has been a fashionable discernment of late. For any who might remain unconvinced, that scholar moved quickly into some passages from the ever-obliging *Moby Dick*, prefaced by the oracular observation that "the erotic part of their friendship may be less unusual in their time than we suppose." In those letters of a couple of Civil War soldiers, then veterans, my eye detects no homosexuality. My eye does discern among such people, however, intimations of the onset of a myriad of independencies of spirit. One sees it dimly in the writings of these unsophisticated women and men; and what Gilman Ostrander styled "filiarchy" waited in the wings as children adopted more fully the emerging modes.[7]

Having decided to move forward from the period of previous study, 1830 to 1860, I faced the question of whether to deal with war sources. Given the classic works of Bell I. Wiley and recent studies by Michael Barton, Randall C. Jimerson, Gerald F. Linderman, Reid Mitchell, and others, I might have felt justified in starting after the war, as I originally planned to do. But the war proved a too inexpun-able part of the late nineteenth-century outlook to be treated as silent prelude. War sources abound, both in manuscript and published form, and many appear in this book. I realized that I must avail myself of a good amount of the original manuscript sources from the war. The very texture and appearance of these war letters and diaries attest, in ways that no reproduction could ever capture, to the chaos, the comparative meaninglessness of that experience. In so many hapless, pitiful cases, they breathe as well the spirit of sadness and suffering. What common people wrote during that violent interlude had to be in the study. Chapter 1 derives almost entirely from such writings; Chapter 6 hinges on them; and they appear generously throughout.[8]

In that classic of our literature that gave one of the abiding names to the late nineteenth century Mark Twain and Charles Dudley Warner noted the pregnant significance of certain "years of destiny that shall fix the current of the century following. . . . Such years were those that followed the double-shotted demand for the surrender of Fort Sumter": "The eight years in America from 1860 to 1868 uprooted institutions that were centuries old, changed the politics of a people, transformed the social life of half the country, and wrought so profoundly upon the entire national character that the influence cannot be measured short of two or three generations." Herman Melville said as much, and so did Henry James. A man who crossed the continent in his lifetime, pausing in that well-trod course to engage in the strife following that "double-shotted demand," entered a marginal "Forest Lake Cal. May 8, 1890" beside his poem titled "Living Oer My Soldier Days." He and so many others did that so much. The father of that country boy in San Jose wrote that poem, and he did not need Mark Twain, Herman Melville, or Henry James to tell him the significance of the war.[9]

Though my original intention had been to use sources from as late as 1900, 1890 came to seem a fitter time to close. The significance of the West is apparent in this study, but Frederick Jackson Turner and what he said and signifies did not enter this decision. Rather, thirty years or a generation simply seemed neater and more coherent. Also, sources seemed sufficiently abundant and representative without including another decade. More important, an intangible matter of tone and texture seemed to create a barrier, providing a cue for termination. An occasional mention of the telephone and here and there a letter done by typewriter intimated an ambience somehow alien to that of the previous thirty, and sixty, years.

To be sure, other and earlier changes of form occurred in those sixty years. Envelopes came into general use in the 1850s, putting an end to folded letters sealed with wax. The spread of the lead pencil after midcentury left more and more sources in irredeemable obscurity. Without it, however, we would have far fewer fragments deriving, for example, from the horror of Andersonville prison. Readier access to paper—often of a lower quality—did much, thankfully, to put an end to cross-writing. In that form the writer filled a page top to bottom, then turned the page sideways and filled it again top to bottom. People who knew each other's script may have had little difficulty in deciphering. To the uninitiated it often appears a maze. Also, common people already had exposure to letterhead stationery, especially in the Civil War, with patriotic motifs, with military unit designations, and with the impress of the United States Sanitary Commission and the United States Christian Commission. And such people now occasionally used postcards. Those changes notwithstanding, the general mode of the 1890s seemed not in keeping with what went before, and the seeming incongruity was avoided.

A brief book notice of my prewar study began its list of the sources from which it derived with "media," leaving "diaries and letters" to the end. Two newspapers appeared in the bibliography of that book, one issue of one and one issue of another. Perhaps some obligatory assumption held that newspapers figured as the foremost avenue to general beliefs. My present study does not neglect or avoid newspapers as fully as did its predecessor, for the simple reason, as discussed in Chapter 7, that common people showed vastly more awareness of newspapers than in the earlier period. Newspapers still play a minor role, entering mostly in incidental and ancillary ways, but they do occasionally appear to buttress or illustrate some point derived from what ordinary people themselves wrote.[10]

In a short story titled "The War Widow" Harold Frederic described Civil War letters of a private soldier, contrasting them with the finely done efforts of an officer whose patriotic effusions often appeared in a local newspaper. Frederic's upstate New York farm laborer, Abel Jones, wrote letters that were "indeed poor misspelled scrawls, about which no one displayed any interest or questioned Aunt Em," and the lack of interest changed little when Aunt Em became a war widow. In the war and out of it a great many letters of the likes of Abel Jones's were written, in many cases "poor misspelled scrawls" yet residing here and there to challenge him who would read them and attempt to distill their gist. Intentionally or not, Frederic presented an allegorical intensification of the matter of semiliteracy and unintelligibility in the figure of Hi Tuckerman. Hi Tuckerman had served in the war until seriously wounded at Gaines Mill. A ball pierced his cheek, took away much of his tongue, and exited the far side. As the boy who narrates the story puts it, "I may mention that when Hi Tuckerman said '*Aah*!—ah—*aah*!—uh,' he meant 'Rappahannock,'and he did this rather better than a good many other words."[11]

It occurred to me that that farm laborer, mute, inglorious Hi Tuckerman, might serve as something of a fictive synecdoche for the imperfections of communication with which one must deal in using such sources. In my treatment of the prewar setting I used a somewhat parallel image from Thomas Gray's "Elegy Written in a Country Church Yard," that being the "mute, inglorious Milton" born, it will be recalled, "to blush unseen." But however compelling Harold Frederic's figure may be, no mute, inglorious Hi Tuckermans will appear here. My sources from the real life of that period posed ample challenges to understanding without invoking Hi Tuckerman. Nor will any "mute, inglorious Miltons" appear here. Unlike sources for prewar study, in which Gray's trope appears fairly frequently in some form or another, sources for the present study yielded only one clearly evident passage from the "Elegy." Tellingly, it was set down in sarcasm rather than solemnity.[12]

Some literary figures of the late nineteenth century do indeed enter this study, and they do so in a way fairly well removed from the way in which some of their predecessors entered my previous study. In the earlier work I juxtaposed the lighter view of Ralph Waldo Emerson with the darker view of Melville and Nathaniel Hawthorne, then offering some thoughts as to which more nearly resembled the essential outlook of those comparatively untutored people, who, most likely, never read any of Emerson, Melville, or Hawthorne. Now, Bret Harte, Mark Twain, and others appear with some frequency, not so much in central roles but to offer supplementary indication of mood and outlook.

As is the case with newspapers, the works of such authors now receive decidedly more mention in the writings of ordinary people.

At least to some degree such people were encountering "The Luck of Roaring Camp," *Roughing It*, Harriet Beecher Stowe's Sam Lawson, and *The Hoosier School-Master*. Whatever one might infer from that growing familiarity, there is as well the fact that these literary exercises partook of a realistic quality. Some of them, to some degree, sought to depict ordinary people. Realism, that effort at verisimilitude, might justify even greater use of the creative literature of that period but for one crucial consideration. However much reality suffused these works, they needed an arresting story and sharply profiled characters. The reality they conveyed was a reality dramatized, sharpened, intensified, and inflated. As we shall see, they paralleled what was occurring in the expressions and attitudes of common people themselves. At least to some degree, that so-called literary realism helped such people to circumvent the humdrum literal reality to which, for more reasons than one, they had previously clung tenaciously. When ordinary people at last got around to tall talk, hyperbole, and sarcasm, they did so, it seems to me, with the prompting and the assistance of journalists and novelists.

A final element which I attempt to relate to my sources—those jottings of unprepossessing people of a hundred years ago—consists of modern historical scholarship. Somewhat to my surprise, that proved a less compelling aspect of the present study than it had when I dealt with the prewar period. Perhaps that old designation the Age of the Common Man ineluctably assured that scholars would venture, in their various studies, something about what common people might have been thinking in that generation before the war. Numerous works of scholarship enter the present work, appropriately, I hope; but there are fewer books such as John W. Ward's *Andrew Jackson: Symbol for an Age*, all but demanding that what is written about popular thought be brought into comparison or contrast with it. Perhaps the most influential book about the thought of this later period, Richard Hofstadter's *Social Darwinism in American Thought*, forgoes the effort, as in this passage from the chapter "The Vogue of Spencer": "Spencer's impact upon the common man in the United States is impossible to gauge, although its effects are dimly perceptible." One gravitates to Rush Welter's recent conclusion; "opinions and beliefs" of that period "have remained a stepchild of historical research."[13]

A brief final chapter conveys impressionistically the outline of persuasions one finds in post–Civil War Americans, but it seems proper to offer here a quick preview of the gravitations in outlook from prewar to postwar settings. Chapters 1 and 2 treat the drift away from the providential outlook, that most rudimentary, common philosophical assumption of the preceding era. Lester H. Cohen has argued convincingly that, for sophisticated people, that cosmology did not survive the eighteenth century. Our humbler sorts needed more time. And here, in noting the move away from a providential view, which foreshadows other alterations treated in the book, it must be remembered that this study derives from what common people themselves wrote, and then, on their own and by the hands of others, managed to preserve. What remains in the manuscript repositories of today involves, beyond all else, the Civil War and the West, phenomena that fill the first two chapters and recur frequently elsewhere. Did these common people whose writings somehow endured neglect important events of their time? Did they fail to perceive changes that strike us as quite significant? Most likely so. For example, the rise of the city and science probably worked large attitudinal changes, but these ordinary people seemed very little inclined to say as much. Sociological theories of modernization may reveal more fully the ingredients of the changes these people experienced, but this book analyzes and describes what common people themselves wrote. This work seeks to follow the urging of Gertrude Himmelfarb that "the ideas, beliefs, principles, perceptions, and opinions" of, in this case common Americans in the late nineteenth century, be treated "as seriously, be assigned the same reality, as facts about production and consumption, income and education, status and mobility."[14]

The first two chapters having laid the groundwork for attitudinal change, Chapter 3 treats the concomitant dissipation of religious spirit and idiom. Chapter 4 moves on to the much lessened role of death as dedicatory and heuristic ritual. Chapter 5 shows common Americans developing both a heightened sense of society and, all but contrarily, a heightened sense of self. Self now emerges in their world with honorific rather than the time-honored, pejorative connotations. In Chapter 6 we see almost modern men and women closely observing the affairs of state and nation, rather as we supposed they had been doing all along. Chapter 7 presents a brief, illustrative coda. All of these themes and subject-matter areas received treatment in my volume on the prewar period. Some have read that work, but reading it is not necessary to an appreciation of the emerging mood of this later period.

When he viewed the abiding spirit of people such as those appearing in this work and in its predecessor, Ben Maddow was moved to speak of "the peasant that endures in everyone: Only survive, that's all that matters." That peasant enduring in us all seems far more at home in prewar America, in that age that knew and internalized the somber aura of Gray's "Elegy," than in the following era. The brasher, breezier, more self-assured American had, as the nineteenth century petered out, come to the place where it was at least thinkable to employ the assertive descriptive terms of Henry Steele Commager in *The American Mind*, terms falling wide of the mark if directed at an earlier age.[15]

The enduring peasant was leaving. Those ordinary Americans of the late nineteenth century were moving at least onto the perimeters of what Peter Gay depicts as, for example, "the modern malady of love." When we get to these people, it would perhaps make some sense, as it would not in treating the generation that preceded them, to adduce, as Gay does, Emile Durkheim and "'anomie,' that old reproachful synonym for the absence of divine regulation." As Gay puts it, Durkheim saw "disorienting phenomena besetting modern society—a sense of uncertainty and unpredictability, the child of overweening, socially fostered egotism."[16]

For the unsophisticated people appearing in this volume, that description stretches the matter somewhat, but the enduring peasant and the enduring Puritan had wended another course. For the people of this study, the bourgeois experience in any full sense lay yet ahead, but they had become believable candidates for that condition. When they expressed themselves about cause and purpose, they did so now in an idiom that was less godly, less providential than that used by their predecessors. They deviated far more frequently from reverential and religious language. Whatever burdens they silently bore, they showed far less open interest in death and the grave. Conversely, they betrayed far more positive concern about themselves and how they might gain satisfaction from the society in which they lived. Individualism—often an exaggerated ingredient in the depictions of our past—now comes in this generation of common people to assume a semblance of its vaunted self.

And these people had come to revel in politics far more than had the preceding generation. Simply, they allowed their attention to be claimed far more by the things of this world, both the material things of gain and consumption and the cultural things such as novels and theater. This general pattern of gravitation should surprise few students of the nineteenth century, but the intricacies of this attitudinal reorientation may prove instructive to a late twentieth-century people who resemble their ancestors of a hundred years ago vastly more than they resemble their ancestors of 150 years ago.

1. *The Waning of Providence: The War*

Common people of the pre–Civil War period had a wearying propensity to see life in terms of the word and the will of God. Much separated those people of the 1830s, 1840s, and 1850s from their Puritan ancestry; but important connections endured. There yet resonated through much of the land a muted and not very thoughtful version of the belief to which Urian Oakes had given classic statement almost two centuries before. Taking his text from Ecclesiastes 9:11, Oakes boldly confronted "the problem of problems," as Perry Miller styled it, "the intelligibility of divine providence within the riot of history." Like many others of his time and persuasion, Oakes brought God's sovereignty, on one hand, and man's endeavors, successes, and failures, on the other, into such neat relation as to conclude that "ascribing things to *Fortune* and *Chance*" is a "piece of *Atheism* and *Heathenism*." Long thereafter, humble Americans continued to internalize and evince that reading, as well as an urging that derived from it: "Labour to be prepared and provided for Disappointments."[1]

What Urian Oakes called the "soveraign efficacy" of Providence had long since been qualified or eclipsed in sophisticated thought; but it remained sovereign, though often blurred, in the attitudes of common people down to the time of the Civil War. Times and moods were changing, however. When the race went to some other than the swift, when the battle went to some other than the strong, deviant and heterodox expressions and observations—if not explanations—were forthcoming. The dangers Oakes and his kind had warned against now entered the discussion far more frequently.

Intellectual changes no doubt played a role in this change, but those common folk often strike one as fairly immune to such influences. Moreover, had humble people reflected sophisticated views, they probably would have done so with banal expressions of scientific law or the orderliness of nature. Such remarks are rare. Of course, an essentially rural people could hardly be oblivious, for example, of the importance of environment, as an Afton, Iowa, woman revealed in a letter to an Indiana sister in 1874: "We are all in a great digree creatures of circumstances. we are what influences around us have made us." Later that same year T. A. Evans of Rice's Crossing, Texas, wrote to a brother with whom he had quarreled over the disposition of their father's property. Evans hearkened back to childhood days before "discord," between North and South as well as between two brothers, "had ever entered to mar our little Eden." Regret shaded into inexorability as he noted that "time must bring its changes" and "the laws of nature must be obeyed."[2]

Nature entered the ruminations of a Colorado miner on his thirty-fifth birthday as he struggled to see some meaning both in his life and in the "volcanic formation" around him. He broke off in frustration; "man cannot comprehend." That conclusion had no novelty except in its neglect of the time-honored insistence that God's sovereignty made all things in some way comprehensible.[3]

Two phenomena, both well known to that Colorado miner, seem to have done the most to move unelevated people away from the habitual language of God's agency—the West and the Civil War. In part, those people said as much; in even larger part, they betrayed as much. Of course, the West involved a long-standing process, and it had figured as a source of spiritual uneasiness from the outset. But the westering process had accelerated prodigiously, and the reverberations and implications had intensified mightily in very recent times, especially since 1846, 1848, and, *annus mirabilis*, 1849. In 1879 Henry James wrote in *Hawthorne* that the Civil War "marks an era in the history of the American mind." Three years earlier Herman Melville's *Clarel* used poetical imagery for the dread moment when war approached and arrived:

True Bridge of Sighs—so yet 'twill be
Esteemed in riper history—
Sad arch between contrasted eras . . .[4]

Common sources, the writings of people who probably would not have read *Hawthorne* and probably could not have read *Clarel*, do a fair amount to bear out James and Melville. Yet other factors must have entered as well. For example, in treating the timeless puzzle of theodicy as it vexed intellectuals in this period, James Turner calls attention especially to the "shockingly unaccustomed forms of suffering" encountered in slums and factories. My sources—deriving largely from America's rural mainstream—reveal very little of that suffering, while the war and the West are writ large, exceedingly so.[5]

In the same year that Henry James penned the line quoted earlier, a western Nebraska cowhand scrawled what was probably the gist of his outlook: "Bad Luck, Good Luck, Failure, Disappointment." (Surely, under some such prescript could be fitted his experience of a couple of weeks later: "Got pissed on by a skunk.") The four-part formulation neglects something, but perhaps the omission is what one might expect from a cowhand who would die at age twenty-nine when accidentally struck in the eye by the popper of a bullwhip. The comparative failure to specify God's will and God's agency appears, however, in the writings of far more than cowhands. For example, Lura Smith, native of the Southold, Long Island, area, who lived in San Francisco in the 1860s, had a tailor-made opportunity to comment on God's mysterious ways when a friend went down on the vessel *Golden Gate*. The circumstances invited remark because the drowned woman had, only at a late moment, decided on the trip home. "She has *indeed* gone home," Smith observed in a way that probably reflects doctrines she encountered at the Second Congregational Church of the city. God's purposes went unremarked. Not long after that omission, Martin Mallett, a Fairfield County, Connecticut, farmer, wrote in his diary: "Walnut Tree Hill school house struck by lightning and four children killed." Though half his entry space remained for an instructive venture into theodicy, this churchgoing man did not oblige us.[6]

Lightning struck elsewhere, as it did on the plains west of Fort Kearney on a night in the 1860s when eight wayfarers huddled soaked and scared in a wagon. Young Hattie Smith of Iowa wrote an account of the near miss that had been felt by all: "Hez felt it in his side, and Homer and Bill in the feet. Unc felt it all over." The only larger construction she placed on this very close call was to remark: "I think that it was a wonder that some of us was not killed." From hard-pressed folk on a demanding trip to Colorado we can perhaps expect little. But consider the case of Margaret Fields, member of a North Carolina family that had moved to Indiana, as she told of her attendance at an outdoor gathering of Sunday schools at a small town west of Indianapolis. She "never saw as many people" in her life, and pleasant excitement reigned. Suddenly, exhilaration gave way to terror when a young horse hitched to a hack bolted and plunged into the crowd. To Margaret, devastation seemed certain, but only three children were run down, none seriously injured. Though she considered it "a wonder" that scores were not killed, Margaret Fields failed to ascribe the outcome to divine purposes. In the setting of massed Sunday schools, that neglect, that resort to the blander, more secular language of "a wonder," seems telling indeed. Her ancestors and predecessors would, most likely, have improved the opportunity far more than she did.[7]

It is, of course, a comparative, not an absolute, matter. Old forms and the old attitudes they conveyed continued to appear, but their frequency had decreased appreciably. And perhaps while illustrating the continuities we can illustrate a couple of demographic concentrations. One involves age; the other involves region. Neither is surprising; but each betokens the configurations lying ahead. Perhaps ever, the aged have greater discernment of the Almighty's sway, and when eighty-seven-year-old William Cheney, a Vermont farmer and woodsman, dictated a memoir in 1874 he could readily espy "the Providence of God" as having had control of his life. Similarly, a Mrs. Blackwell of Bedford, Massachusetts, noted the oddity that she, who had always had "but a slender hold on life," should have lived so long. It involved, she concluded, "a mysterious providence" reflecting the will of her "heavenly father." Inevitably, the old instructed the young. From Warren County, Pennsylvania, the word went to Stillwater, Minnesota, in 1872 reminding the grandchildren in shaky hand, "we little no what we have got to suffer" in this world, but "we must all submit to the hand of providence." That next generation was becoming less and less ready to submit.[8]

Pauline Stratton of Boone County, Missouri, reached age sixty during the wretchedness of the Civil War, and she illustrates a regional consideration as well as one of age. Bushwackers lurked nearby; a son faced the peril of militia service and gravitated toward strong drink; a son-in-law had overtaken strong drink; and the handful of slaves grew ever more "trifling." Little wonder that, at least on occasion, Pauline Stratton could speak of "Gods judgements." This is not to suggest that common people were reacting to crisis as did Julia Ward Howe. Indeed, they wrote peculiarly little that resembles the spirit of "The Battle Hymn of the Republic." The suggestion is rather that proportionally more of the providential utterances came from Virginian-Missourian Pauline Stratton and others farther to the south. Writing from Pontotoc County, Mississippi, in 1869, John and Triphena Henry reported to a niece that it was "through a kind & merciful Providence" that they had been spared so long. Sadly, the daughter upon whom they had hoped to rely in their decline had died: "We had hoped that Providence would otherwise have ordered."[9]

The Henrys were aged southerners, apt counterparts of William Cheney and Mrs. Blackwell; but others in the South seem to have internalized the language of God's will more than did those in the North. Just after the war a former Confederate soldier wrote back to his sister in Missouri from Clarksville, Texas, where the Red River had flooded and "broke" him "flat." Therein, he saw the "afflicting hand of Providence." From Mecklenberg County, North Carolina, came agonizing news of a child's death by brain fever, as well as the conclusion that "hit wose the Lords will." "I ort to be willing," a man in Union County, Mississippi, wrote to an uncle in South Carolina, "to turne thanks to Him that works all things according to his one good will and pleaser." And a carpenter in Fort Worth sent word in 1890 to his native Mississippi of the deathly visitations of typhoid fever: "Dear Pa & Ma It has pleased God to take three of our children from us." That message had the sternness and abruptness of the Calvinistic worldview from which it derived. The carpenter and these other southerners used godly explanations that derived from the distant past. And now, unlike those during the prewar period, they resorted to such explanations rather more than did their northern counterparts.[10]

Of course, in the war many invoked the ancient faith and God who presided in it. Indiana farmer Cicero Sims must have spoken for multitudes when he ended a letter to his son and his son's friends in the following manner: "I must close by commending you all to the care of him who notes the fall of even a sparrow." In January 1863, young James Sims, his Uncle Lew, and the other soldiers from the Middlefork neighborhood no doubt understood the physical challenges yet awaiting them. However James and Uncle Lew fared, they and a host of others like them confronted spiritual challenges of similarly crucial nature. Along with deprivation, disease, injury, wounds, and death, they confronted doubts, perplexities, and confusions of monumental scale, so great as to render moot the question of whether a sparrow fell noted or unnoted. Young James and Uncle Lew stood at a great turning point in this providential matter.[11]

The Civil War apparently served to heighten some thinkers' awareness of the desirability or inevitability of organization, efficiency, and control. In varying ways, Ralph Waldo Emerson, John William Draper, and William James illustrate that view. Common people—soldiers, most centrally—had a different experience and a different reaction. Such people had previously had high regard for organization and control, both public and private. As we shall see later, they came to have greater awareness of government, especially of the United States government and what it meant in their lives, if for no other reason than the Pension Office.[12]

The war itself, however, could hardly serve for such people as object lesson in the orderly or the governed. Simply, for most humble participants and for humble onlookers the war reeked of the chaotic and unpredictable. Whatever the spirit the war breathed, it had immense and immeasurable impact. It figured, to quote a modern assessment that neglects wives, widows, children, parents, brothers, and sisters, as "the *ne plus ultra* of their lives: what came before was paled, what came after was forever changed. The war was a rite of passage. No one escaped its effects. In the wheels of the veterans' lives, the war was a hub—the focus from which everything else in their lives would be defined."[13]

In the documents of the war setting one need not seek long or far to find traditional, providential pronouncements. It could hardly have been otherwise. For Iowa veteran Obadiah Ethelbert Baker, living out his later years in California, the war stood indeed as *ne plus ultra*, and he refought that struggle often. Sometime in the 1880s he employed a mode traditional both in form and meaning when he hearkened back to the conflict:

> The God that stood with Moses
>> When he sought the promised land
> Will be with you all through this war
>> And by you always stand.

This farmer-salesman went on at far greater length than had the Old Testament prophet whose name he bore. Baker also persevered in a matter of form; as did so many of his counterparts in the preceding generation, he imposed the order of meter upon many of his thoughts. As will be discussed in another context, the effort to versify waned markedly, perhaps in part as the perception of order and meaning waned.[14]

Whatever form he used, Baker clearly discerned the "God that stood with Moses." Even more directly in the context of strife, private soldier Charles Ross of Vermont noted that a Sunday sermon in camp came from "Hosiea 6:4" and that it had proved to be a "pretty good sermon." Here again we have a strikingly providential reference. Ross was alluding to God's calling Ephraim and Judah to account for the evanescent quality of their "goodness," for their seeming virtue, which was like the morning dew—"it goeth away." In like manner, the providential ascriptions were going away, and the supply that remained did so usually without the biblical text Charles Ross provided, yet another intimation of a less providential view.[15]

Just embarking upon his military service, another Vermont soldier sought to comfort an anxious mother by noting that "the God that sees all things, will see to my safeness or otherwise, as he sees fit." In treating revolutionary war soldiers Robert Middlekauff finds little reason to suppose they believed that "faith rendered them invulnerable to the enemy's bullets." That rather unnecessary observation would be even less necessary for Civil War participants, as is clear in the remark of that young man from Woodstock, Vermont. Once one was safely removed from battle, however, it often seemed appropriate to note the role of Providence. Thus a North Carolina soldier sent word home that "through the kind hand of Providence" he had so far been saved from "any harm whatever." The fatal wound that lay in store for him shortly ahead at Chancellorsville would not have defied the providential scheme. Gorham Coffin of Massachusetts reported likewise: "Providence has preserved me." When Coffin's head was blown off by a cannonball at Gettysburg a year later, it in no way denied the worldview he had assumed. Also at Gettysburg, Leander Huckaby of Mississippi received a mortal wound in Pickett's charge. Most likely that would not have caused Huckaby to retract the spirit of what he had written after a lesser wound inflicted at Second Manassas. While recovering at a Lynchburg hospital, he informed his father that the "goodness of almighty god" had spared him. Otherwise, "i could not of wrote this for the balls whized around me like hail."[16]

Bell I. Wiley has a fair amount to say about religion and irreligion in *The Life of Johnny Reb* and *The Life of Billy Yank*, particularly about the drift away from religion and, in the case of Johnny Reb, the return to it. But he says little about the central element, the drift away from providential explanations. In discussing the "change of attitude" that came over the South and its soldiers as the grim times got under way with Vicksburg and Gettysburg, however, he offers the following thought about the mood preceding mid-1863: "The favor of God was sought and acknowledged, but extreme confidence in human endeavor tended to belittle reliance on divinity, or make its expression perfunctory." Exhilaration and cocksureness had always had their seasons, and perhaps now as the war went its disastrous way, Johnny Reb was learning humility and was laying aside what may once have been an "extreme confidence in human endeavors."[17]

Regardless of the ebb and flow of the tide of war, the providential view was certainly alive, but it was not as well or as abundant in expression as it had recently been. It often went neglected even in the dreadfulness of a Gettysburg or a Chancellorsville. Given the pervasiveness of the godly outlook in the generation in which these young men had been born and reared, that neglect poses a sizable challenge to our understanding. Would that more of them had given the kind of intimation that Private Charles Ross added to his remark about the "pretty good sermon" that had derived from Hosea 6:4. That sermon had "just hit the case of a great many," and therefore, Ross explained, "it appealed to me." But it appealed to him, the soldier said, "although the doctrin is not sound in my opinion." Just what struck this farmer's son as doctrinally unsound we must leave to surmise, a surmise to which we will need to return.[18]

Active belief in God's Providence involves or even presupposes an ultimately intelligible order. The war seems to have done much to erode that article of faith. Iowa soldier John Sharp maintained the providential view fairly well, certainly better than did the wife he left in poverty at home. But Sharp offered the firmest evidence of that view in May 1865, when he visited the Smithsonian Institution after coming north as a member of Sherman's army. Hummingbirds and ostriches, anacondas and elephants moved him to remark that any who failed to see "the wisdom of God in creation" must be "dumb indeed." John Sharp's faith had endured. Three years before he had espied God's purpose in bringing him through the "leaden hail" at Shiloh; he pronounced it even more emphatically when observing the displays of natural history. For many other soldiers that discernment dimmed or failed.[19]

The aura of confusion overwhelmed many. Of course, the unforeseen had always been there to assail and perplex, but the blighted crop or the dead child posed only a temporary challenge to the sternly providential view. Indeed, in the sense that Perry Miller called "cosmic," that view rendered such events understandable. Understandability failed in war, and even in General William T. Sherman's triumphant drive to the sea his soldiers, as studied by Joseph T. Glatthaar, confronted "utter confusion and pure chance." Even the retrospective rationalizing of God's will came only reluctantly at best to provide common people some sense of the rhyme and reason of it all. Helen Maria Sharp, for example, simply could not understand why her husband, John Sharp, left her and the children to shift for themselves while he went to war. Noting that he had urged her in a letter to tell the children that it was proper for him to leave, she refused to impose that meaning: "i cant teach them that when i know it is not right so i dont teach them anything."[20]

That sullen postscript came after Helen Maria had complained of not receiving a letter, and mail provides a symbol of the general, senseless situation. One can read little of the Civil War correspondence without becoming burdened and confused by the pleas to write sent to people who were, very likely, sending like pleas in the opposite direction, by the gaps betraying letters never received, by the confusions over such things as the names and numbers of military units, by the primitive and pathetic numbering systems meant to keep track of sequence and delivery of letters, by the assurances that money had been sent, could not be sent, or would be pilfered if sent. With excruciating frequency people knew nothing about the most important things in the world to them—husband or son or brother in one direction, wife or children or parents in the other. "Mary why on earth dont you write to me?" Most likely, Mary was doing just that; but the question and Mary's seeming silence resonated across the land. The effect must have been profoundly disturbing, for this Cleveland County, North Carolina, couple and for hosts of others around the country.[21]

Sometimes a mere detail made the situation more manageable, as when a Massachusetts soldier emphasized that his parents must take greater care in addressing him. "Please remember," he urged, "that I am in a *Mass.* regiment, as one letter was directed only to the 46th Regiment." An Indiana father could at least summon a redeeming allusion in telling his soldier son that a couple of letters had arrived from him: "They came according to scripture, last first & first last." Witheringly often, no suggestion of remedy or psychological accommodation forthcame. Worrying about the absence of word from a woman named Ruth in Albany, New York, a Union soldier slipped easily into the emerging language in a diary entry when yet another mail call proved unavailing: "my usual luck." The history of this diary compounds the incalculability. Three weeks after that entry was written, the hand of another wrote, "Found this book this morning on my return from visit to see my brother." The identity of the Albany soldier who brooded about the possibly faithless Ruth lies beyond determination.[22]

The end of the war did not bring the end of unpredictability in communication. The West remained to be regimented, and the South remained in shambles. The former will receive our attention elsewhere, but a word about the latter is in order now. Confusion continued, and an Alabama woman noted in 1868 that the mails had been "so unsirten sence the war." Three years later a North Carolina man grumbled about a particular feature of the generally chaotic situation. Complaining about the inadequacies of mail service, he noted, "There is no dependence to be placed in the postal department since they have so many of the colored persuasion to help carry it on."[23]

If almost nothing was heard from loved ones, almost anything and everything was heard from elsewhere. "We'll start to Texas in about two weeks," a Hoosier soldier reported from Tennessee as the war was ending. He then provided sardonic commentary on the story he had conveyed: "in a pig's eye." In that camp near Nashville, as elsewhere, people faced what that soldier called a "perfect whirl-pool of rumors." As a Georgia soldier put it, "we hear a greateal about the war. we can hear almost anything we wish." Much of the same epistemological futility prevailed at home. A Vermont woman wearily explained that to her husband at a time when, unknown to her, he had been captured in Virginia, "So it has been a thousand stories without any foundation whatever untill I dont pretend to believe anything." Marinda Silsby of Vermont had something in common with Thomas Dooley of Texas, though he used a variant form. Writing from camp in Tishomingo County, Mississippi, some three years before he died in battle, he noted simply, "I believ nothing I hear and half I see." Dooley referred to that remark as "the old saying," and surely such sentiments have been abroad in all times and places. But the skeptical spirit of that old saying and of like expressions received generous reinforcement and intensification in the war setting.[24]

Writing from Alabama at war's end, Iowa soldier Thomas Ball told his wife about the wild oscillation of rumors, and he said he would convey some of them but they would be replaced before he could set them down. And by the time they reached his wife, Serilda, they would have been not only replaced but forgotten as well. Like so many others, he concluded that "a private knows nothing but what he sees come to pass." That pervasive suspension of belief applied to a medium just now coming generally and importantly to the aware-ness of common people, the newspaper. Treatment of this matter will become more important in another section of this study, but it needs quick noting here. The war evidently did much to accelerate the growth of newspapers, and humble people—soldiers or civil-ians—sought them out. People sought them and found them, but they did not rely on them. Newspapers, too, proved untrustwor-thy.[25]

Shortly after the war a former Union soldier wrote to a cousin in Texas telling her that he had served there for a time and had wished that he could have visited her. Now he heard disquieting reports about hostility shown northerners who went to Texas, and he ex-pressed his regret about such a situation. Still, he maintained caution in believing what he read in the papers because he could recall "how they used to lie about what happened" when he was in service. In a no less acidulous expression of that view, a Rhode Island sergeant wrote in 1862: "them nuse paper corspondence are a nusince to the Countrey." A Georgia soldier spoke for many, North and South, in dismissing newspapers as "inreliable" and preferring to believe "nothing we hear."[26]

In 1928 Arthur M. Schlesinger remarked of such sources as these that, though they do not provide a "bird's-eye view of the war," they provide "something that is of greater human interest—an ant's-eye view." A qualification seems to me to be in order: Render that ant drunk or blind. From whatever or whomever he got his inspiration, Stephen Crane captured well the feeling of "apparent aimlessness" borne by the common soldier. Word from loved ones proved painfully inadequate; word of mouth and word of print proved laughably out of keeping with emerging realities. To the individual soldier so much of what happened registered as a riot of senselessness. In the fall of 1862 George Wilkie enlisted in an Iowa unit to help restore the Union. He went north to fight Sioux instead of south to fight rebels, and on October 20 the rather mystified farmer-soldier wrote to his wife from camp near Princeton, Minnesota. He gathered that they were heading for the Mille Lacs area, but beyond that resided guesswork purely. Perhaps they would go to Kentucky, or perhaps anywhere else on the continent, "perhaps Australia or very likely they will send us to Africa to Civilise the hottentots." That flight of fancy had a somewhat unusual quality, but not the sentiment it conveyed.[27]

Another man who found himself marching northwest to fight Indians sourly concluded that "being dashed on to something by surprise" was a constituent part of "military discipline." Most, however, felt in an unadorned way that, as a Union soldier wrote to his sister from Virginia in 1864, it was impossible to "tell any thing with a cirtainty." A Confederate counterpart in the Third Texas Cavalry, a unit that had at the time joined Stand Watie's troops in the Cherokee Nation, attempted to tell his parents what was afoot in November 1861, but he knew he would do it in "a bungled up manner, as Soldiers has only to guess" about the meaning of things. The refrain appears endlessly, and another Confederate put it with disarming simplicity: "ware is very unsertin." A Georgia soldier expressed it in a more complex manner, and he did so without the almost obligatory trappings of irony or sarcasm. He wished, he said, to give his parents "an idea of the proceedings of the war; but they are inscrutable, they elude my mental grasp, lead them into perfect obscurity, and almost reduces them to incomprehensibility."[28]

The Georgian tried hard, and he got considerably beyond what most of his fellows conveyed about the unutterable uncertainty. As he put it in a later letter, "my mental abilities are not capable of penetrating the dark cloud." To defend the South, to restore the Union, to defeat the Sioux, all involved simple purposes, but individual soldiers found the measures taken in pursuit of such goals to be largely indecipherable. Another modern commentator on the writings of "lesser men" in the war remarks that the " 'pointlessness' of an event that becomes totally detached from its purpose is nowhere more evident" than in such documents. In the wake of the debacle at Second Manassas, a Union soldier, probably from Pennsylvania, labored in a letter to a brother and sister through some sixteen small pages that stand as a minor monument to confusion. Marching, countermarching, crossing and recrossing a river, night marching, groping around with little sense of reality other than that the rebels had them cut off, marching all the more madly to get extricated, getting wounded in the hand, having no rations but enjoying a generous supply of abusive officers and misdirections— these and more serve as items in the phantasmagoria experienced by Andrew J. Morrison. Well along in this sorry story, Morrison came upon a man who appeared as if he might know something, and he asked the man a question as fundamental as can be put. He asked him "if he knew the meaning of all this." But all the man knew was that the rebels were behind them: "well I thought that was a fix to be in sure enough." At least, Andrew Morrison had hosts of company in the epistemological "fix" of knowing practically nothing.[29]

When Ransom Perkins wrote home to upstate New York just after the bloodiest action at Spotsylvania, he recognized that those to whom he wrote probably knew more than he did about what was occurring. As for soldiers, "all we know is what we see," he admitted, "and that is not much compared with what is going on." That frustration of discernment begot an insinuating expression that probably betokened in a roundabout way a loss of faith and a growth of skepticism. George Lambert, an Indiana soldier in a brigade band, stated it very neatly. Writing from Virginia to a brother and sister in early 1863, he mentioned yet another matter that beggared his understanding, and he resorted to what seems to have been a new expression—"to use a soldier's phrase 'I just can't see it.' " A young man from Vermont, after having had to " 'skedaddle' *again*" at Fredericksburg, puzzled over the army's movements: "I can't see through them." Months later a newspaper report that his army was on the move surprised him: "Now I can't see it. I guess it is some other army."[30]

Such usages evidently had greatest currency among soldiers, but, as with other expressions, they spread. And it may have been quite apt for Sarah Harlan, a milliner in the bushwhacker country of Clinton County, Missouri, to employ that "soldier's phrase" as well-established hatreds assumed altered forms at war's end. On learning that Ol Shepherd, one of the more notorious members of Quantrill's band, had surrendered at nearby Liberty, Sarah fumed at the thought that "such robbers and murderers" would be freed on taking an oath: "I cannot see it." It may have been a semantic trifle, and, then again, that waxing way of putting things may well have betrayed the acceptance of incomprehensibility that would in logical terms accommodate only very uneasily with the providential faith of the fathers of Sarah and the others.[31]

In such a setting as that suffered by Ransom Perkins, Sarah Harlan, and so many others, the most basic matters of survival came with growing frequency to be discussed in terms of chance and luck rather than God's will. To study, for example, expressions seeking to connect survival of the Union or survival of the Confederacy with God's purposes would involve, by and large, a study in omission. Gerald F. Linderman recently contended that awareness of "God's Plan" was so pervasive in the war that "randomness, meaninglessness, chance, and luck were given no role." That generalization does not much apply to common people, and Linderman's assertion seems based largely on sources more elevated than those used in this study. Moreover, that assertion may not reckon fully with the intensity and thoroughness with which the preceding generation had espied God's purposes in mundane unfoldings. The war did not cause humble people to deny God or God's plan, but it did cause them to say less about such matters.[32]

Early in 1862 an Arkansas private obliged us with words we might expect to find more often. His view from Island No. Ten prompted him to say, "I think God is on our side." Such sentiments are rare in part because common people had not been accustomed to hitching God to their country's destiny nearly as fulsomely as is sometimes insisted and may reflect as well a lessening awareness of God's involvement in human affairs generally. Now there were those such as an Ohio sergeant who could wonder why, if God were so fully involved, "has he not been promoted." A study of the linkage of God and nation would be far better directed at the likes of Julia Ward Howe than at common soldiers such as the Arkansas private and the Ohio sergeant.[33]

When personal survival is concerned, we have vastly more evidence. That Arkansas private expressed tentatively the hope that God would "smile upon" him. Surely, many of these men were sustained through misery by the precepts of traditional Christianity; but, quite as surely, they expressed themselves more and more in terms not fully reconcilable with those precepts. At one level they unthinkingly drifted from one category of explanation or description to another. In May 1864 an Indiana soldier, for example, told his wife that he had put his "hoal faith in the Lord." God's "mursiful power," as that soldier saw it, had spared him "in the batle of mishonary ridge and in the fight at Moores gap and in the battle of Dalton where the shells and grape and Canister and miney balls flew almost as thick as hale." After that powerful testimony to God's dominion, wife Louisa encountered a projection with variant underpinnings, one regarding how military affairs would go "if Grant has good luck at Richmond." A sixteen-year-old Louisianan who bore a soldier's burdens on his slight, five-foot-six frame until death removed them at Vicksburg showed no greater consistency. In April 1862 he, as did others, noted his hope that "providence may smaile upon me"; a month and a half later he wrote that some deaths in his outfit were a matter of "very bad luck."[34]

One wonders if those who read this soldier's letters, or similar ones, saw anything amiss in the nonchalant deviations from sound doctrine. A watch repairman from Peacham, Vermont, entered the war with what appears to be fairly firm religious idiom. He probably never abandoned it, but he did appropriate alternative modes of expression and explanation, as when writing home from City Point, Virginia, on July 4 and 5, 1864. Harvey Marckres could now look back on many "hair breath escapes," and he noted that "the fortunes of war work curiously." Then, when discussing the possibility of locating the grave of his brother Merrill, killed at Cold Harbor, he resorted to the same phrasing: "If the fortunes of war ever makes it possible." Somberly contemplating the disposition of his own remains, the twenty-three-year-old soldier used a variant: "If it should ever be my luck to get killed in battle." Who is to say if the family of this evidently Christian man might have been at all perplexed by Harvey's trafficking in the language of luck?[35]

Though probably as devout as Harvey Marckres, fellow Vermonter Charles Ross showed the same potential for deviation. On a Sunday in May 1863 he heard sound doctrine based on the words: " 'The Lord reigns.' " But "Good luck," not the Lord, had kept him off a "detale," and good things came to him by "a streak of luck" or "a streak of Good fortune." When guard duty fell his lot, he entered the wish that "some cog in the wheel of fortune" might get him out of it. A like agency aided a Rhode Island sergeant whose unit was first to cross one of the pontoon bridges at Fredericksburg. The reception provided by Mississippians proved much less deadly than expected, "as good luck would have it."[36]

Another sergeant, Amory Allen of Loogootee, Indiana, brought religious persuasions to war and probably brought them away from it, but not unchanged. In the comparative calm after Antietam he told his wife of the devastation recently worked on his unit and of his own close calls. At Winchester, for example, enemy fire had torn his canteen from his body, but Antietam proved the worst. There the small-town wagonmaker who had gone to war served as a member of the color guard, a renowned focus of an enemy's attention. During the battle he bore the colors for a while, as others fell or were carried away. Of the six color guards, four received wounds, in two cases fatal. Only a piece of spent shell touched Sergeant Allen. "I have been," he explained, "very lucky and fortunate." In a later letter, brooding over the thought that he might never again see Mary and the children, Allen invoked sounder sentiments, as he expressed his trust "that God will bring me safe home to you again." Even here, as the horror of Winchester and Antietam crowded back into his mind, he could not help remarking that "the chance looks slim," though he tried to trust in God. Before the war ended, that chance appeared even slimmer.[37]

Allen went on trusting in God, or at least he said he did. But the mixture of modes continued to characterize his letters, militating against unalloyed recognition of God's reign. At the Wilderness in May 1864, he suffered a wound that hospitalized him for a time. Again, he resolved to "trust to providence for safety"; again, his description of particulars had a different ring. In the recent fighting he had been struck twice, "and one half inch Difference each time" would have killed him instantly. His belt buckle had stopped one ball that should have killed but only "bruised my belly considerably." "I have been," he concluded, "very lucky . . . I hope I will be as lucky as I have been all along and come out safe."[38]

For those commonsensical Christian monotheists of the preceding generation "every event, however trivial," as Maurice Kendall puts it, "was under the direction of the Almighty or one of his agents. In this sense there was no chance. Everything happened under divine purpose." Now Amory Allen and other Christian men were drifting into neglect of God's central role, and that cannot be viewed as mere attenuation, as a slight variation in form that leaves the gist unchanged. The word *Providence* had become so firmly ensconced in the language as a shorthand term for God's sovereignty that when it stood bereft of qualifiers, such as *divine*, it had lost none of its meaning. Now it appeared less frequently; other words insinuated themselves more centrally into the discourse of common people. Of course, *luck, chance*, and *fortune* were old and eminently usable words, but something new and telling was afoot when they began to usurp the place theretofore jealously reserved for God and God's Providence in the writing of unelevated men such as private soldiers.[39]

Profound challenges confronted the assumptions that humble men and women harbored about the purpose and design of things. War struck them often as the quintessence of confusion and meaninglessness. The chanciness or chaos of war beggared the faith that divine reign superintended. A minié ball turned by a belt buckle might leave one not only with a bruised belly but, as well, with a heightened sense that fortuity prevailed. Beyond the minor detail of a busted belt buckle stood the awesome fact of destruction and death on massive scale. Chance loomed all the larger; odds could appear stupefying. Amory Allen saw them as "slim"; another Indiana soldier calculated that "a man has three chances to die where he has one to live in the army." That vastly overstated the case, but the impression is certainly understandable.[40]

Earlier I noted James Turner's depiction of the emergence of "shockingly unaccustomed forms of suffering" and the intellectual and attitudinal reactions to them. "Such horrors," he continues, "could make an individual ask whether any God could have created such a world." This "shift in perception," he allows, "possibly owed something to the war itself," though he sees fit to keep his attention on socioeconomic conditions other than war.[41]

For the people appearing in this study that shift in perception indeed owed something to the mind-boggling enormities encountered in conflict or occasioned elsewhere by the conflict. To be sure, most of these people had had close acquaintance with deprivation and suffering, and their fathers' faith seems not to have suffered much for that acquaintance. But a couple of elements in the changing situation, as analyzed by James Turner, clarify the corrosive effect that war had on religious persuasions, even of humble men and women who bore slight resemblance to the enlightened and elevated Christians he discusses.

First, the contention that the intricacies of nature necessarily presupposed a designer and creator had become a mainstay of much of Christianity. "Rage for design," as Turner puts it, "peaked in the 1850s," just in time to run headlong into the monumental shambles of the Civil War. Earlier we saw an Iowa private prating a simplified gist of William Paley as he admired the array of life forms at the Smithsonian Institution. But for so many, design, in however vague form, fell afoul of the mysteries and fortuities of war. It did so in a way vaguely parallel to the way in which design would, for intellectuals, founder on the shoals of Darwinian chance survivals.[42]

Second, the orderly God of design—ever more susceptible to human understanding—came to be perceived as more benevolent, more humanely inclined. Wholesale untidiness and butchery such as that at Antietam could only with painful effort be teased into accommodation with a loving God's intentions, rather as, for others, the colossal waste of individuals and species in the Darwinian view defied notions of a kindly, godly economy. Even to some degree for common people, God was being pleasantly redefined in such a way as to make His presence inappropriate to some important, though ugly, sectors of human affairs. Little wonder that in horrific Civil War settings the invocations of God and the expressions of godliness should take on an uncertain cast.

In March 1864 a twenty-year-old soldier addressed his eight-year-old sister, and, inevitably, he broached the subject of when he might return to see her. In doing so he employed two expressions that registered somewhere between widespread and hackneyed. If the "God of battles" saw fit to preserve him, he wrote, he would see her when this "'cruel'" war ended. That particular God—the God of battles—appears frequently in such sources; the description of the war as "cruel" appears so frequently that this soldier employed quotation marks. *Cruel* became a byword.[43]

One must use caution in drawing significance from these usages. But it seems fair to surmise that that God of battles—that God of suffering and horror who presided over a dreadful struggle ritually regarded as cruel—was a God with whom an ever more humanely inclined people felt ever more ill at ease. "God," as James Turner described the ironic unfolding, "became the victim of those who insisted on his humane tenderness." Though humble people probably had greater reluctance to take umbrage at the thought of a wrathful and cruel God than had their sophisticated counterparts, they may well have downplayed godly idiom in the context of unprecedented messiness.[44]

Though Frank Wilkeson entered the Union army as a private soldier, he rose to officer rank, and after the war he wrote extensively for newspapers and published a book based on his Civil War experiences. He will not do as a direct source for this study, but a wonderment that arises from reading a tense and pathetic chapter of that book has pertinence. The book, published in 1886, contains a discussion of the conduct of wounded and dying men, much of which is appalling. There is nothing of the godly, but there is a compelling illustration of the resort to language discussed heretofore. Wilkeson recalled an advance under fire in which he came into line beside a man who had just been hit in the leg. That soldier pressed on and, shortly, received a slight wound in the arm. Wilkeson urged him to go to the rear: "'You are fighting in bad luck to-day.' He turned his head to answer me. His head jerked, he staggered, then fell, then regained his feet. A tiny fountain of blood and teeth and bone and bits of tongue burst out of his mouth. He had been shot through the jaws; the lower one was broken and hung down. I looked directly into his open mouth, which was ragged and bloody and tongueless. He cast his rifle furiously on the ground and staggered off."[45]

Here we have the ease of expression almost never found in the on-the-scene writing of common soldiers. We have, as well, the resort to the language of luck and—even in the setting of agony and death—nothing to register spiritual ultimates. Soldiers writing in the midst of death did not ordinarily go so far in neglect, but they too make us wonder. In August 1864 Thomas Colman wrote home from besieged Atlanta. He pondered why, in the Yankee shelling, one died, another lived. "Tis God who is most kind and just directs the deadly missive [sic] ought not I to be thankful[?]" Young Colman had lost most of his playful streak by this time, and he might not have appreciated inquiries regarding that "most kind and just" deity who directed the "deadly missive." It sufficed for him to say that "every one puts his trust in god and is resigned to his fate." God in lowercase probably involves a meaningless slip, but some significant transformations were taking place, especially the intermingling of "god" and fate.[46]

Andersonville prison, that apotheosis of agony, provides illustrations of that intermingling of God's agency with those deemed atheistic by Urian Oakes and other ancestors, perhaps begetting a profound change of focus. In the account of Vermonter Charles Ross, as in others, one feels that something is missing, or muted. Sentiments that would seem to be supremely obligatory surface less often than expected. For a point of departure we can begin with an expression of a member of the previous generation, Charles Ross's mother. Ten days before her son's capture, Mrs. Ross wrote in terms reinforcing the godly outlook so characteristic of the prewar years, even to adducing Psalms 34:7. We have, she continued, "great encouragement" to trust in God, and "very little" to trust in man.[47]

His mother's letter stayed folded in his diary during his captivity, and Sergeant Ross found little reason at Andersonville to put trust in man, whether captors or fellow prisoners. "Divine Providence" duly informed the brief will he wrote in his diary, but circumstances soon altered its provisions. The watch willed to his brother, for example, was sold in the struggle for survival. Only a week into his prison stay the sergeant from Vermont recognized that those around him were "rough swearing fellows" who did not "look to Him for strength." In that same entry he reaffirmed the faith that "God only can support me," but as time passed he and others perceived that luck, wits, and cunning might help.[48]

As measures falling short of "exact honesty" grew acceptable, as men died around him by the excruciating path of disease, exposure, and malnutrition, as rumors swept the camp only to die and reappear, as this twenty-five-year-old man, all but crippled by rheumatism, struggled to endure, the invocations of God, though continuing, became more cursory. And luck entered the picture more frequently, as when he had the "good luck" to obtain an old waistcoat, or as it fell his "luck" (not necessarily good) to enter the prison hospital, or as he wondered on the day he was chosen to leave whether that made him one of "the luckey or the unluckey." It proved the former. Aboard ship bound for Annapolis an even five months from the day he had been captured, Ross reduced prayerfulness to convention: "thank God today I am out of their power."[49]

Corporal Joseph Flower served in the Sixteenth Connecticut, a unit that surrendered at Plymouth, North Carolina, in April 1864. His diary account of degeneration that led to camp grave number 5122 at Andersonville makes painful reading, the last entry of which ends as follows: "My only trust is in Christ." That pronouncement probably reflected Corporal Flower's most basic belief, but his diary, like other documents from that setting, mentions such things far less frequently than had previously been customary. On only one occasion during those ninety-four days of captivity and suffering did clearly religious sentiments intrude upon the stoical and secular flavor of, for example, his recognition that the place was a "miserable hog pen—but I will try and have patience and endure it, as there is no help for it." Another corporal in the ill-fated Sixteenth Connecticut, Henry H. Adams of East Windsor, lived to leave Andersonville, but only to go to a similar camp at Florence, South Carolina, where he succumbed. His last entry tells that a sermon had been preached. The next day another hand brought the document to its close: "The writer of the foregoing died at 9 o'clock PM." Hardly more than the unadorned mention of a sermon betrays that Henry H. Adams probably believed in God's reign.[50]

Private Albert Shatzel of upstate New York provides a variant focus on the message emanating from Andersonville, that quintessence of suffering. He survived, and so did his diary. The scholar who edited that diary called attention to "a well preserved four-leaf clover pressed between its pages" as attesting to the care taken with it. That clover, found at a spring at Andersonville, has another implication that stands in contrast with a part of cavalryman Shatzel's entry for August 30, 1864: "Finished reading the testament for the first time in my Natchrel life." That seems a wonderfully natural thing to be doing under the circumstances, but it does not rest comfortably with that once-proscribed charm. In fact, Shatzel seems more attuned to that four-leaf clover which, his editor surmises, he may well have found at Providence Spring, so named because its appearance supposedly struck some as divinely inspired. That spring got its name from the likes of Boston Corbett, onetime Andersonville prisoner, later the killer of John Wilkes Booth and full-time religious fanatic. But simply, Shatzel found a symbol of luck, and it would be idle to speculate as to whether he felt it helped to preserve him, or whether he valued it above that book he had gotten around to reading.[51]

It is at least curious that people confronted with the most wretched and ruinous conditions did not unburden themselves in the way that had come so readily to their fathers and mothers. God was playing a considerably smaller role in these men's writings about their situations. In what may have been his last letter, an Ohio soldier wrote from "Camp Anderson" to alert his wife to the gravity of what he faced and to assure her: "as for my part I feel reconciled to my fate let it be good or bad." This pitiable missive, penciled on a double sheet torn from a three-by-five diary, ended as follows: "I leave you hopeing for the best." Short of his signature, those may have been the last words written by Clemens L. Clendenen of Beverley, Ohio, who remained permanently at Andersonville. Men such as Clendenen may well have been expressing Christian fatalism, but they leave one to surmise that. Similar Americans of a moment before in history imposed no such burden of inference upon their readers. In their depictions, a Christian God figured prominently and unmistakably.[52]

With a deserter's death awaiting him the next day, Hellkiah McHenry of Illinois addressed "Friends and Fellow Soldiers" at Fort Donelson in the summer of 1863. "I am now sentenced to die," he began, "and I hope that you will all have a soldier's love for me and my grieved Parents at home." He remarked about "that good old flag" under which he had served; he outlined his army service; and he described the circumstances that brought him to a "disgraceful" end. But from "Friends and Fellow Soldiers" to "Farewell, all of you," hardly a word betrayed spiritual condition and not a word bespoke divine purpose or lack thereof. Probably no amount of effort could now determine if young McHenry died, to use James Turner's words, "without God, without creed." Still, there resides power if not eloquence in what this doomed soldier neglected to say.[53]

Such people may have been gravitating away from providential ascriptions in part because the redefined, more loving God seemed inappropriate to the horrors of war. Perhaps even for these humble and long-suffering folk, God had become, as James Turner puts it, "the victim of those who insisted on His humane tenderness." The God of battles in a cruel war may have proved too much for some believers to assimilate. In August 1865 Lizzie Fentriss of Guilford, North Carolina, surveyed the ruin of the "cruel war" in a letter to a sister. She supplied a wide variety of dolorous details such as deaths, physical ruin, and, not least, that only one of her several brothers remained a "professor" of Christianity. She did not specifically connect that last sad fact with the war, but there was ample reason to pronounce: "Oh what a cruel war it was." And in her most general effort to make sense of it all, Lizzie Fentriss showed caution in offering what would previously have been standard obligatory explanation: "perhaps it was the Lord will."[54]

One might simply contend that those unstudied explanations and expressions betoken a more earthy and less reverential society and that soldiers especially could be relied upon to evince such qualities. That would only make the basic point in a slightly different way. In what they wrote about others and betrayed in their own locutions, Civil War soldiers foreshadowed a less restrained modernity. "*This war*," nineteen-year-old George Mellish from Woodstock, Vermont, informed his mother, "has fairly *ruined* many a young man." Little wonder that he was given to calling it this " 'cruel war.' " Here, he had gambling in mind, but a host of other topics received attention. Private Harry Morgan of Louisiana had a penchant for the older ways; as he advised his wife on one occasion, "stick to your belief like a sick kiten to a hot rock." So sticking, Private Morgan protested against grumblers in a way that was plummeting out of fashion: "If it is the will of God then we have no rite to say a word."

Right or otherwise, many failed to heed Morgan. He bemoaned that he had not heard "a sermont" since leaving home: "It seems like the soaldiers has forgotten that they are a-countable to God fore the deeds done in the boddy. I am astinished at them. When they are sick anuf to dye all most they dont forget to sware." Indiana soldier Benjamin Mabrey had in mind not Private Morgan but Confederate General John Hunt Morgan when he wrote to his wife from near Nashville in November 1862: "well my dear we have had another Chase after oald morgan but did not have the luck to ketch the oald sun of a bitch." Pre–Civil War writings of common people have little of this casual resort to the explanation by luck. They have even less of what to us is the tepidly indecorous reference to "oald morgan." If not yet great, unrestraint was certainly growing. Reflecting on the experiences and influences soldiers encountered, a Massachusetts private used general terms that must have occurred widely and frequently: "many of the boys, if thay live to come home they will not be the same fellows as they was before."[55]

"If whisky and revelry will save the country," a Michigan farmer-turned-soldier sourly remarked, "we are safe." The reckless aura prompted John Ransdell of the Seventh Indiana to appropriate what he called an "oald saying," probably meaning that he had heard it a good deal in the army: " 'we will eat when we are hungry, we will drink when we are dry, and if nobody dont kill us we will live untill we die.' " Such nonchalance seems to have a timeless quality, but it is well to bear in mind that the immediate predecessors of John Ransdell did not traffic at all heavily in that commodity. It may indeed have been an "oald saying," but it was being visited upon people who had not theretofore internalized it.[56]

And now common men took to playing fast and loose with Scripture itself. "Sherman is our guide," a Wisconsin soldier put it as the war was ending, "like Moses of old." But Sherman did not "smote the waters of the Chattahoocha as Moses did the red sea," and so the crossing proved less convenient. And there was another touch or two wherein Sherman differed from his predecessor of yore: "In place of smoting the rock for water, he smotes the seller doors, and the wine, brandy, gin, and whiskey flows in the place of water. Sherman is rather ahead of Moses if he gets us through the wilderness all rite, I think." The fourteenth chapter of Job served as point of departure for parody sent home by Abraham Runshe, a twenty-year-old laborer who had become a private in the Sixteenth Indiana Volunteers: "Man that is born of woman and enlisteth as a Solger in the Ind. Sixteenth is of few days and short of rations." The particulars of high jinks that follow end, appropriately, at number 13: "He playeth seven up with the chaplain whether there shall be preaching in the camp on the sabbath and by dextrously turning a jack from the bottom postponeth the service."[57]

It all sounds so innocent to a modern ear, accustomed to hearing so much worse so much more. But those contrivances that parodied Job and cheated the chaplain at seven-up reveal a culture attitudinally on the move. Humble people of a later age might well delight in contemplating a chaplain cozened at high-low-jack; similar people of an earlier age would have been more disgusted than amused.

Jonathan Labrant of Company G, Fifty-eighth Illinois Volunteer Infantry, will serve as a summary case study. The young carpenter who went to war loved his country, and he loved his wife and child. Moreover, Jonathan Labrant feared God. In late summer of 1862 near Danville, Mississippi, he spent a night on picket guard, and he suffered a rude awakening when rebel fire tore up a cartridge box he was using for a pillow. He had ample reason to tell his wife that "the intervention of the Divine providence of Almighty God" had saved him. But Corporal Labrant assumed other postures. His well-developed capacity to moralize suffered atrophy. In January 1864, his regiment went by boat from Paducah to Cairo, the last trip for Private John Guthier of Company F. According to Labrant, that ill-fated soldier had been drinking whiskey when he attempted to draw a bucket of water from over the side. The whiskey and the water took Private Guthier from the boat to eternity. Corporal Labrant offered no comment other than description. The war had become a matter of "guessing," and as the conflict wore on, that aura of uncertainty intensified. In April 1864, writing from near Natchitoches, Louisiana, while a member of General Nathaniel Banks's Red River expedition, he offered a standard line about the superabundant rumors he heard. They proved so burdensome that Labrant had come to believe "only what I see & only half of that."[58]

That Red River campaign tested Corporal Labrant's spirit more than his body. He saw combat, but the soldiering itself proved comparatively easy. Perhaps that helped to seduce the carpenter from Illinois into neglect of Urian Oakes's admonition to soldiers:

"Labour to be prepared and provided for Disappointments." At Alexandria in late March Labrant reasoned that the Confederates would make a stand somewhere, but "we will be Quoncoror for I think we have an army that is invincible." A letter of May 1 from the same area placed a far different construction on the situation, though he could still thank God that he had survived. "My head," he complained to his wife, Mary, "is so confused with the failures & drawbacks of this army that I hardly know what to say or where to begin." Corporal Labrant faced the unfathomable. Everything had "appeared favorable," but "Quoncoror" Banks proved less than invincible. Indeed, when the "confution" ended, Banks had assumed the role of "Rebel Commissary," he who came to conquer now issuing, per wagon train disaster, rations to the enemy. Writing and brooding aboard the boat *Adriatica* at Vicksburg in late May, Corporal Labrant described military operations as "so misterious," thereupon adopting the language of luck in thinking of what might lie ahead.[59]

Little or nothing indicated that Jonathan Labrant abandoned the conduct of a "goodman," to use the term Michael Barton appropriates from Proverbs to designate the character of Civil War soldiers. That way of viewing things has much to commend it, but the traits of character Barton discusses—especially order, control, and self-denial—derive very much from what went immediately before and what was, here in the war and the years after it, altering appreciably. In his concluding passages Barton addresses us rather firmly about appreciating what people of the Civil War era endured, in combat and out. They had not yet become "a relaxed, tolerant, spontaneous people," but we should respect them nonetheless: "Only our arrogance or innocence would allow us to claim that we, in their place, would have done a little better, or that now we do much better. We should have a decent respect for their necessary troubles and their sufficient sanity."[60]

In this, Barton gets my agreement, as does Walt Whitman's assessment of the " 'decorum of the common soldier, his good manners, his quiet heroism, his generosity, even his good, real grammar.' " In what they wrote, those common soldiers did indeed reveal themselves as, in some general sense, goodmen; but they were changing. They were starting to talk our language. Some of them seem to have been changing a good deal more than blue-eyed, brown-haired, five-foot-eight-inch Corporal Jonathan Labrant of

Company G, Fifty-eighth Illinois. Some of them were neglecting far more than he the godly language of the preceding generation, and surely that betokened a consequential drift in outlook. They were drifting into nonchalance and even avoidance of the philosophical basis of the worldview of their predecessors. The idea of Providence had sustained that worldview, and that idea was moving toward eclipse. That change did much to lay the groundwork for their becoming the kind of people modernity—if not Michael Barton and some others—would prefer, "relaxed, tolerant, spontaneous people."[61]

2. *The Waning of Providence: The West*

In December 1880 an Arizona schoolmarm went by stagecoach from Wickenburg to Prescott. Coming off Antelope Mountain the drunken driver lost control of the horses and then tumbled off the stage, leaving coach and occupants to career wildly beside the precipices. According to Angeline Brown, who made that chaotic trip, one of those passengers had "'been West'" and therefore had command of a "varied vocabulary of oaths," and "he spun them out at a rate of speed" that amazed her. A greenhorn—"the eastern expert," as she styled him—"prayed with the same wonderful flow of language." And so they went "swearing & praying," while a hysterical woman "wept & screamed & shrieked." Thus in a dazzling display of the fortuitous, came the unlikely assemblage off Antelope Mountain. Fortune—or perhaps the prayers of the "eastern expert"—served them well. Once on level ground, the horses slowed and then were stopped when one of the passengers climbed over the stage and onto the tongue. The driver, somehow unscathed by his tumble, overtook them and shepherded them into Prescott. This vignette, as rendered by a sprightly woman who found the West both terrifying and invigorating, seems somewhat trite, but it does incorporate much of the aura that common people evinced and reported, an aura that bears much resemblance to the aura of the war.[1]

As the preceding chapter sought to show, the Civil War struck common people as the epitome of pointlessness and confusion. The West impressed them much the same way. In a general sense, the West provided an equivalent for war, though hardly a moral one. Both arenas reeked of disruption, of separation, of wild oscillation between utter boredom and terrible excitement, of frantic and indecipherable movement, of hardship, suffering, sudden death, opportunity, chance, and, for the lucky, quick and large rewards. J. S. Holliday has depicted the gold rush—that catalyst and symbol of all of the West—as amounting to a "national tragedy, much like a war." He did not pursue the analogy; but in the war and the West, "the world rushed in," to use his title. Things of the world rushed in to threaten and violate the spiritual haven which common people had sought to defend and maintain. God's Providence had given meaning and purpose to that haven, but meaning and purpose got short shrift in what Holliday calls "The Great California Lottery." "Luck Is All." That legacy endured and prospered.[2]

The relation between the West, that quintessential land of luck, and the ambience of war bears emphasis. In part at least, the relationship occurred because people who had gone to one or the other had exposed themselves to hardship and danger and had often exposed others to hardship by so doing. Explanation seemed in order, and it could, of course, forthcome quite readily for soldiers, most of whom were volunteers. Ira Butterfield joined a Wisconsin artillery regiment and then injured his back and spent time as a hospital orderly at Milliken's Bend on the Mississippi, service providing abundant opportunity to see, as he put it, "the dark side of the picture." With the sardonic breeziness that was becoming so much more characteristic of common people, Corporal Butterfield told his foster mother of the final disposition of many soldiers. Those who died at the hospital were "decently buried," that is, they got a coffin and "their regular land warrant" of "six feet by two." Those killed in battle often "get cheated a little in their land warrant." Perhaps the talk of land warrants anticipated his envisioning the end of war in a way that he set down a few days later. When again a "free man," he would have "a glorious old time a hunting a new home in the wilderness. I don't know how it is but there is a strange fantasy hanging to me that it seems to me that nothing will do me but a trip out west to hunt a new home."[3]

Probably very few used words like "strange fantasy," but many regarded the West as ineluctably attractive and infectious. Moreover, in one way or another, they perceived that the West changed people and made them uncomfortable with the ways they left behind. Though they often suffered and often repined, they showed reluctance to abandon the unrestrained and gamey ways, just as soldiers, though bemoaning intensely many situations in which they found themselves, so often doubted that they could ever resume the staid pace to which they had previously been accustomed. In large part this probably involved unintended consequences. That many, though certainly not all, sought assiduously to perpetuate and to improve the ways and views of the areas from which they came seems undeniable. Though discouraging words could occasionally be heard in Stearns County, Minnesota, in 1870, young Albert Bugbie could happily report that "every year brings us nearer and neare[r] to the manners and customes of the East." He and others probably did all they could in that regard, but Paynesville, Minnesota, would never be exactly the same as Belchertown, Massachusetts.[4]

In 1863 Everitt Judson of Tulare County, California, wrote home to his wife in New York, whom he had left eleven years before, to tell that finally he had hit upon a plan to "make a fortune." Sadly, that vegetable-growing scheme did not pan out, and he returned to his wife apparently broke and certainly about to die. Six months later Sophia Smith of Visalia, whose husband had pursued the vegetable venture with Judson, wrote to the widow to inform her that her deceased spouse had left no other holdings in California and that he had made a mistake in not taking three hundred dollars for what he had when he had the chance. She explained his error in part by his having become accustomed to the Far West existence and wishing to have something awaiting him should he return. Sophia Smith used an exceedingly common theme in explaining Everitt Judson's retaining a stake in the Far West: "there was so many went home came back did not seem satisfied he thought he would be the same."[5]

Everitt Judson would certainly have agreed with fellow argonaut William Carroll, another easterner in quest of western fortune, who observed that "very much depends on luck and chance." Throughout the West this truism took on the guise of doctrine. In the spring of 1869 George G. Tilden left Rochester, Vermont, where his father, an unprosperous miller, had raised the family. Young Tilden was scouting Iowa, where his father and a younger brother had already located, for a likely place to try his hand at the mercantile business. Before locating at Ames, Tilden visited his father and brother at Manchester in the eastern part of the state, and he wrote that their situation left much to be desired. "Eastern people," he noted, "would think it most impossible to live as they do." But, he continued, they would have comfortable surroundings before long "if they have good luck." As William Carroll noted when he worried about the onset of the ague season, one "must trust to luck." That trust is distinctly different from that which most such people would have expressed in the previous generation.[6]

"The western country is a great section," Leonard Dibble happily informed the folks back on the Connecticut farm shortly after arriving in southern Minnesota. The "western habits," he added, are "peculiar institutions." This twenty-two-year-old Yankee may have meant nothing special in that last expression, but there is a southern dimension to this general perception of the West. That southern aspect of the West might involve little more than encountering too many southerners there, "Southern Chivalry," as New Yorker William Carroll disparagingly styled this "very ignorant rough kind of people." In 1867 a Massachusetts man found far too many southerners in San Diego, all of whom "smoke, chew, drink & gamble." However fair that assessment, it was all but standard.[7]

This assessment involves the long-held notion that southerners bore fewer restraints than their northern counterparts and thus could accommodate more readily with the ways of the West, the land of "unrestraint," as Frederick Jackson Turner called it. In the cartography of the American mind no clear line of demarcation separated West from South. More particularly, one of the clearest defiances of providential sway and restraint typified, at least in the eyes of many beholders, this southern-by-western tilt. That last item in Ephraim Morse's list of San Diego offenses—gambling—has been, of course, widespread if not endemic for Americans, this "people of chance," as John Findlay styles them. "The qualities that identified Americans as a people of chance," he writes, "stood out most boldly on western frontiers where gambling tended to flourish and where distinctly American betting games emerged for the first time." Indeed, the story of America's gambling has a decidedly southwestern direction. The epicenter moved from the southern Mississippi to gold-rush California, the land of "a fast people," before settling in Nevada.[8]

Here again, the Civil War and the West appear in conjunction or in parallel. What people said of one they frequently said of the other. Writing from Alabama late in the war, an astounded Indiana soldier, John Carmine, for example, told of returning to his quarters after a Sunday evening "praier meeting" to find "several of our boys playing cardes they would wrather play cardes as go to meeting." Few could portray the cultural drift of the times so succinctly. Time and again similar things would be said of the South and of the West, bearing out the attitudes and perceptions of lesser Americans as they moved toward the West and toward modernity.[9]

As did the war, the West abounded in the misleading and the illusory. Little could be believed, and the plethora of stories about gold have only the most legendary quality, "Bilk," as one discouraged miner described the golden fantasy that had driven him around the West. Far more things than mining proved deceiving. As in the war, the newspapers in the West had a notorious capacity to exaggerate and misinform. Near Central City, Colorado Territory, in 1866 Zina W. Chase, a Maine man by way of Minnesota, wrote in his diary of newspaper estimates of ore that would come from the territory that year, estimates ten and more times greater than what reliable people believed. "So much for News Paper Reports," he concluded, "they ought to be suppressed." George Loring left Boston as a member of a colonizing organization that made an effort to establish itself near where Flagstaff, Arizona, would shortly take root. In mid–1876 Loring left the apparently mismanaged colony, but not before he had alerted his wife and mother to the deceptions he had encountered. Only two of the colonists, he noted, yet had any faith in the project, one the old chaplain of the company, "whose mind is affected." As for the captain, he "would have been strung to a tree long ago" had not the members of the organization been such decent people. "Dont believe a single word you hear in Boston about the company or the country," he warned, "two thirds you hear in Boston is a dam lie."[10]

The West possessed an almost intrinsically misleading quality. As with the war, people could not always see the reality of the West, even when looking directly at that reality. All were awed by its distances. They could see a long way, but they suffered confusion and perplexity over what they saw and how far they were actually seeing. For a sophisticated visitor and observer in the West, the historian John Fiske, that phenomenon of having mountains appear to be only a small fraction of their actual distance away had the happy effect of giving "a more powerful sense of the Infinite" than he had ever felt. Lesser mortals did not share Fiske's view. Joseph Nevins, the son of an Adams County, Illinois, farmer, traveled across the West in 1874 to look for work in California. He invites juxtaposition with Fiske because his son Allan would become a historian. "On the side of a hill that seems to be not more than 40 rds away, antelopes appear no larger than rabbits. And little houses among the rocks, apparently within a stone's throw, look not much larger than Frisk's kennel." To Joseph Nevins, that did not involve the "Infinite"; it involved the "very deceptive." A puzzled young Iowa woman concluded simply that the West was "a very disceatful country in that respect." Another Illinois man knew that the clearness of the atmosphere accounted for the "very deceitful" effect, but nevertheless he and his party were "continually being deceived." In the West one did not trust appearances any more than one trusted rumors, boomers, or newspapers.[11]

James Jones's years in California—some of them as bartender for Sam Brannan—had prepared him to spot what he called a "humbug" when in September 1869 he made a trip from San Francisco to the eastern slope of the Sierra Nevada. "Rum or women," as he remarked to a sister, had taken everything but a mining claim he was going to check. His health had failed badly, and James Jones probably knew that he neared the end of his pursuit of Dame Fortune or of a "humbug" as he wrote to another sister from Lone Pine, telling that the hotel in which he now stayed was very near where he and his fellow prospectors had camped seven years before. The Indians they had then feared now were wearing stovepipe hats and paper collars, "playing seven up and bucking at a Faro Bank against a Texas gambler—such a change in nature I can scarcely comprehend." If pressed, the former bartender might have admitted that he was a walking repository of the altered ways, but he too could bemoan the emergence and dominance of "a fast people," to use John Findlay's term. He too could hearken back longingly to "old fashioned people such as we used to know and mingle with in our young days." In less than three months James Jones died. His letters powerfully register the changing ways and the changing language of California and the West. And we can rely on a California woman—Minnie Harney of Shasta County—to interject the newer modes into a long, detailed account of her suffering in a difficult childbirth that killed the child: "I came very near passing in my checks." Like many others, Minnie Harney had appropriated gambling's ways of talking and perhaps its ways of thinking.[12]

California epitomized the emergent outlook, but it was not confined to that state. The language of gambling came easiest to those engaged in the gamble of mining, as was the case with William Pritchard, who was in northeast Oregon in the late 1860s mining, as he put it, "on my own Luck." Orthodox expressions recurred to Pritchard on need, as when a relative died: "it's God's will, and we must submit." Elsewhere he resorted to other terms, as he did in discussing various setbacks he had suffered: "I shall have to get married or do something desperit to see if it will change my luck." John Grannis, a Colorado cowpoke, suffered domestic difficulties, lost his wife, and turned to mining. As he set out for gold he assumed a proper philosophical stance: "(I am the creature of fortune)." In an entry for December 31, in a space often previously used for setting down one's perceptions of God's dealing with him, this native of Indiana summed up briefly and dejectedly: "this year has been Bad luck to me from the first to last."[13]

In fact, all of the West involved a gamble, and many more than miners availed themselves of proper linguistic trappings. Leonard Dibble, a Connecticut Yankee in southern Minnesota, employed the emerging modes of expression often and well. Writing from Le Sueur in 1868, he told his father that he meant to "take all the chances in sight & make them win if possible." Shortly, he moved on to St. Peter and then claimed an eighty-acre plot on the Minnesota River near Redwood Falls, where he sought to start a ferry. The West had "more chances," and, as Dibble put it, "I propose to take as many as possible, and run them Broad gague [sic], and I think some of them will win." Young Dibble may have been employing an innocent surrogate for such ancestral expressions as "improving the opportunity," but, consciously or unconsciously, he used the gaming language, to take chances rather than improve opportunities. Ideas and attitudes have consequences, and words and expressions betray them.[14]

A more extended examination of an individual case may prove illuminating. Donald W. Davis was a Forty-niner, having been born in that year on a farm in Londonderry Town(ship), Windham County, Vermont. In childhood and youth he labored on the farm and went to school, but his destiny lay elsewhere. Perhaps the year of his birth betokened that. Outside of war, 1849 provided America more excitement than any other year, and California did not do it all. In studying the social changes that came to Vermont around midcentury David Ludlum used the year 1849 as the focal point in the development of the state's railroads, "the symbol of the new age," a development which, according to another student of Vermont history, "reoriented everything it touched." And "it touched nearly everything."[15]

Donald W. Davis, born at a magic moment in the history of the state and the nation, started his westward drift at age eighteen. Writing home from a job he had in upstate New York he pronounced: "I am bound to go west the lord only knows how far." The Lord stayed in lowercase here in His one intrusion, a conventional one at that, into Davis's surviving letters home. In fact, the Lord seems to have played precious little part in what followed. Young Davis relied on other agencies. Having followed his job as far west as Cleveland, the youth, who stood five feet, ten inches, and had hazel eyes, dark hair, and dark complexion, enlisted in the army. That would take him much farther west and to excitement, as when the steamboat *Nora*, aboard which he rode up the Missouri, sank above Omaha. But neither that "bad luck" nor his belonging to the Thirteenth United States Infantry would prevent Davis from enjoying himself and doing well in the Sun River area of Montana Territory, an exciting place on the southern perimeter of the fabled Whoop-Up country.[16]

Davis spent most of his three-year enlistment at Fort Shaw, and three letters he wrote during that time survive. Perhaps the most compelling item in them involves an event about which he said little, the attack on a Piegan Indian camp in January 1870 by a force drawn partly from the Thirteenth Infantry. As usual, construing silence, or near silence, poses a great challenge, and Davis's cryptic mention of an episode that has generally been considered deplorable seems peculiarly out of proportion. He assumed that his mother had seen newspaper accounts of the raid, which he casually referred to as "a big thing." One might suppose that that unsatisfactory passing reference registers his awareness that no words could move his mother, or others in the East, to see such horrors from the angle of vision of a westerner. New Englanders in New England might well become incensed, but our New Englander at Fort Shaw had his mind mostly on other things.[17]

A year before the sanguinary episode, Davis told his father that he planned to have a thousand dollars saved when his enlistment expired in 1870. He minced no words in explaining how he was going to do it: "my surplus money I speculate on . . . by discounting vouchers checks &c. . . . And then every pay day I calculate to make some by gambling on poker Bluff [?] & chuckluck or in fact anything to keep up excitement know matter what it is." He remarked that "good luck" was all he needed, and he got it. Most of his three years as a soldier went to keeping military stores at Fort Shaw, work that prepared him to step into the dramatic and tawdry liquor trade of the area. He became in time the trader at Fort Whoop-Up, later a founder of Calgary, and later yet the first member of the Canadian Parliament from the Alberta District of the North West Territories, all a far cry from the unprepossessing setting of the Windham County farm.[18]

There comes to mind Herman Melville's often-quoted depiction of another Vermonter, Ethan Allen: "Though born in New England, he exhibited no trace of her character. . . . His spirit was essentially Western; and herein is his peculiar Americanism; for the Western spirit is, or will yet be (for no other is, or can be) the true American one." Some might use less flattering terms. Davis's half-breed children, for example, who go unmentioned in the extant letters home, and who would be, with their mother, displaced in time by a white woman and children, as well as the malodorous aura of the whiskey trade in which Davis participated, might move some to view him as a New England renegade, pure and simple, a Simon Legree gone northwest rather than southwest. However understandable, that view would not completely satisfy because it leaves Davis unduly isolated. Many people were assuming—intentionally or unintentionally and to whatever degree—the posture of renegadism. To go west almost inevitably involved so doing. People went west, as Rodman Paul put it, out of "ruthless pursuit of private gain." Unlike most, Davis secured it. In the process, he employed language and attitudes that were becoming widespread, and not just in the West. As David Ludlum wrote about Vermont in the years after 1849, "The Forty-Niners seemingly put the stamp of approval on the spirit of acquisitiveness which had formerly met with a latent hostility." Our young man from Vermont figures doubly as a Forty-niner, in one sense figuratively, in one sense literally.[19]

The impact of 1849 and what it symbolized receives more powerful and more impressionistic statements by Ben Maddow, poet, novelist, screenwriter, director, producer, and historian. In *A Sunday between Wars*, a work using some sources similar to those used for this book, Maddow depicted gold as "the spark that set off the great engine of our present lives." Indeed, "this mania for gold" amounted to "a recurrent mental illness." That interpretation does not quite reckon with the likes of Donald W. Davis, for whom the lure of the West was "private gain" but not gold per se. Maddow's concluding imagery enlarges the scope to encompass the West in more than its gold-rush dimension, the war as well, and that other "engine" of emerging reality, the railroad.

> Such dislocations: the massive Civil War that moved two million men from their homes and the successive gold rushes that moved a million more in the next half century were the stimuli that conditioned men to settle elsewhere from where their fathers had lived, moved them from their job and landscape, released their energy in fresh views and fresh applications, and became the force that broke, several times in every generation, the ossification which any society tends to form inside itself. So the last half of the nineteenth century was for America a symbolic rush with inadequate brakes down a glittering, seemingly infinite track with gold glimmering ahead like the sheen of lanterns against the valley mist.[20]

Surely, poetry resides in Maddow's remarks, but they put a construction on things that bears a resemblance to what common people showed more and more inclination to write. Of course, the West had figured in American existence from the outset, and we are dealing with comparative and emergent matters, not absolute and precise ones. Still, humble expressions from and about the West written after 1860 show more of the spirit depicted by Maddow than do those written before 1860. Many things were changing, and the railroad must have done much to allow for a departure from the sober and even querulous tone that pervaded what was written in the West earlier. Going to the Far West in a handful of fairly comfortable days stood in exhilarating contrast with what had been endured on the trails before. The trek of Joseph Nevins in 1874 bears almost no resemblance to the ambience of, for example, his fellow Illinoisans of the Donner party of 1846. In Nevins's account entries made first early in the day and then late in the day of January 14, 1874, tell of Ogden, Utah Territory, and then of eastern Nevada. This rate of movement probably heightened his sense of erratic perceptions in that very deceptive western country. On the next day in the Humboldt country of western Nevada, he exclaimed: "One week since we left home!" The historian's father made that pronouncement at roughly the point it required the Donner party half a year to reach.[21]

When David Ludlum informs us that the Forty-niners somehow "put the stamp of approval on the spirit of acquisitiveness," we immediately remind ourselves that acquisitiveness was nothing new. Still, that spirit does surface more frequently and unabashedly in humble sources of the late nineteenth century than it had in the generation before. Donald W. Davis provides a classic instance, but, whether attended with success or failure, the mood abounded and grew. Writing back to California from Helena, Montana Territory, W. H. Taylor, sometime doctor, told about "multitudes" of such practitioners in the gold camp, one waiting tables, another using pick and shovel, and so on. "I have several prospects in view for making money," he remarked, then added sourly, "but of course, all will fail, as they have always done." The one thing needful could be elusive, and Taylor was already prepared to write off the Helena rush as a "humbug." A couple of years later he appeared in such places as Treasure City, Nevada, bartending, then awaiting the roulette wheel, which might redeem things, and, one can fairly well surmise, recurrently operating pretty much as a drug dealer, a calling rendered far more common by the agony of the Civil War. That spirit of acquisitiveness more boldly accosts the eye of the researcher when he gets into the later stretches of the nineteenth century.[22]

So, for example, do some usages that might, in the fictive world of Edgar Allan Poe, be thought of as "simple if not altogether innocent expletives—imaginative phrases wherewith to round off a sentence." Poe probably meant to parody traits he espied in the Transcendentalists when he created Toby Dammit in "Never Bet the Devil Your Head: A Tale with a Moral." Toby's cocksure references to betting this and betting that came to the pinnacle in "'I'll bet the Devil my head,'" a proposal he neglected to keep in the abstract.

The long-suffering and unimaginative narrator in the story be-seeched Toby to recognize that the language of betting was "vulgar," "immoral," "discountenanced by society," and "forbidden by Act of Congress." The hyperbole aside, that simple and moralizing narra-tor spoke for a society that spurned, however successfully, those "not altogether innocent expletives." Poe left the American scene as California entered it. In time the danger that his Toby Dammit personified was ignored, and the avoidance that his nonplused narrator urged fell by the way.[23]

California and the West led the way in such regards. There the new spirit and the unshackled language could be apostrophized by naming a mine "You Bet." That name breathed the aura of the changing times, and the expression itself was not confined to mining operations. A decade after California statehood, Andrew Jackson Stone wrote home from Placer County to expatiate on the destiny of "the best state on broad platform of this great and mighty creation; You Bet." That expletive involved attenuation. Sometimes full form and specifics appeared. George Loring wrote to his mother not long after leaving the Flagstaff area to tell her of the promising situation into which he had settled in Phoenix. Another of the Flagstaff colo-nists had recently arrived with the intention of making money, "and he will make it you can bet your life." But could she? That that man would surely prosper in Phoenix involved a suppositious certainty even beyond what Urian Oakes had warned against and almost as great as Poe impishly paraded in Toby Dammit, headless at the end of the story.[24]

America's long and rich history of gambling featured countervail-ing inhibitions that now neared exhaustion. Near the end of the seventeenth century Increase Mather availed himself of Proverbs 16:33, for example, to warn against lotteries, "a serious thing not to be trifled with." Near the end of the nineteenth century that inhibi-tion had become little more than vestigial. And in the late twentieth century the telephone directory of the former mining town of Grass Valley, California, has an entry for a place of worship that would, one assumes, astound Increase Mather: Mission Beth'El—The You Bet Red-Dog Community Church, located on You Win Court.[25]

The latent hostility that had kept the language of gambling in check was relaxing elsewhere. Other subjects that had been almost totally absent in humble writings were doing their parts to diminish the godly spirit, especially in the West. We recall that when Minnie Harney of Shasta County told of an agonizing and dangerous child-birth she resorted to the language of the gaming table. She nearly cashed in her checks. Minnie Harney had appropriated other modes of outré expression, and she employed them forcefully in that same letter. After urging the friend to whom she wrote never to have children, Minnie expressed the resolve to have no more herself, "even if I have to cut off my old mans Pod or sew mine up." The circumstances help explain that venture into the indecorous, but they do not explain the gratuitous coarseness that follows. Simply, the rough and tumble language that some would have expected all along now starts to appear in at least appreciable amounts in such sources as these. Sut Lovingood had been ahead of his time. When George Washington Harris created him in the 1850s, his Rabelaisian approach to reality seems to have reflected the spirit of precious few Americans of modest circumstances. Minnie Harney and others were helping them catch up.[26]

Nahum T. Wood did his share also. This New Englander herded sheep in southern California, especially in the hills between San Juan Capistrano and Anaheim. On New Year's Day of 1871 he spent the time in the former drinking and playing billiards, and that estab-lished the tone. A week later he went to Los Angeles to appear as witness in court, and we can only wonder to what he referred when he reported having seen "a front view of the Elephant" during some idle time. That figure of speech had appeared very commonly before the war to refer to the hardships of the overland trail, but now it was going into partial eclipse. It could, of course, apply to almost any-thing, and one wonders if the man for whom Wood was named, Nahum the Elkoshite, might not have found behind this veil of metaphor yet added reason to cry, "Woe to the bloody city!" though Los Angeles in 1871 had not yet equaled Nineveh.[27]

Shortly, Nahum T. Wood boarded the stage for Anaheim, and during that trip one rider fell out and was run over while the coach was "under full headway." Happily, he proved "too drunk to get hurt." And so it went. When a Sunday came, the sheepherder noted that it had been observed "partly as the Lord's Day and partly as the Devil's," and a full two days later Wood's partner was still in "high glee." Indeed, "Pard" had been seen on "the high road to Debt—to Anaheim with a Biped,—if I mistake it not it will turn to a quadruped before morning." Billiards, a biped, whiskey, and the Omaha Lottery—these things and others like them seem to have provided the informing spirit of the country around San Juan Capistrano and Anaheim. And when old Mister Hipwell was found dead on the road, apparently victim of intemperance and exposure, no providential language forthcame: "Poor old man! his troubles are at an end."[28]

Godly language sometimes enters Wood's account, but, as in the case of the passage regarding the "Lord's Day," one cannot construe his remarks with certainty. In mid-May he and others headed their sheep south toward the San Diego area, apparently to escape dry weather farther north. The pitiful remnants of "crazy" efforts to do dry-land farming in the scorched area gave visual punctuation to the searing misery as they labored southward. "The Lord," Wood observed, "has not allotted any day for the sheep man." It would get worse as they moved past San Diego and across the Mexican line into the Hapa Valley "(The devil has it mortgaged)." That assessment came in late June; near Tecate in early September, shearing time, the situation was "Hell in two volumes." Mostly, the suffering sheepherder maintained a secular and sometimes coarse tone. "Why not!" he noted of a lottery ticket transaction that could not be neglected even during "Hell in two volumes."[29]

This man occasionally wrote in something other than the doggedly literal way that his predecessors of a generation before had maintained. On a blazing day near Tecate at the beginning of September he wrote: "I love this country, and intend to settle here," then added after a dash, "Sarchasm." That commodity was nothing new, and one supposes that ordinary people had long employed it often in the spoken word. In the written word, however, it appeared far less frequently in prewar than in postwar sources. Nahum Wood did not leave us to wonder about his intention, and now and again in other sources one encounters such usages as "Ha Ha" to signal a lapse in the literal. Often, one needs no such help. Another Californian urged a friend to return to the Little York and Dutch Flat area from somewhere nearby. "I am afraid if you stay there," he remarked, "you will forget your catechism."[30]

No irony or even sarcasm informed a letter which a pair of playful young San Francisco women wrote a friend in the 1870s. It closed this way: "Well this is enough dirtiness so good-bye—." Josie and

Kate had provided enough for many. (In a letter Kate wrote to Josie I had my first encounter in humble sources with the usage Tom Wolfe put at the epithetic center of "The Street Fighters" a century later.)[31]

Deviation from accepted ways—godly or otherwise—appears more pronounced in the West, and a young man named Hooper, a friend or relative of Josie and Kate, attested to that when he visited in De Witt County, Illinois, in 1880. A week after leaving his California friends, he wrote back from Farmer City, noting the differences he encountered. He found things comfortable and nice, but, as he put it figuratively, he "dispise[d] to have to walk so straight one here is doing a great wrong if they use an improper word." Why, "some of them are so nice they dont know they have got any." Any what went unspecified, but it may be illustrated by the following anecdote. On the street one day westerner Hooper met a young and pretty woman who so steadfastly looked ahead, knowing she should not acknowledge a stranger, that she failed to avoid a loose board in the sidewalk: "Well the plank came up & she came down flat on her—well it didn't hurt her any I guess." Hooper did not specify that on which she came down, and the young lady may not, if Hooper is to be believed, have known she had that anyway. "Its a funny world this," he philosophized, "you western folks don't know how the eastern folks live & they don't know how you live. Do you know I haven't heard an oath since I got to Ill. They are all church going folks here I am trying to get on my most solom look." This young man expressed himself in arch and impressionistic terms, but there is accuracy in what he had to say.[32]

One must not exaggerate California's accountability. Even back in Illinois people were getting abreast of the times. In that area too letters now begin to reveal some "treason against God," to use the title of Leonard Levy's book on blasphemy. "You shant loose a cent," George Mooers insisted to a New York friend who had loaned him money. To be sure, Mooers was "busted up" in Lee County, Illinois, country that was, of course, the West to these people. In pressing on from fact to explanation, Mooers ventured into treasonous terms: "if the god damb wheat had have done anything" and if some other "god damb" business "had have been in hell I would have been all right." Surely, we need not be aghast at this language. We casually and comfortably suppose that a George Mooers has been in every village and on every block, perhaps for quite some time. Having

recognized that, however, we must recognize as well that significance attaches to the growing readiness to indulge in the unrestrained ways and to abandon or at least alloy the abiding tone of
earnestness and dedication—dedication especially to God—that
had previously informed humble writings. And there at Nelson,
Illinois, in the fall of 1876, George Mooers, a New Yorker who had
gone west, offered this summary statement, replete with curse and
luck: "I have had more god damb bad luck than would patch hell a
mile." From God's Providence we arrive at "god damb bad luck,"
truly in the realm of profane Esau.[33]

The literary realists of the era served us fairly well as indicators of
the changing ways. Thus James Turner refers to Harriet Beecher
Stowe's 1859 novel *The Minister's Wooing* as "the literary *coup de grace*
of American Calvinism." Certainly, Stowe did much to reflect and
perhaps to accelerate the emergent moods. In 1878 her *Poganuc
People* gently but firmly put "what was in those days spoken of as the
'doctrine of divine sovereignty'" in comfortably bygone days,
roughly those of her childhood. Her fictive Sam Lawson, brought to
fullest form in 1872, proved an ideal device for tempering the stern
and ancient godly precepts. When, for example, the children ran
afoul of churchly expectations in "Laughin' in Meetin'," they went to
Sam for "indulgence and patronage." Though "rigidly moral and
instructive in his turn of mind," Stowe's Sam Lawson "had that
fellow-feeling for transgressors which is characteristic of the loose-
jointed, easy-going style of his individuality."[34]

That "loose-jointed, easy-going style" was waxing, especially
among westerners. Mark Twain often epitomized that outlook, and
in "The Man That Corrupted Hadleyburg" his "loafing, good-
natured, no-account" Jack Halliday appears as the "typical 'Sam
Lawson' of the town." The story of Hadleyburg has much that
pertains to Providence, most appropriately in the old and rather
pathetic couple, Mr. and Mrs. Richards. Appropriately also, it is Jack
Halliday who perceives at one point that "'Providence is off duty
today.'" Unlike Stowe, Mark Twain generally betrayed no gentle-
ness in parodying the doctrine of Providence into an off-duty condition. *Roughing It* provides a fine western illustration in the performance of the bibulous storyteller who pronounces that "Prov'dence
don't fire no blank ca'tridges, boys." He establishes that theme in
telling of the demise of a besotted uncle who had been killed when

an Irishman and a hod full of bricks fell on him from third-floor construction. Though Uncle Lem died, the Irishman lived, and that satisfied the storyteller as to why his uncle had been leaning against the scaffolding just where he did: "Uncle Lem's dog was there. Why didn't the Irishman fall on the dog? Becuz the dog would 'a' seen him a-coming and stood from under. That's the reason the dog warn't app'inted. A dog can't be depended on to carry out a special prov'dence."[35]

Where Mark Twain resorted to parody in flaying the sound doctrines of an older outlook, Bret Harte, his immediate predecessor in the fame of the western genre, simply preempted the ground of the ancient notion. In "The Luck of Roaring Camp," when Cherokee Sal, after giving birth, cashed in her chips, Stumpy spoke as follows: "'we're here for a christening, and we'll have it. I proclaim you Thomas Luck, according to the laws of the United States and the State of California, so help me God.'" Stumpy observed punctilio in that closing invocation, and what he had christened, though it be the orphaned offspring of a camp prostitute, had a lively future, if not in the fictive Roaring Camp then in the West and the nation at large. "The Luck," as the babe was commonly called, came to exercise full sway over those hundred miners. When he left, he did so in such fashion as to reinforce his centrality in Harte's microcosmic camp. The tale closes in the aftermath of a flood, when the miner Kentuck is found dying but still holding the "Ingin baby" that the miners "worship." That "Ingin baby" was dead, and Kentuck left with these words: "'Tell the boys I've got The Luck with me now'; and the strong man, clinging to the frail babe as a drowning man is said to cling to a straw, drifted away into the shadowy river that flows forever to the unknown sea."[36]

The same spirit intrudes into literature even less elevated than this. John Wallace Crawford had been a boy hero of the Civil War, accompanying his Irish immigrant father into the conflict. A nurse who cared for him after he received serious wounds taught him to read and write, a favor he returned by becoming a poet. He also became a frontier scout, Indian fighter, and actor. During the Black Hills gold rush he heard the story of Monte Bill and Rattlin' Joe, dear friends who revered their mothers and little else. Indeed, each spared his mother's feelings by telling that he was involved in banking, neglecting to note that the banks in question were faro banks. When Monte Bill died, Rattlin' Joe had the obligation of providing a Christian burial, which Bill insisted on for his mother's sake. "Thar' war' no gospel sharps" in such settings. So Rattlin' Joe had to make do with a deck of cards:

> "The ace, that reminds us o' one God,
>> The deuce o' the Father an' Son,
> The tray o' the Father and Son, Holy Ghost,
>> For ye see all them Three are but One."

And so Rattlin' Joe went through to the knave,

> ". . . that's the devil,—an' God if ye please,
>> Jist keep his hands off'n poor Bill.
> An' now, lads, git down on yer bended knees
>> Till I draw, and perhaps I kin fill . . ."[37]

Crawford had a flair for reciting his poetry, and, according to him, "Rattlin' Joe's Prayer" was "first recited in Henry Ward Beecher's church, old Plymouth, Brooklyn, at a Ladies' Fair." Beecher and Crawford would have made an arresting pair, one hesitates to say a pair to draw to. "God and Man in Brooklyn," to use Paul Carter's term, were, at least for the Crawford moment, taking on a western cast. According to the poet scout, Beecher "smilingly pronounced" the poem " 'most innocently sacrilegious.' "[38]

Stanley Huntley, another Brooklyn figure of the 1880s, had been west as a journalist and as a scapegrace for any season. After noteworthy antics on the Dakota frontier he returned to his native Brooklyn to grace the *Daily Eagle* with his wit, especially his juxtapositions of the ways of Bismarck with those of Brooklyn. He held orthodox religion in contempt, and that may have congruence with the warm and friendly tone of an interview he had with Beecher, which appeared in the *Eagle*. Perhaps Huntley perceived in Beecher what historian Paul Carter did—the "gospel of exuberance, of spontaneity." And perhaps if Beecher read Huntley's humorous material in the *Eagle* he may have found some of it "innocently sacrilegious."[39]

One of Huntley's best-known efforts treated "the first sermon" in Bismarck, which novelty seemed unlikely to win favor.

> There were murmurings in Bismarck,
>> When the dealer of a bank
> Announced that Parson Miller
>> Had brought his gospel tank.

But when the parson took his place at the faro table, now serving as pulpit, the boys observed the "solemn rule,"

> Whatever game may be proposed
>> To always take a hand.

When, for example, the parson called for a hymn, the boys obliged, but only with the closest thing to a hymn they knew, "Whoa, Emma." "And the very bottles rang."

At last Parson Miller passed his "battered hat," and it returned heavy with chips.

> The Parson, all bewildered, asked
>> What he should do with those,
> And learned that he might play 'em in,
>> Or cash 'em as he chose.

So religion had ventured even into Stanley Huntley's Bismarck, and God's ways would, at least in part, now be observed.

> And each faro-table has a slit,
>> In which each man has got
> To drop a part of what he wins,
>> Which slit is called "God's Pot."[40]

One could, of course, contend that such things as a gambler's prayer partake of the conventional so much as to be timeless. But if they were there in the generation before the war, they figured far less prominently in the writing of lesser sorts, perhaps being confined to subcultural, gambling lacunae, or, fully as likely, to the comparatively sophisticated who read the likes of *Spirit of the Times*. Humble Americans of that earlier generation would have inclined more to the seventeenth-century view identified by Thomas Shepard's expression "God's Plot"—another term for the whole providential schema—than to a waggish journalist's condescending depiction of "God's Pot" at the faro tables of Bismarck. Henry Ward Beecher of the 1840s, author of *Seven Lectures to Young Men*, could hardly have taken a tolerant view of "Rattlin' Joe's Prayer." Lecture V, "Gamblers and Gambling," began with text from John 19:23–24 with soldiers casting lots for the coat of Jesus, and it closed the "Mighty Game" with the reader "the stake, and Satan the winner," leaving no room for levity and latitudinarianism. Those things were coming, partly under the auspices of a changing Henry Ward Beecher. The task at hand is to suggest how lesser Americans were changing with him.[41]

Part of that task involves depicting the people of the late nineteenth century as appreciably more conversant with the likes of Mark Twain and Bret Harte, with popular literature and journalism, than had been the preceding generation. The fuller attention this matter deserves will come later, but a couple of instances pertaining to authors just discussed may be in order now. Wilmot Sanford of New Hampshire enlisted in the army for a five-year term in 1872, and he spent much of that time in the frequently unutterable boredom of Fort Buford in northwestern Dakota Territory. He read a great deal, and one would love to know what he thought of Henry Ward Beecher's *Norwood* when he read it in 1874. Neither that novel, of which William G. McLoughlin has made much, nor anything else begot commentary from Private Sanford. He offered only the unadorned facts, such as that on April 15, 1875, he finished "Luck of the Camp" and that on May 8 following he was "Reading Roughing It by M. Twain." Lemuel Hazzard served us better. In the summer of 1873 his wife went back to Indiana for a visit, leaving Lem to continue his carpentry work in Salem, Missouri. Like so many others, former soldier Hazzard was appropriating breezier modes, as he evinced in remarking playfully about all the letters he was sending to Indiana. Bret Harte would have been irritated to know that yet another person was absorbing "Plain Language from Truthful James" ("Truthful James" most likely being California journalist "Lying Jim" Townsend) rather than what its author considered more important. And Lemuel Hazzard could puckishly refer to the letters to his wife as being "almost equal to the cards that fell out of the 'heathen Chinees' sleeve 'and I state but the facts.' "[42]

Surely, more than the Civil War and the West contributed to the erosion of the godly terms humble people had been accustomed to using. One thinks quickly of the spirit of business which supposedly pervaded the period. Eric Goldman opened *Rendezvous with Destiny* with a short chapter of impressionistic flourish titled "Bejabers, I'm Worth Me Thousands," and it begins with the words an Indiana farmer once pronounced to Charles Beard's father: "Everybody and everything's goin' places." As will be discussed further in another context, the intonations of enterprise do more to color diaries and family correspondence than had been the case previously. One has less difficulty finding letters such as those written by Henry Queripel in New York City in 1864 and 1865. Late in the former year he told a friend that he was "just barely earning enough to live." Not long thereafter he had better news to report. He had secured a position as a secretary in "a large stock company" capitalized at $500,000. That, he observed, looked very impressive to "a fellow who has not got a dime to his name."[43]

This young man had an active interest in religion, and here, embarking on a new venture, he hoped—he did not say he prayed—to have "the smiles of Providence upon my undertakings." But the nature of his "undertakings" seemed to trouble him because he belabored a theme he first put in mercenary terms deriving from an old play: " 'Money makes the mare go.' " Money had become "the God of the present generation." Little wonder that people were saying less about God and more about such a god as Henry Queripel specified shortly, the "Oil Barrel" or " 'Petrolium.' "[44]

This juxtaposition of Providence with petroleum admits of commentary. First, perceptions of creeping if not runaway godlessness seem wearyingly timeless. Second, a western dimension lurks in the background here, and as James Bryce in his chapter "The Temper of the West" noted, along with scores of others, the enterprising spirit approached the status of religion in the western reaches. Henry Queripel had had an involvement in the West, and the friend to whom he wrote still lived there. Necessity had driven Queripel back to New York, but, if circumstances allowed, his song would again be " 'To the West.' 'to the West.' " Indeed, not long before his ruminations about "the God of the present generation" Queripel tried to interest his Wisconsin friend in a small merchandising arrangement that would allow the two to take advantage of the western connection.[45]

Perhaps nothing came of their efforts, but the spirit behind those efforts was a common one. As new Minnesotan Leonard Dibble, whom we encountered before, wrote from Blue Earth City at about the time of Henry Queripel's letters to Wisconsin, one must not suppose that the western people were not "sharp in regard to their own interests." Those "Pioneers of Civilization," as Dibble styled them, stay "on the alert for any chance that will tend to that end in fact it may be said that they all came here for the purpose of showing their shrewdness." Whatever the West may have signified to thinkers such as those studied by Henry Nash Smith, to common folk it meant a better "chance" to tend their "own interests." The West smacked of the aura of business and the main chance—or the great spec or the next racket—which we earlier saw Leonard Dibble so assiduously pursuing. That Dibble failed and returned to Connecticut to live out a "rather pathetic" life does not detract from his perception of the chancy and often frenzied spirit of enterprise suffusing the West.[46]

Scientific developments must have had a corrosive effect on the providential view, even among the unelevated. Scholarly obligation would seem to involve determining the degree of that effect in this generation after *Origin of Species*. Such determination would probably defy the best efforts, but it does seem fairly clear that that degree was small, verging on the unappreciable. By the same token, the notion as offered, for example, by Martin Marty that some scientific law of Progress preempted the ground of the providential view has no pertinence for a study such as this. However much intellectuals may have made such a transfer, common people, though they thought and talked in more secular terms, offered next to nothing that would connect with a law of Progress, Herbert Spencer's or anyone else's.[47]

Some evidence might suggest that, in scientific terms, nothing had happened at all. Inveterate versifier Obadiah Ethelbert Baker, a man who appears more conversant with affairs of the world than most of his peers, wrote a poem titled "The Creation" in 1891. It contains no intimation that men such as Charles Lyell or Charles Darwin had been at work and had raised some questions. Providence appears less frequently, but little, if anything, suggests that science had anything to do with it. No mention of Charles Darwin and no unmistakable mention of evolutionary theories came to my attention. A Colorado miner momentarily pondered the age of a volcanic formation and left the subject abruptly with "man cannot comprehend," and a Texan allowed that "the laws of nature must be obeyed." Probably no one would have troubled to quarrel with the banal conclusion of the man who had gone west from Maine and the other who had gone west from Mississippi.[48]

Getting beyond such unarguable constructions as those imposes the need for some thimble-rigging. It would hardly do, for example, to perceive natural law translated into social law in a letter of outlaw Bill Longley headed "Devils Pass Hells half acre September 41st 7777." The Texas gunman said God damn to "the world and evry son of a bitch that dont like me." With godliness thus served, young Longley suggested that things be considered "dog eat dog . . . and let the bigest dog eat the most." This is simply the tempestuousness of a young man who neared his rendezvous with the gallows, and providential content, or lack thereof, is beside the point. As Bill Longley put it in noting his neglect of an opportunity to kill the man to whom he wrote, "I cursed my week minded soul and treated myself to a drink of good old brandy and wrode on."[49]

Brandy seems susceptible to naturalistic constructions, and in his book *The Spiritual Crisis of the Gilded Age* Paul Carter availed himself of the story about the dying U. S. Grant, periodically jolted into semiconsciousness by injections of brandy into his veins. A zealous Methodist minister baptized the unconscious man and watched in awe as he momentarily revived. " 'It is Providence!' " " 'No,' " a man of medicine remarked, " 'it was the brandy!' " That telling interplay of Providence and brandy brings to mind a story one sometimes encounters in Civil War letters, especially in Yankee efforts to fathom rebel actions. In explaining to his wife why the South almost won at Shiloh, Leonard Hawley of Ohio said nothing about God or Providence, but he did end his summary of natural causes with the report that every rebel "had to drink so mutch whiskey with gun powder in it." In some form or another, such a tale seems all but inevitable, but great hazard would reside in presenting it as naturalistic replacement for providential notions. Those notions seemed to be going into eclipse, but science, whether Bill Longley's, Leonard Hawley's, or Charles Darwin's, seems to explain that fact almost not at all. Published in the centennial year, the dour Melville's *Clarel* conjured many troubling images, including this one:

Man disennobled—brutalized
By popular science—Atheized.

However well that serves as poetry, or as projection, it seems fairly wide of the mark as historical description.[50]

It would probably have puzzled humble people to learn that philosophers were resorting to the element of chance in Darwin's evolutionary theory to avoid deterministic readings of human affairs. Perhaps nothing could have been as far from their minds as, say, tychism or chanceism. To them, science would have meant, in commonsensical terms, certainties and predictabilities. So there seems to be no direct causal connection between the rejection of design by Darwin and the lessening propensity of common Americans to speak of the design of Providence. That both sophisticated thinkers and people far removed from them saw a much greater role for the fortuitous, however, has both interest and significance.

God was not entirely the loser in these developments. If His vaunted sovereignty had been diminished, He gained in love. In the previous chapter we considered, in the context of war, James Turner's contention that "the defenders of God slowly strangled him." To modulate the metaphor, God found Himself painted into a theological corner by those who emphasized His love, almost to the exclusion of other attributes. When Civil War soldier Benjamin Harris wrote home to Nebraska in December 1862, he urged the children to "due what is rite," then invoked "the God of peace and love." But in the untidiness of the Nashville area from which he wrote it might well have occurred to him that a God so described was either a trifle neglectful or something other than omnicompetent. Surely, Harris's personal fate—wound, capture, imprisonment, and death aboard a hospital ship far from Sarah and the children—could have reinforced such a thought. Whatever the problems, that Nebraska soldier's way of referring to God was growing.[51]

Just after the war Mrs. George Ingraham wrote some "Home Musings" upon her return to the scenes of childhood and youth in Pembroke, Maine. Ingraham had been west, to San Francisco and even beyond. Now her musings had much to do with changes that had occurred in the years since she left her home area. Her sister and mother were in graves there. A brother lay in a battlefield grave, and her husband, who had been a teacher, occupied a grave in Hawaii. These dolorous items in the melancholy tale did not prevent the widow from concluding, however logically: "My ways are ordered by a God of love."[52]

James E. Glazier of Salem, Massachusetts, fought through the war as a private in the Twenty-third Massachusetts Infantry, and after the war he went west. For several years he did carpentry work, small farming, and various other odd jobs in northern California. At the end of the 1870s he took his family to The Dalles area of Oregon, where his wife died. The heartsick widower recrossed the nation, depositing children variously with families and institutions while keeping the two oldest boys with him. Efforts in his native area proved unproductive, and in the early 1880s he went south, seeking work in such places as St. Augustine and Tallahassee. Work there proved sporadic, and he and the two boys lived hand-to-mouth. The lure of the West remained, and at mid-decade he found the wherewithal to return to California, still shuffling seven children around in a way that beggars clear understanding. Slowly, he managed to get his life back into a semblance of order and to get all of the children near him and in at least acceptable circumstances. At the end of 1891, he penned his usual summary statement for the year, a practice now widely neglected by his fellow diarykeepers, in terms vastly removed from the litany of pain of the previous, wretched decade. "So ends 1891," he wrote, "I am in more pleasant & prosperous circumstances than heretofore. God is good. God is love."[53]

Those "more pleasant & prosperous circumstances" issuing in the conclusion that "God is love" may serve as emblem or illustration of very basic cultural and religious developments. But this smiling theological construction had the drawback of leaving God, implicitly at least, in the role of part-time player, of sunshine soldier. James E. Glazier was a consistently godly man, and it took him a good while to equate God and love. In other cases, however, the muting of the providential language seems almost to have been a result of the altered image of God. For example, in the summer of 1873 Mary Carpenter, with husband and small children, left a rented farm near Rochester, Minnesota, to try to get land of their own in the largely unsettled area near Marshall, far across the state to the west. Shortly after the two-hundred-mile trip by wagon, Mary Carpenter wrote an aunt of the deprivation she and her family were suffering. The thirty-two-year-old woman came pitifully near begging, and the one reference to God in that letter had a noteworthy qualification: "I try to trust in God's promises, but we can't expect him to work miracles nowadays."[54]

Somehow, God did not fully pertain. In one sense the age of

miracles was long past. In another, the wretchedness in and around that "leaky ten foot shanty" must have seemed out of keeping with the notion that God is love. And in noting her efforts to keep from worrying about whether they would be able to survive the winter situated as they were, Mary Carpenter resorted to a text quite alien in spirit from the emerging sunnier views, Matthew 6:34: "Sufficient to the day is the evil thereof." The Carpenters were having to make do without their few books, apparently including the Bible, as well as a good many other things.[55]

Many such people were yet prepared to see their benefactions as deriving from God's purposes. Schoolboy Harry Cooley committed metered moral instruction to his diary, including this standard senti- ment entered probably in the earliest days of 1876:

And lift my heart to God above
In praise for all his wondrous love.

Likewise, when some money came to an Iowa farm couple at the settlement of an estate in Indiana, they acknowledged it "with thanks to God who gives us every good." On a Sunday early in 1873, Uriah Oblinger wrote home from Fillmore County, Nebraska, where he was readying a farm home for his family. He wished he were at church with them, "but our lot is cast otherwise[,] it seems as though we are destined to help make (what was once called the great ameri- can desert) blossom as the rose." The "lot is cast" and "we are destined," but the prospect proved so rapturous that the former soldier turned frontier farmer soon offered this piece of enthusiasm: "surely the hand of Providence must be in this." Surely, the ortho- dox view would have held just that; but it could not have accepted the unstated premise to which Oblinger and the others were drift- ing, that God's purposes did not pertain to the hurtful or ugly.[56]

To equate God with love and good, to exclude the hardship, the suffering, and such problems as Mary Carpenter's "leaky ten foot shanty" from His dominion, amounted to circumscription and denial, however unthinking. Consider the case of a soldier from Brooklyn, a prisoner of war at Andersonville, and the way he misremembered a famous couplet from William Cowper regarding God:

"Behind a smiling Providence
He hides a smiling face."

Perhaps George Hegeman had sometime been exposed to Henry Ward Beecher. His peers of a preceding generation would have been far less likely to make such a slip. To them, it would have come as second nature that it was "frowning Providence" behind which God hid a "smiling face." The upshot of the slips and the shifts could hardly fail to be, to some degree or another, a constricted employment of the godly language.[57]

All in all, that godly language had been appreciably muted, and the war and the West seem to have figured most prominently in working that change. Whatever the causes, the results can be put under two heads, closely related but separable for quick illustration and summary. On one hand, God's agency or Providence suffered neglect; on the other, it suffered at least partial replacement.

Civil War soldiers and westerners showed greatest neglect in ascribing things to God's purposes, but they had ever more company as time passed. In the 1880s Rose Williams and her husband tried settling on the Dakota frontier but soon left for their home area in Ohio. In February 1888, while her husband was away, Rose visited her mother and decided to spend the night. "And O," she wrote to a Dakota friend, "if I had only went home then how different it might be now for now I don't have any home to go to." Their little house at Raccoon Island had been unpretentious at best, but to have it and almost everything they owned destroyed by fire was a disaster indeed. "It seems sometimes I could not stand it." And thus Rose ended the pitiful account, leaving God's purposes to take care of themselves. In 1872 Eliza Nutting of Michigan wrote to a daughter in California brooding because they were so far apart: "we ask why these things must be & echo only answers why." The Massachusetts of Eliza's childhood would have provided a more satisfactory answer than that echo.[58]

In the evening of October 8, 1878, a young mother near Memphis addressed some lines to "My Darling Little Daughter," who lay asleep in a cradle nearby. Julia Raine explained to the baby that mother, father, and child had fled the river city when yellow fever ravaged it. They had gone only as far as Macon, and, alas, the "Grim Distroyer" had now covered the thirty miles to that village. They did not have sufficient money to obtain a team for further flight, and railroad travel was as dangerous as remaining where they were. "Frost," the distraught woman explained to the unheeding baby, "is our only hope which seems far in the distance as to night is as warm

as the middle of July. . . . This is our position to-night, my Baby."
After noting that tomorrow they too might be dead, Julia Raine
began another paragraph: "I cannot bear the thought, darling that I
should be taken away forever without leaving some message for
you, something that when you are grown you can read and think of
as direct from the Mother that you never knew." The poignance
continued, as the mother told her child of the love and care both
parents had lavished upon it. Only very late in this remarkable letter
did God enter, and then only by way of the prayer "that God will
always keep you as innocent as you are now." Julia Raine seems to
have been a religious woman, but here, in most distressing circumstances, God's purposes entered the picture hardly at all.[59]

Other terms and other categories to some degree insinuated
themselves into the place once occupied by God's purposes. Chance,
luck, fortune, fate, destiny—however ill they might comport with
one another—appear far more frequently than before as modes of
expression and explanation. Writing from near Vandalia, Illinois,
Louisa Jane Phifer informed her soldier husband that they had had
"some very bad luck" at the farm she tended in his absence. After
prolonged rain, she heard a crack and looked out to see that the
curbing of the well had given way and windlass and platform were
on their way down. She managed to save some of the rigging, but the
well was ruined. It was, indeed, as she noted again, "awful bad
luck." But then this farm wife called attention to another aspect of the
matter: "it is good luck for Just before I heard it I had thought of going
after water but I did not. And it was good luck for Just about the time I
could have got out there it went down & if I had been on the platform
we would have all went down together." Before closing, Louisa Jane
Phifer invoked roundabout comfort by noting that "we are not the
only ones that has bad luck." Bad luck had preempted the place of
frowning Providence, and good luck appeared clearer than His smiling face.[60]

In the wake of the yellow fever scourge another Memphis woman
penned a poetic relation of the hazards faced by her and her family,
one verse of which tells of her tardiness in getting away from the city:

I was to have followed my Sister
But alas such is fate
Theres many a slip twixt the Cup and the lip
I made up my mind too late.

She fell ill but recovered to poeticize about fate and accident. Amelda Arrowsmith of Burlington, Iowa, wrote her last letter on October 6, 1886, eight days before she died at age thirty. Stationery had by that time come occasionally to bear illustration and embossing. The dying Amelda's displayed a mark of the emergent times, a wishbone crossed by a four-leaf clover. Such decorative touches had a breezy spirit, but a far different tone informs the fervent hope of a destitute farmer-teacher in Arkansas that the Louisiana lottery might ease things somewhat—"a little luck in lottery[,] what a difference it would make."[61]

Early in a new year a young man in Indianapolis wrote to a woman in whom he had more than passing interest to express regret that "fate" had prevented his visiting at holiday season. One sentence in particular figures as a fine surrogate for the sound doctrine of a yesteryear, a performance that calls to mind the often remarked *Hamlet* without the Prince of Denmark. "It was my fate to be sick," he explained, "& wee should never grumble at fortune but meet life with a smile." Ages before Allenson Study crafted that line, the bishop of Hippo lectured Christianity to the effect that the fall of the Roman Empire was "neither fortuitous" nor a matter of "the position of the stars." "Divine providence" handled such matters, as well as everything else: "And if any one attributes their existence to fate, because he calls the will or the power of God itself by the name of fate, let him keep his opinion, but correct his language." The spirit of that urging had been echoed in America by Urian Oakes and many others, and common people had evinced such a view until the Civil War era. By then the providential worldview could not be reasserted by a lecture from Augustine, or from Oakes, Jonathan Edwards, or anyone else. Common Americans remained overwhelmingly a religious people, but that religion no longer rested so firmly and comfortably on the unquestioned assumption that God's purposes were being played out in all that occurred. They found it appreciably more difficult to handle the "problem of problems," as Perry Miller put it, perceiving "the intelligibility of divine providence within the riot of history."[62]

3. *The Drift from the Temple*

The most fundamental aspect of the Christian worldview—the belief in Providence—was waning among common people, and it
followed inexorably that the expressions and practices of religion
would take on a less intense cast. In 1838, when Emerson depicted a
"decaying church and a wasting unbelief" with a gravitation from
the "temple" to the "market" and the "senate," he seems, insofar as
humble Americans were concerned, to have missed the mark somewhat. He made that dark assessment too soon. Had he waited thirty
or forty years he would have been describing the common people, as
well as the elevated among whom he moved. This chapter seeks to
show how the common man's religion, considered as the spirit and
the rituals of accommodation with the stern realities of Providence,
diminished in keeping with that lessened awareness of the role of
Providence in human affairs.[1]

   A. P. Tannehill of Osceola, Missouri, described religion in inel-
egant but time-honored terms in the summer of 1860. He farmed,
taught school, and tried keeping tavern, all of which allowed him to
enjoy "the sweets of poverty." He may have had a cantankerous
streak, and, surely, he saw turbulence looming ever closer for the
nation. Still, religion seemed to endure: "Religion is the sam it all
ways has been[,] that religion that Smooths the paths of life[,]
Supports the totering frame in old age[,] blunts the sting of death[,]

Supports and cheers the troubles and sufferings of a sick bead and furnishes us with delightful and glorious Anticipations of a future world and puts an end to all our Sorrow." One wonders if this man may have later reconsidered. Surely, in almost the same setting he recognized some dangers to religion, especially some of "Yanky dom's" pernicious influences headed by the "Deavle." Whether or not A. P. Tannehill came to hold a darker view, religion as it appeared generally in these humble sources was undergoing appreciable changes. The background, if not precisely the cause, of the two key factors in this unfolding were considered in the two previous chapters—the Civil War and the West.[2]

First, we can note the prevalence of specific observations about the deleterious effect that the war and the West had on religion. As Charles Flanders wrote from camp in Virginia to a friend in upstate New York, "it is posable to live a Christian" in the army, but the very phrasing betokened the "great deal of effort" necessary to do it. Soldiers hit upon this theme times without number, especially on Sundays, which might or might not be days of comparative rest. "In plase of preaching of sabbath morning," an Indiana soldier wrote home, "wee have inspection of arms and in stead of evening meeting wee have battalion drill." Very frequently, such men employed a usage of the past in referring to religious matters in terms of privileges. Elias M. Wood tried to "swim against the curent to live a religious life in the army," and so it pleased him much to have a brief stay in Cairo, Illinois, where he had the "great privalage to be where I can attend meeting." But, as we shall see later, the very connotation of privilege and meeting were making the alteration to modern secularity, so much so that one young man assured the woman he would later marry that, although a soldier, he did not "hate" the "holy word" she taught in her Sunday school at home.[3]

Spiritual things did not always go swimmingly at home either in these times. From Locke, New York, came the disheartening report not only of sickness and death among children in the first war winter but also of the inability of the Methodists "to keep up a Sunday school" for want of attendants. The war, Annis Pierce reminded her relative in Wisconsin, "takes the place of every thing els in the mind." Later in the war, when protracted meeting time came to Hendrysburg, Ohio, a resident there ruefully reported that many in the community "thinks our meeting will not do much good for this hole country is nothing but war." The situation must have been much the same in many other places. As has been noted, such a perception needs to be qualified when considering the South. Still, in general terms, people saw the war as disrupting religion, and probably they were right.[4]

They saw much the same in the West. In 1864 a Michigan black-smith's daughter wrote her sister about a brother's imminent marriage. These people had gone west from Massachusetts only a few years before, and so Nellie Nutting, herself not a practicing Christian, slipped easily into the ritual comparison of "how much harder it is to live a Christian life than at home down east there it was expected you would hear religion talked of and we did but here it is very seldom you ever hear it excepting sabbaths of course." That refrain sounded almost endlessly. In 1872 a North Carolina couple wrote home from Neosho County, Kansas, to report among other things their "greatest objection" to the new home—that the western people "dont appear to know when sunday comes only to go fishing and hunting and spending the sabbath vainly and unholy." And a man in Factoryville, Pennsylvania, whose son had become a railroad worker in the West, received a similar report of the situation at Grand Island Station in Nebraska in 1867. Sunday, Benjamin Smith learned from his son, "is not respected at all" there. California epitomized the phenomenon, and, as one argonaut put it in 1860, "how quick a man looses his vows and love of Religion in this land of crime and gold."[5]

Of course, that smacks of what Herman Melville had put in dolorous terms a decade earlier and of what Mark Twain expressed more nearly in levity a decade later. It partakes of that "temper of the West" depicted by visitor James Bryce a bit later yet and by various others. When realistic novelist Harold Frederic completed the story of *The Damnation of Theron Ware*, he had that fallen Methodist minister making a perfectly understandable move in exchanging upstate New York for Seattle, Washington Territory. There, Theron Ware would work for a land and real estate company and keep an eye on political opportunities. What figures importantly for us is that changing religious reality caught the attention of common people as well. They perceived it clearly.

Some common people, encountering the most intense drama of their times, pronounced it baneful to religion. Many others con-

veyed that view not in denotative assertion of reality but in connota-
tive betrayal of reality. Religion and the privileges it involved—to
use the term so frequently employed theretofore—were waning and
undergoing alteration. The changing use of terms and expressions
betokens what was afoot.

The word *privilege* had very often been used as a general covering
term for religious observance of some formal or sanctioned nature.
With various qualifiers, of course, the word could apply to many
things; but standing alone, it betokened the religious dimension of
existence. This usage was changing. Far less frequently does one
find it used as Sarah Morse did in writing to relatives from the new
home near Genoa Bluffs, Iowa, in 1862. Things were starting to look
"*deasant*" for her family, especially, as Sarah pointed out, because
now they could "improve" their "precious privileges." The context
leaves no doubt whatever as to what Sarah Morse had in mind; she
spoke as the generation before her had spoken. Almost needless to
say, such things endured as objects of regard and solicitude, and it
may not be stretching the matter too far to illustrate with a diary kept
by a Texas cowhand on a trail drive in 1871. Nearing the destination
of Schuyler, Nebraska, T. C. Oatts encountered a standard difficulty
with a farmer who resented Oatts's bringing a part of the herd to
water that the farmer wanted for his own livestock. The cowhand
met the diplomatic challenge first by pretending not to hear the
farmer's protestations. Instead, he began to ask questions about this
"naborhood": "do you have Sabith Schools & Preaching and all
sutch questions as thease and stil riding on & the cattle folowg me."
Soon the farmer was "in good umer," evidently enjoying that discussion of what had been known as privileges. The trail hand got his
cattle watered, and the farmer had a good conversation.[6]

Things did not always work out so satisfactorily. As indicated
very generally before, the army experience taught people to get
along without privileges. For an extreme case we can look over the
shoulder of a Connecticut prisoner in what he styled that "God
forsaken place," Andersonville. "One cant help but think," Henry
Savage wrote on a Sunday in June 1864, "of home and the priveleges
there on the Sabbath while here we have to lay in idleness." Confederate soldier H. J. Hightower suffered little idleness while serving in
General James Longstreet's command in early 1864, but he too bemoaned in characteristic way the loss of those "blessed priviledges
which we use to injoy."[7]

Soldiers often made such complaints, but they also tended to alter the acceptation of the word *privilege*. It came to connote things other than the "blessed." Those men who served however long during the Civil War appropriated some of the language of that highly secular setting. That language often had a formal or quasi-legal tone, and the widely adopted expression for something of importance—the order of the day—provides a handy illustration. In telling his wife that there was no chance of getting a substitute to serve in his place, a Mississippi soldier put it in terms that probably involved official restriction: "We are debarred of all Such privilleges." Illinois soldier James Forbes used less formal terminology when he went on temporary duty with an Ohio artillery unit near Nashville, an assignment that pleased him much. He now had "good officers" and a "tip top set of boys" with whom to serve: "besides that we have more privileges. we can run around as much as we please and have horses to ride." In the army it became easy to think of privileges as a matter more of being able to "run around as much as we please" than of churchly function and even obligation.[8]

Soldiers led the way, but others soon followed as *privilege* was drawn more and more into the language of secular discourse. At the end of an 1868 diary, a Seneca County, New York, woman wished for an easier way to exchange thoughts than by letter writing, but, she concluded, "we must make the best use we can of the pen, and be thankful for the privelege." In Chariton, Iowa, five years later a woman referred to a recent letter as "cheering to the mind and a great privalige." Writing from a North Carolina camp meeting in the summer of 1882, Callie Coble bemoaned not having seen the sister to whom she wrote when that sister made a visit in the area. For all the privilege that Callie must have been enjoying, she used the word to apply to the unrealized chance to see her sister. That had been the "privilege," and she had missed it.[9]

Though acceptable, these usages show that a particular word, so often confined by common people to the realm of spiritual benefaction, was being used far more indiscriminately. Perhaps humble people were becoming more aware of the significance of what the very word *privilege*, or private right, meant. The idea of the individual was growing among these lesser sorts, and their rights and liberties, which they were coming to perceive and pronounce, at least hesitantly, comported more with the dictionary definition of *privilege* than did the spiritual obligations and activities of a previous time.

Privilege was becoming just another secular word. Looking back from the 1880s on her difficult early years in Michigan, Lettie Pennoyer wrote of having lost her "school priveleges" when the family had made a move to a new home. Now also, the word sometimes appeared to mean no more than opportunity or chance. Prompted by Federal troops, renegade Manson Jolly fled the troubled Anderson area of South Carolina in 1866. Writing as "R. E. D. Horse" while on his way to Shreveport, Jolly told his sister that he had the "priveledge" to let her know that he was well, meaning apparently that an opportunity had presented itself to get off a few lines during his trek to the West. By the same token, when one wished to specify the religious arena, one felt more and more the need to attach some qualifier to the word *privilege*. Former soldier Uriah Oblinger left Indiana in 1872 for Nebraska with an eye to making a new home for his small family. After lengthy description of the chosen location in Fillmore County, Uriah discussed the religious condition so that wife Mattie could see what "church privileges" awaited her. Previously, such people needed the qualifier only when something other than church was involved.[10]

Uriah Oblinger was foreshadowing the view of the "secular modern" as depicted by Joseph Haroutunian in 1932. Oblinger offered a premonition of the inclination to speak of the " 'religious interpretation of life,' " to quote Haroutunian, as if it were only one among several or many. Other terms of less central significance than *privilege* underwent similar transformations, generally losing the distinctly spiritual resonance they had previously had. Times of spiritual lassitude, for example, had often been referred to as dull, but now that word applied more to the marketplace than the temple. In 1869 the word was used in typical fashion in far northern California. As C. H. Essy of Cottonwood described it, "times are quite dull here at this time. produce is very low." California might lead the way in such secularization of language, but people elsewhere were not far behind. Joel Triplett reported much the same from northern Missouri in the dull year of 1874: "Times pretty dull health good money scarce." *Dull*—so commonly employed theretofore to castigate spiritual lethargy—was moving from that frame of reference to that of produce and scarce money.[11]

An antonym of *dull* was making a similar move. Previously, the word *interesting*, applicable, of course, to almost anything, had appeared in special concentration in the religious sphere. An interesting condition in another person might well involve that person's having come under spiritual conviction. An interesting child often proved to be one brought face to face with ultimate matters by serious illness or imminent death. To be sure, religion yet had interesting facets, as an "interesting prayer meeting" attended by an upstate New York village postmaster in 1861. But the term *interesting* no longer had particular aptness and application in discussion of religion; it was moving elsewhere. Nothing serves better to illustrate than discussion of children. Such matters will bear treatment elsewhere, and one illustration will suffice here. In an after Christmas letter of 1883, a man in Superior, Wisconsin, waxed happily about his two little girls: "I tell you Susie and Flossie are getting to be quite interesting. Susie is so sharp about everything and Flossie is beginning to talk considerable." Previously, the child that was dying had been seen as particularly interesting; now it was the one that was considered "sharp," or active, or alert, or, least supportable to this modern reader, cunning.[12]

The religious connotation of very simple ways of speaking was giving way. The most rudimentary solicitude or informative urge required a remark or a question as to how the writers or recipients of letters were enjoying themselves. There, too, resided a religious resonance. Previously, that had involved soul and spirit, but that dimension was decreasing appreciably. An 1868 letter from an Indiana woman to a cousin in North Carolina clearly echoes the old form. The writer assured her relative: "we are trying to do the best we can to live and not forget god and his promises," and "we are trying to enjoying [sic] our selves as christian people." That tone was giving way to a breezier one. Civil War soldiers showed an especial adeptness at noting how they enjoyed themselves, providing unadorned and not always candid assurances to loved ones. Only rarely does one find the intimation of religion that once colored such comments. A Vermont soldier followed standard form in leaving a trail of descriptions of enjoyment from enlistment camp in Burlington to camp near Richmond in the peninsula campaign: "I am in good health, generally enjoy myself pretty well."[13]

Across the continent in El Monte, California, Jane Whiteman Dallas informed a sister of how she was getting along in her new setting. "I have," she wrote, "enjoied myself to my satisfaction since

I came here." In bringing *enjoy* and *satisfy* together, this writer compounded the potential for religious commentary, but that potential went unrealized. *Satisfied*, too, had had an important place in the spiritual vocabulary, and a very devout Alabama soldier struck that chord in a letter to his wife. After some advice about the farm and urging that she kiss the children for him, Elijah Odom asked wife Sarah to write soon to tell how things were at home "& how you are satisfied in particular." That matter of a satisfied mind attesting to spiritual resignation was falling into disuse; being satisfied was coming to connote a simple fact of the world. Unlike Elijah Odom, who retained the older association, some Confederate soldiers at Richmond gave lip service to the older usage. In a group letter each man in turn professed to be "well satisfied" or even "verry well satisfied," but Bennet Parten indicated in his part of the letter how he might become even more so. If he had some of that "good old peatch brandy" made by the man to whom he wrote, he would "gest mak hit fly." Indeed, if he and his friends had a barrel of that brandy they could "snatch evry yankee in the north baldhedded."[14]

Satisfaction, enjoyment, and the other expressions discussed above would not qualify as "keywords," to use Raymond Williams's collapsed term. The changed usage, however, might well qualify as what Williams refers to as "a process quite central in the development of a language when, in certain words, tones and rhythms, meanings are offered, felt for, tested, confirmed, asserted, qualified, changed." Surely, in the case of the people used for this study the "critical encounters" of meaning did not take place at a "very conscious" level, as Williams notes that they can. Rather, those encounters occurred in such a way as to "be felt only as a certain strangeness and unease" by the modern reader who finds that common words were shifting in their acceptations. As they shifted, they registered not just "the process quite central in the development of a language" but also the process quite central in the alteration of basic attitudes and patterns of thought. The meaning of words can hardly change without changing the way we view the world.[15]

For example, the seeming near abandonment of the most basic division of reality into the realm of the spiritual and the realm of the temporal has significance. Writing to the husband who had unwisely followed his son into the Union army, Elizabeth Stevens of Oskaloosa, Iowa, offered a blend of encouragement and sermon incorporating the old duality: "o, my dear Simeon, if you [k]now the anxiety I feel both for your spiritual and temperal wellfare, it would stimulate you to duty." Mrs. Stevens employed a usage that had become rare. One might contend that that usage remained firmly in mind but had become neglected in statement, possibly because it seemed self-evident. This construction does not satisfy because these people had little if any dread of the trite. Somehow, it was not occurring to them to make that rudimentary separation. The word *spiritual* remained in common use, but not in the formulation that Mrs. Stevens employed, or that the present author employed as the organizational framework for a book on pre–Civil War popular thought. Now the word *spiritual* generally stood alone, not in dominance over its lesser vis-à-vis or even in equipoise with it. *Spiritual* meant no more than an aspect of existence, an aspect suffering ever greater confinement.[16]

The word *temporal* slipped, by and large, from common use, no longer having to serve as the dark, logical counterweight to what had been, as the biblical allusion of the previous generation had so often put it, the one thing needful. Noah Webster, that guide and monitor of American language and thought, gave the following as the primary definition of the adjective *temporal*: "Pertaining to this life, or this world, or the body only; as *temporal* concerns; *temporal* affairs. In this sense, it is opposed to SPIRITUAL. Let not *temporal* affairs or employments divert the mind from spiritual concerns, which are far more important." As late as the 1862 edition, Webster's wisdom and piety echoed that refrain. Dictionaries change, and the vestiges of Webster's values that would inform the spirit of a later age place this definition—"In this sense, it is opposed to SPIRIT-UAL."—in a secondary position, duly deprived, of course, of the moralizing the master had attached to it.

Changes of definition betoken larger changes, and those larger changes become more evident when attention is directed to the ways in which common people wrote about spiritual events and practices. Here we are dealing not with subtle shifts of verbal usage but with the content and intensity of what unsophisticated people wrote about religious occasions. Religious observances continued, of course, in some ways with even greater frequency than before. They did not, however, command the attention they previously had. From being nearly the raison d'être of much humble writing, religion sank to the level of a subject frequently mentioned, for some, of course, dutifully mentioned. As ever, there was a season to all things. In the earlier period one occasionally finds the word *season* standing alone and unqualified, simply to designate a time of spiritual intensity. Research for the present study uncovered no such usage. There was yet a season to all things, but now there were many things.

Innumerable religious gatherings continued much as before, and the very word *meeting* by itself probably would have still been taken as referring to the religious dimension. Surely, that had been the case in the prewar generation. The old form still appears, as when Angeline Van Scyoc of Ohio told her brother that she would "always expect to attend my meeting as long as I have my health," or as when Sarah Clendenen of Troy, Iowa, happily reported that her husband, James, had become "a grait hand for meettings." But there were fewer of those "grait hands for meettings" than there had once been. Here again, the war and the West were doing their work. From frontier Phoenix in 1876 George Loring wrote home to New England to tell, among other things, of a meeting he had attended the previous evening. James Bryce would have nodded knowingly at Loring's remark that "we had quite a long chat about business . . . before we got to religion."[17]

Young Loring was not an irreligious man, but he failed here to give any religious intimation of the spirit informing that ostensibly religious gathering. Here as elsewhere a casual and even at times flippant tone surfaced in such accounts. When a young woman in Trousdale County, Tennessee, told a friend of the "fine time" she meant to have at a forthcoming meeting, the context left no doubt that she referred to a realm other than the spiritual. A couple of her counterparts in Indiana playfully told a third of the "distracted" meeting that was under way in one of the local churches, then urged that third person to join them. They would go to a night meeting "and ——— git ——— a ——— beau." With Christmas and the three fights precipitated by its celebration now past in Plainview, Minnesota, young farmer and part-time frontier soldier Austin Carrell noted in his diary that he had attended meeting. He probably felt no uneasiness in punctuating that revelation with the droll question, "hant I good?"[18]

People had less to say about their meetings. What they did say has a less earnest and reverent tone. More and more, other considerations intruded upon or overlapped with the strictly devotional. The religious sphere is perhaps never free from adulterations, but the adulterations certainly seem to have been increasing. The young watchmaker just starting on the road to success in Phoenix encountered that situation, as business made good its claim before religion received its due. Things other than business diminished the Argus-eyed attention that had once been given to the enhancement of the spiritual condition.

On an April Sunday in 1879 in Broome County, New York, young Clifford Pierce wrote in his diary: "Went to Temperance Prayer meeting at the lodge rooms in afternoon." Categories were becoming complicated. Pierce had to designate the gathering as a prayer meeting because it was held in the quarters of a village lodge he had joined. He had to qualify further because the prayer was being channeled to a specific and not precisely spiritual purpose, temperance. A YMCA meeting at the lodge rooms a couple of months later might well have occasioned similar wonderment as to just what purpose was foremost. Four days after that YMCA meeting, when another Sunday entry appears, we are not certain what construction to place upon the passage: "lay around the house went down and opened the Lodge room for the meeting." What was the nature of that meeting? Was it lodge, temperance, prayer, or all three? If the writings of such people as these yielded anything more than the dimmest prefigurings, if that, of the Social Gospel movement, those might also be channeled into this wonderment. As it is, we can see that the crucial imperative was yielding to intrusions. Ruben Abbott of Creston, Iowa, went too far in grumbling about the state of meetings in his area at what should have been the revival time at the end of 1870. "Meating at dances is the topic of the day," he complained; "Religion is al most out of fashion." He may have exaggerated, but what he said was not entirely out of keeping with what others were saying or betraying.[19]

The discussion of meetings suffered attenuation, and the specifying of the central feature of most of those meetings—the sermon text—waned accordingly. When working in prewar sources I quickly formed the habit of keeping a King James Version of the Bible at hand at all times. Biblical citations made that desirable, and the propensity for specifying sermon texts made it all but necessary. In the present research that habit gave way to an occasional resort to a Bible, a concordance, or a book of quotations. Changes in a researcher's habits offer some roundabout testimony to alterations in patterns of thought.

Some people, of course, did what they could to defy the alterations. On the evening of December 6, 1868, carpenter and millworker John K. Baldwin of rural Bladen County, North Carolina, married Susan Cain. Earlier on that Sunday he attended church, and he duly recorded the text of the "sermond," 2 Timothy 4:2. It was probably James Cashwell, the man who performed the marriage ceremony that evening, who dilated on that challenging passage: "Preach the word; be instant in season, out of season; reprove, rebuke, exhort with all longsuffering and doctrine." Twenty-two-year-old former soldier Baldwin did far more than most in remaining "instant," or, in modern terms, constant. According to Timothy's next verse, "the time will come when they will not endure sound doctrine," apparently a needless worry in John K. Baldwin's case but not in others. Preacher James Cashwell had a growingly unfashionable orientation to the Old Testament, and in the months thereafter he used Jeremiah, Proverbs, and Ecclesiastes to edify the Baldwins and others. A conclusive urging of the May 2, 1869, "surmond" came from Ecclesiastes 12:13, "Fear God, and keep his commandments: for this is the whole duty of men."[20]

On a Saturday evening nearly two years later, Baldwin went to "Preaching," but he did not arrive "in time to here the text." The previous generation had deemed it important to make those specifications, though many times a telling blank betrayed the difficulty of getting the text home and committed to writing. In the spring of 1878, a farmer in Madison County, New York, wrote "the text" and then left a space that never got filled. His next lines provide the slightly misquoted gist of what he had failed to identify: "Little foxes spoil the vines." Just how his preacher had embroidered upon that passage from Song of Solomon 2:15 would be interesting to know. The diarist, Benjamin Cloyes, sought in his faulted way to maintain the old form. So many more were now doing so much less.[21]

Insofar as one can generalize about the ever-lessening textual citations, it seems safe to offer three guarded observations. First, as was suggested earlier, the emphasis seems to have been more and more on New Testament passages. Some years before he had had that chance to contemplate the Old Testament text from Song of Solomon, farmer Benjamin Cloyes entered a sermon text that perhaps better suited emergent times, John 8:11: "Neither do I condemn thee: go, and sin no more." In Seneca County, not far to the west, young housewife Mary Jacacks delighted in hearing sermons in the nearby village. In 1868 a visit to relatives in New Jersey provided a chance to hear Henry Ward Beecher in his Brooklyn church. Jacacks duly specified the text, one that avoids even the partial untidiness of John 8:11. Beecher enlarged upon Titus 2:14 wherein we are called to recognize Him "Who gave himself for us, that he might redeem us from all iniquity, and purify unto himself a peculiar people, zealous of good works." That involved a prospect so pleasing as often to have escaped an earlier, more dour generation of unelevated Americans.[22]

In turn, it seems that texts were coming more often to reflect immediate circumstances than had been the case before. Doctrine— most centrally the residue of Calvinistic orthodoxy, which nearly all of these people had imbibed—was in retreat. A pragmatic and heuristic sanction seems now more often to have influenced the choice of the text. Of course, from the earliest moments of our history preachers occasionally selected texts pregnant with meaning for the moment. But they also had a strong inclination to put their flocks over doctrinal hurdles, just to keep them lean and limber in a way that Moses Coit Tyler sadly saw in abrupt decline in the late nineteenth century.[23]

The war may well have hastened that development. Impatient people who came to question many things most likely expected practical messages. In September 1862 a disheartened Mary Labrant wrote to her soldier husband, including word of a Methodist meeting she had recently attended. With war news "so discuraging," Mary probably found it all the more appropriate to offer details of what may have been Exodus 33:14: "the text read as folows but i cant tel where it is. and he said unto him i will be with you and my presance shall give you rest." Perhaps Jonathan Labrant would need such comfort. Amos Ames, a captured Iowa corporal on his way to Andersonville, wrote very little about religion in his diary, but when a "rebel preacher" addressed the prisoners on "*Daniel in the lion's den*" Ames judged it "*very appropriate*." Andersonville diaries do not have the fullness of spiritual content one might expect, but William

H. Jackson of Connecticut, who seems to have recorded more than he internalized, kept a diary that reflects the instructive nature of what he heard. In July 1864 he heard, for example, sermons from 1 Timothy 6:12, "Fight the good fight of faith," and from Romans 14:12, "So then every one of us shall give account of himself to God."[24]

The timeliness of such messages suggests a final aspect of the sermonizing of this period as it is reflected in humble writings. That involves, to use the words of David S. Reynolds, a "shift in homiletic style" from "doctrine" to "narrative." In Iowa, for example, both ends of the Protestant spectrum revealed the change essentially in the way that Reynolds's depiction of more elevated sources suggests. In Belle Plaine late in 1870 Anna Furnas told of the new preacher and his attractive ways. She showed no uneasiness that the newcomer had gained the sobriquet "the clown" because of his once having been a circus performer. He had, she continued, a voice "like thunder," and he told "a good many stories &c &c." Fifty miles to the east in Iowa City, the university town, one had access to more refined fare. Adaline Jones, wife of a grocery store employee, heard some of that more liberal religion on Sundays in March 1880, a good sermon on the life of William Ellery Channing and a "grand sermon" on the life of Theodore Parker.[25]

Milo Cooley, a Connecticut soldier turned Iowa carpenter, had a chance to hear a noteworthy visitor at the "Oppera" house at Independence in 1878. T. De Witt Talmage of Central Presbyterian Church of Brooklyn, New York, had come to town to say a bit about "The bright side of things." The sometimes sensational Talmage figured prominently in a bevy of "Princes of the Pulpit," making Brooklyn almost a showplace as well as a focal point for that "shift in homiletic style" to which Reynolds refers. Sadly, we know nothing of how Milo Cooley reacted to "The bright side of things." This Iowa triangulation of Belle Plaine, Iowa City, and Independence—of "the clown," the Reverend Mr. Clute, and visitor Talmage—has, for all its seeming variety, a decided commonality in its leisurely drift from doctrine.[26]

Some four years later, Milo Cooley, now returned to his native Connecticut, again had an opportunity to hear Talmage and others who made Brooklyn a homiletic hotbed. At the end of 1882 carpenter Cooley took a temporary job in that city, and he brought the year to a close by hearing, on New Year's eve, Talmage in the morning and Henry Ward Beecher in the afternoon. In the weeks ahead he heard both of them again, and he added to the list of notable sermonizers by hearing Beecher's son-in-law Samuel Scoville, apparently visiting from his church in Norwich, Connecticut. After hearing Scoville in the morning, he listened in the afternoon to Hugh Pentecost, a preacher not yet embarked on an erratic course into Christian social- ism. Cooley also heard Richard Salter Storrs of the Church of the Pilgrims, who had difficulty accommodating fully with the breezier, more spontaneous ways. Perhaps that helps explain how Storrs eventually became president of the American Historical Association, addressing in 1896 some remarks to that body on the significance of the "modest, unnoticed men" of America. Unfortunately, Storrs neglected Cooley, who had come to hear him on January 28, 1883.[27]

The drift away from sound doctrine and toward sunnier mes- sages and stories seems apparent among the comfortable and so- phisticated. Evidently, much of the same was occurring among "modest, unnoticed" Americans. Thus on the first Sunday of 1884 another Connecticut worker, mill worker Hattie Mason, heard a sermon on "fools of the bible." Not far away in time and place, Nettie Comins heard sermons on Absalom, "the fast young man of the bible," and on Samson, "the physical giant and moral dwarf of the bible." Whether in Iowa, Brooklyn, or Connecticut that shift in hom- iletic style continued. Though well meant and perhaps invigorating, it might be seen by some as all the more reason why one Brother Childers in Callaway County, Missouri, chose to preach from Acts 2:40: "save yourselves from this untoward generation." Diarist Nancy Holeman took pains to specify that text, but she had also to note that her husband had "staid at home." As it was recorded in 2 Timothy 4:3, "the time will come when they will not endure sound doctrine."[28]

In the devotional realm of prayer much the same was occurring. Of course, genuinely prayerful material in diaries and letters is, ordinarily, not great. Thus it might appear that these people were, on the face of it, no less devout than their predecessors. One might even incline to the opposite conclusion in reckoning with the supera- bundant appeals to God to bring an end to the Civil War. But given the circumstances, what they did falls short of what Tennyson re- ferred to as "battering the gates of heaven with storms of prayer."

Also, these appeals had as their purpose not accommodation but amelioration. They sought to end suffering more than they sought the means to endure it.

Here also, one occasionally encounters words suggesting that feminization, as analyzed by Ann Douglas, was beginning to have some currency among people less sophisticated than those she studied. Writing from Petersburg, Virginia, in July 1864, a Union soldier told his sister of the much-remarked uncertainties of war, including one's own survival. "I am thankful I am spaired and can say so in words," he noted, "but not in prayer. I have a mother who will and can say so in prayer and feel she is not a hipocrit by so doing which I could not do." Such items do not abound, but perhaps they betray the beginning of a separation of spheres that did not characterize humble writings in the prewar period. In those one does not get the impression that women were seen as speaking the language of prayer while men were seen as speaking the language of words, even the words of a "hipocrit." Ann Douglas has contended that between 1820 and 1875 "American culture seemed bent on establishing a perpetual Mother's Day." Surely, she overstates the case of common people, especially in the early part of that period, but intimations had started to appear. In 1887 a man whose father had died at Andersonville wrote from Ashland, Kansas, back to the woman he sought to marry. He told her that one of his employers had recently gone to Kentucky for his mother's funeral. That man returned to Kansas a more religious man, and the writer noted how the two of them now got together to discuss their "mothers and religion."[29]

Whatever the significance of such items, a less arguable alteration can be seen in the decrease in soulful and prayerful exercises when a diary or letter marked the end of a year or a birthday. Upstate New York farmer Benjamin Cloyes, whom we saw trying to salvage a recollection of a passage regarding little foxes, had sufficient years behind him to recall and to some degree practice that December 31 spiritual accounting. At age sixty in 1878 he ended the year with literal prayer: "our father in heaven I desire to come ni to the at this time to render my thanks unto the for thy watchful care . . . all prases be renderd Amen." Down in Delaware County, Alonzo Teed had come on the scene far later, and his generation showed much more inclination to bring a diary year to a close with simply "the end of the year." A Hoosier's "Good-by 1880" has the emerging ring.[30]

Such abruptness seems all the more telling because the turn of the year had added spiritual attraction for being located within the season of revival and protracted meeting. For an essentially agricultural people economic demands lessened, and the availability of time and the rigors of the season combined to put people in a proper frame of mind to get themselves in spiritual order. The peaks and valleys of American religious life retained a seasonal pattern, with the wintry protracted meeting and, to a lesser degree, the late summer or early fall camp meeting still figuring as the central events. Those oscillations still appear in this period from 1860 to 1890, but the pattern traced has a lower profile year-round and less abrupt and intense peaks where once those protracted meetings and camp meetings had lifted so many to rapture. Regarding these central events of spiritual enhancement, perfunctoriness was settling upon the land.

As 1873 commenced, a twenty-six-year-old farm laborer near Johnstown, New York, mentioned in his diary the onset of some prayer meetings and then a protracted meeting that got under way on the sixth day of the new year. Marvin Snell was dying, and, whether because of or in spite of that fact, he recorded what so many others had recorded before him. What effect some few opium pills, secured for him by a glovemaking sister, may have had upon Marvin Snell's religious awareness must be left to conjecture. That difficult winter along the Mohawk hastened Snell to his grave, though until very near the end he made brief notes in the diary that may well have been bought to relieve his idleness. Life was somewhat more pleasant in a small town in southern Iowa that winter and spring. A woman there happily reported to a sister that they had had "a big time" with "religious revivals," though not without some difficulty and frustration. It appears that the various churches of the neighborhood had "tried it separate and couldn't seem to get much excitement." Then, concluding that "thare was strength in Union," they held combined meetings for three weeks with generally salutary effect.[31]

People yet kept an appreciative eye on such matters, but the vigor and intensity were departing. More and more the reports appear in low-keyed if not quite nonchalant form, and they appear less frequently. Perhaps that attitude reflected, at least in part, the growing awareness and intrusion of the attractions of the outside world that dwarfed and trivialized local events and meetings taking place in

Johnstown, New York, or Afton, Iowa. Main Street, whether of the middle border or elsewhere, still had great vitality, but, as will be discussed more fully later, its denizens showed markedly increased interest in such essentially national figures as Henry Ward Beecher.

In the centennial year a California woman went east to visit her family and made a brief stop at the Philadelphia Exposition. A relative of modest means secured tickets to an evening performance of "the great German composer Offenbach and his celebrated band of one hundred." That event at the Hippodrome impressed Lois Dane as "very fine and grand," but she confessed that she "would much rather have heard" Moody and Sankey, who had recently held a "great meeting" there. The fare in small towns in Massachusetts, Michigan, and California that Lois Dane knew would have suffered severely in comparison to that offered by that "Prince of the Pulpit" Dwight L. Moody and the sacred songster Ira D. Sankey. In Topeka, Kansas, Mattie Shaw, a newly wed and recent arrival from a rural area, heard the *"great"* evangelist Moody at least three times when he visited there in 1889, and she judged his farewell sermon to be "just splendid." On a sad visit to Chicago five months later to see her gravely ill husband, Mattie Shaw became ill herself, so much so that she was a semiformal occupant of the hospital where her husband convalesced. Tonsillitis was no laughing matter, and Mattie Shaw knew that she took "a big risk" when she "slipped away" to walk to where Moody performed on his home ground.[32]

While Mattie Shaw was in Chicago, a "great protracted meeting" was entering its third week and was moving to larger quarters in Fort Worth, Texas. Surely, as Mrs. T. W. Chapman pointed out, the presiding preacher was doing much good: "I think he is a little ahead of Mr. Sam. Jones." Very likely he had yet a way to go to overtake that Georgia Methodist, who had come to be known as the "Moody of the South." Mrs. Dane and Mrs. Chapman were coming to know the benchmarks of their time. What they saw immediately about them they judged against larger-than-life models, with whatever corrosive effect.[33]

The Chapmans and Danes illustrate another of the emergent realities of the religious situation as it is reflected in humble writings. Unlike the pre-war period, men's writings seem less concerned with the spiritual dimension than they previously were and than were those of their female counterparts in the war and postwar years. At summer's end of 1868 Robert E. Chapman of Mississippi heard from a friend or relative in Franklin County, Arkansas. In that letter Charles W. Hicks awkwardly reported a barbecue he had attended and a "democrat speach" he had heard. In treating these exciting matters, Hicks did not limit himself to events immediately at hand. He went afield to "frogbio" to an event of which he had heard but had not attended: "They had good speaking their they turned some of the rads to democracy." Such matters will be treated more later, but here we can note Hicks's turning from converting some "rads" to a more noncommittal report of religious action: "Their is a presbyterion protrakted meting a going to comence here to morrow I hope it wil be a good meting." Hicks not only reported that protracted meeting; he wished it well and meant to attend. His fuller involvement, however, went to those barbecues and speeches whereby "rads" might be brought to the true faith.[34]

In that same summer Lois Dane received a sister's account of religious affairs in Decatur, Michigan, where a revival was being enjoyed. Ada Baker took pains to specify that it had affected the women of her congregation, and "such *good* meetings" were being held: "we have *very* few male members in our church & that makes so much difference & we do have such good female prayer meetings." Far more appreciably than before the war, we can see that much-remarked feminization of religion, or at least that separation of spheres so relentlessly remarked by late twentieth-century historians if not always practiced by their nineteenth-century ancestors.[35]

However imperative it may have seemed to convert some of those "rads" in northwest Arkansas, people wrote little about religious conversion itself. Time and again, the previous generation betrayed its fascination with that matter by references to an individual's being in an "interesting" condition, or a "thoughtful" condition, or some such. Those and similar usages betokening a spiritual situation hanging in the balance become exceedingly rare in the postwar period. Whatever people might now write about religion contained next to nothing of those telltale signs by which an earlier age gauged a person's readiness for full spiritual involvement. Now, to a far greater degree, we find, for example, bare numbers, "fifteen converts I beleave," at a spring revival at Afton, Iowa. On a January first in California James Colby admonished a son to "commence a New Life." He did not mean a spiritual rebirth but rather the simple matter of whether young John would become "a good man or a bad man." Colby wrote in secular terms, and transcendent categories entered only by way of "God forbid" that John should become other than a good man. Now and again, also, we find the theme of male imperviousness, and Ada Baker pronounced it well a few months after that religious excitement in Decatur, Michigan. "Why is it," she asked, "that after so many years of life together our influence for Christ is not manifest by our husbands coming & walking with us— perhaps it is to learn us a lesson of patience 'Learn to labor & wait.'" Interestingly, Ada Baker here appropriated, not a holy text but a line from Longfellow's famous "A Psalm of Life."[36]

Holy texts became less evident, and so did strictures directed at other sects or denominations. In general terms, the more vague and vestigial the once Puritan Protestantism became, the less intense the suspicion of ancient enemies. Universalism, for example, received fewer animadversions, most likely because others were semiconsciously gravitating to the very position for which Universalists had once been reviled. "D——n the place and Mormons too," a small-time freighter wrote from the country east of Salt Lake, "I am getting disgusted with the whole institution." Lorenzo Chillson may not have been the only disgusted observer, but most people managed to write a good deal without damning the Mormons or anyone else.[37]

Spiritualism seems to have aroused less intense interest than it did in the prewar years, except perhaps in the far West. James Bryce betrayed awe if not admiration at the readiness of "shrewd" westerners to "relapse into the oldest and most childish forms of superstition. Fortune-telling, clairvoyance, attempts to pry by the help of 'mediums' into the book of fate, are so common in parts of the West that newspapers devote a special column, headed 'astrologers,' to the advertisements of these wizards and pythonesses." "Enough about spirits," an exasperated John Hyde wrote to his father in 1868 from Sonora, California. Hyde had had enough because his partner had come to rely, not wisely but too well, on the guidance of spirits, much to the detriment of their business. Bryce summed up the matter with the old formula "the less faith the more superstition."[38]

If one cannot discern more superstition, one can at least detect more observance of holidays. In some superficial way those observances, or at least references, might suggest a greater religious vitality. Evidently, that was not the case. The observance of Sunday, for example, was now taking on for many the added dimension of Sunday school, a fairly new development for humble people and one that was lauded widely and generously. It is well to remember, however, that Sunday schools represented a mixture and an accommodation. They did more, other, or less than propagate truth and sound doctrine. That churchly functions should act in such a way is hardly new, and a young man in Bullock County, Alabama, was not writing in an untoward way in asking an acquaintance in Texas about pretty girls out there and moving immediately from that subject into a question about Sunday schools. The austere and contemplative Sunday so cherished by some was giving way, and the Sunday school legitimized the change. In San Francisco, Rebecca Colby happily reported that at her next Sunday school meeting there would be a picnic, then added the comforting information, "they are always having picnics and parties."[39]

A noteworthy illustration of the blend that Sunday schools involved appears in a long letter of an Indiana woman in 1868. Margaret Fields informed friends and family back in North Carolina, not just about a single Sunday school but about a gathering of Sunday schools. She told of banners, of decorated horses and carriages, and of the bands of music accompanying the displays of the various communities in that area west of Indianapolis. She gave details of the Sunday school her own family attended near Clayton. Evidently, more than the purely spiritual was served, and Fields proudly told of her own son's progress: "he spells in the class at sonday scool by hart . . . they ar taking the most pains to educate children here i ever saw rich and poor." That would strike most of us as laudable, as perhaps would the patriotic motifs such as displays of "stairs and stripes" and speeches by the "scollars."[40]

Religion itself must have received some attention, but that was difficult in gatherings where, as Anne M. Boylan notes, participants "avoided doctrine as much as possible." Little wonder that some worried about dilution or worse, and, just three days before Margaret Fields wrote at Clayton, Moses Puterbaugh reported a discouraging word from Peru to the northeast. He opened one paragraph enthusiastically: "Sabbath School—We organized one." That involved singing, indeed "splendid singing." That, in turn, involved such a "fuss" that one beholder said the singing was "fit for nothing but the ball room" and would "lead the children to hell." Though

Moses Puterbaugh called it "superstition," that criticism was perfectly understandable. These lines of tension at Peru, Indiana, were as old as Christianity and probably as old as religion.[41]

Long before this "fuss" at Peru, Paul lectured the Galatians on similar matters, bemoaning that, after they had come to know God, still they turned to "weak and beggarly" ways. "Ye observe days, and months, and times, and years," as Paul put it in Galatians 4:9–10. Whether or not those ways were styled "weak and beggarly," our latter-day Galatians were coming to observe days more and more. In by far the most important development in this story, Christmas quickly emerged from obscurity among common people to something resembling its twentieth-century form and, in so doing, left Thanksgiving far behind in humble awareness. Some, especially New Englanders, both recognized and regretted that the spiritual credentials rendering Thanksgiving comfortably more than mockery no longer obtained.

In 1869 a woman born in Massachusetts and now living in California reminisced about the separations her life so vividly reflected, conjuring for the sister to whom she wrote the "scenes and associations" of childhood, including Thanksgiving. "We always keep that day," she noted, "it seems so much like home to both of us. It was the one great holiday of our childhood." Two years later a native of Connecticut writing from Silver City, Nevada, pronounced it "impossible for people here to celebrate Thanksgiving . . . like they do at home." Insofar as westerners observed that day, Dwight Bartlett sourly continued, they did so by getting drunk. In 1873 a Massachusetts man in California plowed and grubbed in a vineyard on December 25, and, as so many did in the years before the war, he offered no indication of what that day represented. Back on November 27 James Glazier was laboring just as hard, "same as yesterday." But this religious and hard-pressed man could at least identify the day if he could not keep it: "Thanksgiving day." The acids of western modernity had not entirely effaced the ancient ways, and in transmogrified form Thanksgiving would in time do splendidly as a prolonged weekend.[42]

In the same year that that California woman wrote about "the one great holiday of our childhood," Harriet Beecher Stowe offered confirmation of that assessment in the thinly veiled Connecticut village that served as setting for *Oldtown Folks*. Chapter 27, "How We Kept

Thanksgiving at Oldtown," presented that day as "king and high priest of all festivals." In the context of Thanksgiving's primacy, Christmas got no mention; but few people could have done more to legitimize and popularize Christmas than Stowe. A decade after the retrospective *Oldtown Folks* she wrote *Poganuc People: Their Loves and Lives*, and it chronicles the erosion of the vestigial Puritanism she had known in her youth. The first chapter, "Dissolving Views," sets the tone, and little Dolly, who is destined for liberation, soon confronts the dilemma of Christmas. Dolly's maturation and the dissolution of the old views appear against the backdrop of three Christmases, on the last of which Dolly, now a young woman, wishes her parents " 'a happy Christmas!' " Long spurned as one of the "old cast-off rags of the scarlet woman," Christmas had been disinfected and domesticated. Happily ignoring what had theretofore been seen as Christmas's association with Catholicism, common people soon availed themselves of the unaccustomed delights.[43]

The damnation of Theron Ware, Harold Frederic's fictive Methodist preacher, came about, not because of Darwin and scientific naturalism but because of an awakening in Ware of an aesthetic quest fed especially by a beautiful young Roman Catholic woman. She played the church organ, and that only symbolized a variety of allurements. Realist Frederic pushed to a dark conclusion what Harriet Beecher Stowe skirted. In *Poganuc People*, Dolly slipped out to see the Christmas illumination at the Episcopal church, and, though she fell asleep beneath a Christmas tree, she was no worse for her experience. On a Christmas Day in Topeka, Kansas, a newly married woman went with her mother-in-law to a 4:00 A.M. Catholic service: "Church beautifully decorated and fine music." Mattie Shaw did not oblige us with further comment on this nexus of Christmas, Catholicism, and aesthetic display. This Disciple of Christ appears as oblivious of possible dangers in the aesthetic quest as she does of the fact that a man named Darwin was disturbing the religious peace. Not yet four months into married life, Shaw had already reaped heartache from it. She probably sought some relief in the loveliness and dignity of that Catholic service.[44]

Relief and comfort are ever in demand, rarely more intensely than in the Civil War. Perhaps ironically, that conflict did a great deal to naturalize Christmas. Even in those four years of devastation there were seasons to different things. Combat came and went, and winter imposed comparative inaction on the armies, allowing mail a better chance to reach its destination. Whether or not soldiers had observed Christmas at home, they found it tailor-made for replenishing clothing or getting a few cherished food items. They had such desires year-round, but Christmas provided a ritual intensification of their needs and of the efforts of others to succor them. On the day after Christmas of 1862 a New England soldier wrote his mother that the box she had sent had arrived on the twenty-fourth, and it proved "a fine Christmas Present." Such boxes received great attention, and a Connecticut soldier at Andersonville noted in his diary in early October 1864 that "lots of the men are writing home for boxes." The pitiable condition of those captives did not stand on the formalities of the birthday of Jesus some ten weeks away, but that holy day, especially in the South, where it had been better known all along, might enhance the chances that a precious box would get through a multitude of vagaries.[45]

Andersonville aside, the lives of weary and endangered men slowed in winter so that Christmas provided an occasion, often ignored before, for people to demonstrate their love in a material way. Also, when armies went into dormancy, soldiers had more chance for leave. If a soldier happened to be home in late December, surely the most would be made of it, as evidently was the case at Shelbyville, Tennessee, during a wartime Christmas. Kattie Rowzee, a young woman who lived there, informed a sister that it was an especially fine Christmas because several of the boys, including her sweetheart, were home from the camps. That young man left Kattie after Christmas urging that she cry no more, drying his own tears to assure her that "he would come back again." Surely, Rowzee and others throughout the land would have done their all to make it a memorable Christmas. Rowzee would have left it to fanatical Yankees to " 'abhor the arrant whore of Rome' " and her "cast-off rags" such as Christmas. Those Yankees had better credentials for doing such work, but their aptness for it was, through the efforts of such as Stowe, falling into some disrepair.[46]

America had embarked on the course that would lead to the hypostasizing of the December carnival of consumption, but among humble people it probably had its most important beginnings in the wartime aura of deprivation and sorrow. Whatever the setting, the details of this emergent festival proved not altogether clear. Having accepted Christmas, common people hardly knew what they had or what to do with it. Talk about Christmas trees, for example, now entered the vernacular, but it did so in a way that seems to us off the mark. A Christmas tree was an event, something one attended, and one might attend several. Thus a milliner in Webster, Massachusetts, reported in 1876 that "there were lots of Christmas trees but I could not go to any of them." Evidently, doing so involved financial considerations. The trees served as points of exchange for small gifts such as autograph albums. Hattie the milliner had not had the means to send anything to the friends to whom she wrote, and that straitened condition kept her from the Christmas trees. Johnny Parrott, an arch Mississippian who in other seasons indulged a fondness for attending "nigger baptizings," would not miss a "Christmas tree" at nearby Mastodon in 1887, but he "Did not put anything on or take anything off."[47]

Only rarely did trees appear in humble homes. Insofar as they had a churchly place, it was ordinarily in that ancillary arena the Sunday school. There some arresting blends and accommodations might occur, as at a December 24 gathering featuring "Mother Goose," another similar but sadly illegible figure, as well as "Santa Claus and the White Pony." The situation all but begged clarification, as it did at an Iowa village in 1874 when those attending were treated to "chirades and tabloos." With indiscriminateness so rampant, yet other categories sought involvement in the newly popularized celebration, and Mamie James's Christmas Day letter of 1876 from Burnside, Connecticut, instances that well. After telling that she had received "a pair of mittens and a good time," young Mamie related what else had marked the day: "We had two torchlight processions here one Republican and one Democrat. . . . We lighted up with candles for the Republican one."[48]

Some may find it disturbing that political parties intruded upon a religious observation, but that only shows that Christmas was for most of these new observers a religious occasion in name only. Those who have waxed longingly about getting Christ back into Christmas would do well to consider that as Christmas emerged among common people in this country, Jesus often had little to do with the business, even when the setting seemed more devotional than "chirades and tabloos" and torchlight parades. "Christmas,

1876" at the "Baptist Sunday School of Farmer Village" in the Ovid, New York, area bears that out nicely. A small, nicely done printed memento survives in the form of a song "Inscribed to Superintendent B. E. Bassette. Air—'America'":

> As round our Christmas Tree,
> With happy hearts and free,
>   We stand to-night:
> May we rejoice to raise
> A song of grateful praise
> To Him who crowns our days
>   With blessings bright.[49]

Jesus duly enters verses two and three, but somewhat tardily and not by way of a manger or the like:

> God bless our Sunday School,
> Each heart may Jesus rule,
> Forevermore!

Verse two has not ended before the scene shifts to heaven with Christ presiding: "There Christmas comes each day." The concluding stanza returns to the motif established at the outset:

> Lord, bless the land we love,
> Let concord from above,—
>   Let peace descend!
> May "*love*" our motto be,
> Bless us with liberty,
> Help us to trust in Thee,
>   Till time shall end!

In Farmer Village, now known as Interlaken, God yet presided, though far more smilingly than had been His wont. Perhaps the Farmer Villagers gave voice to what has been so much discussed in our own time as "civil religion." Whatever the case, those rural folk suffered some uncertainty as to how to handle Christmas.[50]

Many Americans had no better grasp of the strict meaning of Christmas than did little Johnny in Bret Harte's "How Santa Claus Came to Simpson's Bar." "Wot's Chrismiss, anyway?" Johnny asked the Old Man. "Oh, it's a day," came the "exhaustive definition." "Why do they call it Chrismiss?" Johnny persisted. Only a hush came in response, and "Chrismiss" was indeed a "mighty cur'o's" matter. Christmas came to unelevated folk of this land as something of an open charter, and political parties in torchlight parades and patriotic airs had no more of the anomalous than did Mother Goose, or the White Pony, or, for that matter, Dick Bullen's ride back to Simpson's Bar with a gift for little Johnny.[51]

Common people's Christmas was preeminently, almost exclusively, a social occasion, so much so that one might almost applaud rather than bemoan the transformation of Christmas in the past hundred years. From Placerville, California, in 1878, for example, came the discouraging word that "Whit" Hall got a black eye in a fight, and the only redeeming feature of that Christmas Day activity was, according to Josie Beckman, that it was "darn good" for "such a dog gone fool any how." Perhaps one should not expect a great deal of Placerville, or of Company D, Sixth United States Infantry, at Fort Buford on the upper Missouri, where, after a "good dinner" on Christmas Day of 1874, several fights broke out. But even considering the source in these cases, it disconcerts one to see the frequency with which "a hell of a time" was expected or reported on December 25. On the eve of that day in 1871, for example, Donald W. Davis anticipated "a hell of a time" the next day at Anoka, Minnesota. A couple of days after one Christmas a man in Kellogg, Iowa, looked back on the "hell of a time" they had just had. Jesus intruded into this account but only by way of blasphemous exclamation.[52]

So it went around the land. A young man from Illinois who was hunting buffalo on the Kansas plains had the opportunity to play the fiddle at a "stag dance in a dugout" on Christmas Day, and all apparently went smoothly because or in spite of the presence of two of the Masterson brothers, Bat being elsewhere. A year earlier and over a hundred miles to the north on the Kansas plains, Luna Warner did a bit better than a dance in a dugout. On Christmas Day of 1871 Luna, member of a homesteading family, attended a wedding and a dinner, and then she went to a hall where she "danced the schottisch like everything with Mr. Phillips," not getting home until 5:00 A.M. In Topeka on the Christmas Day that Mattie Shaw began at 4:00 A.M. Catholic services came to a close for her many hours later at the annual mail carriers' ball. The tuberculosis that would kill her postman husband before long rendered him too weak to dance, but neither solicitude for him nor an admonition against dancing she once received from a Disciples of Christ deacon could keep Shaw off the dance floor: "Home at 2 o'clock A.M."[53]

Dancing was the order of Christmas Day, and not all would be satisfied with that. At the South reports of untoward conduct often featured blacks. On December 18, 1870, an overworked store clerk in Georgia approached exhaustion, grumbling that "as it is near Xmas the niggers are as careless and saucy as well they can be." A North Carolinian retained more decorum in a Christmas Day letter to his father. After telling that he had "laid out for Miriam $2., and she is the only one among us that got anything at all," William Garland complained that Christmas was a day for "drunken men and rowdies (I should have said Negroes for I did not see a white man who was under the influence of liquor)." However accurate that report, December 25 had little reputation for the devotional. For most it meant, along with the exchange of very modest gifts, dancing and frolic, often inordinately so. In June 1866 Zina W. Chase of Maine by way of Minnesota reached the mining town of Breckinridge, Colorado Territory. Near that community he saw a grave with an inscribed board nailed to a tree: "D M Martin—frozen Dec 26 1861—found May 21 1862." Chase concluded that it "would indicate Chrismas drunk."[54]

More and more people flouted Paul's warning against observing days, and, as in other things, the West did its part in accelerating the change. At the outset of our period Sarah Colby, sometime garment factory worker, wrote from San Francisco indicating the greater emphasis on such festivities. In a January 4 letter she mentioned Christmas, then noted that "folk keep new years out here just the same as they do any other holidays." The war probably did even more than the West, and not just for Christmas. In 1864, March 17 came on Thursday, and Union soldier Alonzo Teed's diary indicates a day off, "It being St Patricks day." That day and a few others were now coming to the attention of people who had previously neglected them.[55]

The very notion of holiday—in either sacred or secular terms—had a fairly novel aspect to these people, and they did not always handle that notion adroitly. A Nebraska farm wife, herself only six weeks from the grave, wrote to her parents at the outset of 1880 mentioning the recent "holly days." Mattie Oblinger made a slip here that is eminently understandable, but one finds worse misconstructions of holy day. "It being St Patricks day to day," Alonzo

Teed's full observation reads, "we have a hollow day." Nothing suggests that Teed was indulging whimsy. Alice Watson seems to have been even freer of playfulness when she wrote to her sister Ida just before Christmas in 1889. After noting that a "green Christmas" seemed likely, she gave an account of the death less than a week before of another sister's twenty-two-year-old daughter. That event probably assured that nothing but earnestness informed the reference to the onset of the "hollow days."[56]

Alice Watson may have committed artfulness rather than error, though that seems unlikely. But a certain aptness might occur to some. Though Harriet Beecher Stowe did much to encourage the more relaxed ways, she could wax eloquent about contriving celebrations and "fiddling and dancing" to serve as "sops" to keep people content. At the outset of her description of a traditional Thanksgiving she set it down as a "general axiom, that people feel the need of amusements less and less, precisely in proportion as they have solid reasons for being happy." Such a view allows one to see a sardonic quality in "hollow days," whatever the writers' intent. "Hollow days" or holy days, they had little to do with religion.[57]

If, in general, the writings of common people reveal less of the religious, one noteworthy qualification needs mention. It received brief attention in a previous chapter and deserves fuller treatment here. Contrary to the prewar period, the diaries and letters of southern people in the war and postwar years seem more replete with religious content and idiom than do those of northern people. Of course, some modern readers feel that such writings are almost wearyingly spiritual, whether North or South, but that reaction fails to reckon with what had gone before. One editor of a northern soldier's diary concluded that the man's religion had been "deepened by his sufferings," but that was not at all apparent to me. In fact, compared with diaries of the previous generation, his did not strike me as much inclined to the devotional. Now and again, also, editors seem to find religious matter insupportable, and, as one explained, the "omitted portions of the correspondence deal principally with comments about religion," an omission that probably would have horrified the writer of those letters. Whatever the case, these people after 1860 did not burden us so fully or frequently with their religious discussions and soliloquies, though a good many in the South made an effort.[58]

Before the war had ended, for example, Johnny Reb had surpassed Billy Yank in religious intensity. Bell I. Wiley wrote persuasively of this matter, but he does not convince me that the southern soldier *entered* the war a more devout man than his northern counterpart, as he seems to suggest. Wiley's calling attention to the desperation that came upon the South after midwar, however, seems altogether likely in explaining revivals in southern armies and the increasing amount of religious fare in what southern soldiers and others wrote. Of course, as all would recognize, many Union soldiers practiced their religion and relied on it for sustenance, but religion intruded less and less. Thus a Connecticut Yankee in Florida complained late in the war: "We are apt to trust the arm of flesh. We want more faith in God, and less of man worship." They may have wanted it, that is, needed it, but they seem not to have received it.[59]

When they did it often proved transient. Benjamin Mabrey of the Eighty-second Indiana Volunteers maintained an earthy tone in letters to his wife until the intense unpleasantness that dragged bloodily across north Georgia in the spring of 1864. Near Ringgold in March, Private Mabrey assured his wife about his general good conduct, then added: "i do not profess to be a Christone." Then the situation took deplorable turns, such as Mabrey's report that "they have got to cilling prisners on both sides now." Now, too, other considerations began to enter the picture. The Hoosier's letters now mention "meatings" and thoughts about that realm "Whare parting is no more." And Mabrey's wife, Lou, received an injunction for which she may not have been entirely prepared: "Deare Wife pray for me and I will pray for you." Benjamin Mabrey had become a "Christone," and, with Dalton, Georgia, looming menacingly ahead, he told his brother-in-law, "i have seen more hapiness since i gave myself to the lord than i ever did before in my life." But the hell encountered at places such as Dalton gave way to the comparative ease of a year later, when Mabrey wrote from Goldsboro, North Carolina. Campaigning had become almost a breeze. Mabrey reported that he had become a corporal; he could send some money home; and he found no place for religion in his letter of April 1, 1865. The feelings he had appropriated in north Georgia fell into disuse on the easier road north.[60]

Private Mabrey had found deliverance from the wretched conditions that had made him a "Christone." His nation's cause had prevailed. He went home in triumph, and the degree to which religion informed his forty-seven remaining years probably lies beyond determination. Mabrey's southern counterparts found no such deliverance. Balm for their miseries would have to be found elsewhere, and revivals swept the southern armies. From the camps near Atlanta across the line from Private Mabrey of Indiana, Robert T. Wood sent word to his wife and children a hundred miles to the southeast in Washington County, Georgia, that there was "a great revival of religion gowing on around hear . . . preching evary day & a most evary night." Wood brought his letter to a close to go and see a comrade baptized.[61]

In mid-July 1864 Robert T. Wood could have found few things apter to do, and he evidently had much company. A Texas cavalryman, for example, writing from Arkansas in early 1864, provided what seems as close as we can get to a conversion experience written by a common person in this period. "I feel," he concluded his brief account, "like a different man as much so as if I was not the same." A Louisiana soldier attested more to changes in others than in himself. He carried on a religious dialogue with his wife through much of the war, especially after having been "perfectly thunder struck" to learn that she had become a Baptist. Baptists added to illness and war seemed "a nuff to make a man go crazy," but Methodist Harry Morgan worried especially about godlessness among his fellow soldiers. That changed. Against the appalling backdrop near war's end he reported different conduct in his comrades: "wee see them nelt down all about in the woods praying for pease." On hearing a report that religion did not prosper in his home area, Morgan admonished his wife, "if thare ever was a time that peopal needed religion it is now." Private Morgan brought that letter of February 19, 1865, to a close by firing another round or two at the Baptists, but his general assessment has much to commend it.[62]

However numerous the Harry Morgans, his humble expressions illustrate the emergence of the South, far later in the nation's history than we sometimes suppose, as the section having greatest religious fervor. The war and its sorry aftermath catalyzed that development. Confederate soldier Thomas H. Colman blended reality, myth, and synecdoche in writing from besieged Atlanta on an August 1864 Sunday when southern guns remained silent while those of the invaders thundered away "as usual." He served reality by noting that some soldiers were needlessly killed for having become so inured to the noise of the bombardment as to grow neglectful of their own safety. He served myth in the invidious allusion to what might have been fleshed out into grossly utilitarian Yankees. He served synecdoche in portraying southerners keeping the Sabbath rather than keeping the guns firing. It would have added only an incidental refinement had Colman noted that his southerners no longer had the wherewithal to keep those guns firing.[63]

As Confederate guns fell silent, other modes of expression emerged. Relief would come from another quarter, and so it became more customary for the southerner to say, as a North Carolinian wrote to his father in 1871, the "Lord will help us soon." According to William Garland, 2 Corinthians 6:18 said as much, and he tossed in Revelation 21:7 for good measure. Perhaps the changing times are illustrated by the elder Garland's invocation of Shakespearean imagery regarding "the winter of our discontent." Richard III received response from 2 Corinthians and Revelation in January, and near the end of the year the son adduced the near ultimate consolation—the Twenty-third Psalm. "The Lord has promised," as a Greeneville, Tennessee, couple assured a woman whose husband had not survived Confederate service, "to be a husband to the widow & a father to the fatherless."[64]

William Garland of Laurinburg, North Carolina, neglected to note that Paul, immediately before the verse Garland had adduced for his father's benefit, urged the Corinthians to "come out from among them, and be ye separate. " The Garlands and many others had tried just that in 1861, and their failure came full in 1865. That failure notwithstanding, the previously mentioned couple in Greeneville, Tennessee, doing what they could for the spiritual comfort of widow Mary Ann Wilson, told her also that they admired her "rebelism." Perhaps such a combination or juxtaposition could have caused W. J. Cash to portray the intensification of religion in the postwar South as, in part, "a pole for patriotic pride and a shield for the South's defense." That interpretation would probably read too much into the unpretentious writing of people such as these. They knew hatred and defiance of the North, but, straitened and sorrowful, they wrote in the even more direct terms of disconsolateness and deprivation.[65]

As the war ended, a Georgia woman had the "profound" pleasure of getting a letter from her husband and learning that he was well, his "small rashings" notwithstanding. "The health of this settlement is tolerably good," she continued, "and all the people are getting a long after the old sort, temperaly, but we are all getting a long much better spiritualy." Mrs. E. P. Henslee did not fall into the neglect that so many others were showing; she drove directly to that fundamental separation between the temporal and the spiritual. Nor did she lose sight of the admonition, so ceaselessly emphasized by the preceding generation, that the spiritual took precedence over the temporal. To put it another way, with "rashings" (a fairly common southern corruption of rations) as short as they were for many of the people in her land, spiritually was about the only way folk could get "a long." Little wonder that, as Henslee reported, a revival broke out at the last meeting, and Brother Carter and Brother Martin "held on for twelve days and twelve nights."[66]

Only now, with the Civil War behind us, do we find talk of revivals and their trappings more readily in the letters and diaries of common southerners than in those of common northerners. Its tone is shrill and its imagery is strained, but Chard Powers Smith's morose story *Yankees and God* has much to commend it in seeing certain consequences "flowing out of the Civil War and drawing much of Greater New England away from the Puritan tradition." For religious intensity one now must look to such places as the Pleasant Garden–Randleman area of North Carolina, where in September 1882 a "splendid revival" was recorded by Bonds, Cobles, Erwins, and Rosses. Fannie Ross designated it "splendid," and at its conclusion Lizzie Coble declared that "the church was revived and it seemed like they had a good old time of it."[67]

No doubt they did indeed have a good "old" time of it, but, insofar as common writings betray common values, they had, as it were, a good "new" time of it. Though he presses on to complexities that are unnecessary here, W. J. Cash nicely sums up the contrasting spiritual directions in the aftermath of the war: "And everywhere north of the Potomac and Ohio rivers piety, remaining always a mighty force, would nevertheless grow steadily more gentle, more vague, and at the same time more rational." In the South, however, "the movement was to the opposite quarter."[68]

That the drift to the "opposite quarter" had little of the "gentle," the "vague," or even the "rational" may be seen in the case of "Big Wah," one of the farming McIlwains who moved west from Mississippi in the postwar years. Cash might have enjoyed this vignette, and it provides also an intimation of the abiding consanguinity between the ways of the South and the ways of the West. John "Big Wah" McIlwain wrote from Mount Vernon, Arkansas, in 1881: "I went into a bar to get me a drink and a big, double-fisted Divil asked me to treat him. I said I would but it would be like a dog, and he lit into me. I takined my knife handle as a pair of nucks and I made a map of Texas on his face." "Big Wah's" way came up short in the gentle, vague, and rational categories as he made his way into Oklahoma and into being a Cumberland Presbyterian preacher.[69]

"Big Wah" and the southern salient aside, humble people found religion a less absorbing part of human affairs in this generation than they had in the preceding one. Of course, Cash's qualifier—"remaining always a mighty force"—must be borne in mind. We are dealing with a comparative matter, and one wonders how some scholars can neglect as much as they do the religious dimension of this later period. How is it, for example, that Michael Barton could do a content analysis of the writings of Civil War soldiers that virtually ignores religion? His index contains no religious terms per se other than a subentry—"and religion, 75"—which falls under the rubric "Emotions, control of." Insofar as those soldiers were "goodmen," it derived in large part from their being religious, and the innocent reader ought not to be allowed the supposition that things of that nature appear only on page 75. Or, turning to other settings, one wonders how Elizabeth Hampsten could say so little about the religion of the women she discussed in *Read This Only to Yourself*, even if she believed that religion "might well be thought a plausible explanation for many ills" they suffered.[70]

Religion remained that "mighty force." On that front many of these humble people were, to appropriate the language of Longfellow's "A Psalm of Life," up and doing, but the tone and content of their expressions had decidedly changed. Prayerfulness enters less frequently, as does spiritual self-assessment and soliloquy. Revivals get more routine treatment. Conversion enters the written discussion far less frequently and intensely than before. Millennial notions, which seemed to lay very little claim on the attention of the prewar generation, seem, in turn, to have laid almost no claim at all on the attention of the succeeding generation. Days of ostensible religious observation proved more hollow than hallowed or holy. Historically recognizable religious figures grace the scene far more than they had previously, but they seem to have done little to intensify in others the spirit they seemed to embody.

Religion figured as the very essence of much of what common people wrote before the war. In the war and after, excluding the South, religion appears with less frequency and in desiccated form. The gravitation "from sacred to profane America," to use William A. Clebsch's formulation regarding the country's emergence "outside the temple," came, of course, over a long period; but for unelevated people, the change admits of some concentration. However profane, however much "outside the temple" they would become in time, the groundwork was firmly laid in the period from 1860 to 1890. Earlier we saw Ruben Abbott of Creston, Iowa, grumbling that, instead of "meatings" in the traditional mode, folk gathered for dances in December 1870. Warming to his theme, Abbott concluded: "Religion is al most out of fashion Practical religion is al most extinct." Abbott took a much too dour view of the situation, but we can understand why, older man that he was, he waxed so gloomily.[71]

4. *The Dying of Death*

When Knut Hamsun visited America in the 1880s, he made sport of the writings of Ralph Waldo Emerson, whom he designated "the Aesop of the American mob of moralists." The Norwegian's comments partook of parody more than fairness, but an Emersonian assertion about the place of death in pre–Civil War America tempts one to join Hamsun in the ridicule. In surveying that spiritual ruin brought on by a "decaying church and a wasting unbelief," the sage arrived at one final item of the sorry situation: "and when men die, we do not mention them." One hardly knows what to make of that line. Considered in a literal sense, the remark seems laughably amiss. As anticipation, however, it has a certain aptness. As with other subjects such as narcissism, Emerson heralded a time yet fairly far removed a good deal more than he described his own time. That pronouncement about death was premature but not entirely wrong. Death—the focal point of profound religious concern—was "dying," to use James J. Farrell's way of putting it. Humble Americans modified their religious expressions, generally in the direction of atrophy. What they had to say about death changed accordingly.[1]

Of course, the old and mordant ways, what might strike us a near obsessional pall in common writings of the prewar period, did not depart abruptly or completely. In the same year that Emerson spoke the words quoted above, Longfellow published "A Psalm of Life," pronouncing emphatically that "Life is real! Life is earnest!" Such an appraisal of life would have surprised no one. That "the grave is not its goal" would have admitted of greater wonderment. That latter proposition might not have gained full acceptance from a milliner in Connersville, Indiana. In 1864 Eunice Brown informed a brother that Jenny Newkirk was "dead and buried she was happy and willing to go." After some pensive remarks about other departures, Eunice Brown offered the time-honored fact which no amount of poetry could obscure: "truly in the midst of life we are in death." Eunice Brown had reached no more than her twenty-seventh year. The sentiments she expressed generally came from people of greater age, people harboring persuasions inculcated in a more distant past and now themselves more directly conversant with death. A month before the Indiana seamstress wrote to her brother, an older woman in Chittenango, New York, penned some lines to a relative serving in the Union army. Four deaths in one week in the Chittenango neighborhood moved Mrs. John Colyer to pronounce what that soldier had abundant reason to know: "sur[e]ly while we are in life we are in Death."[2]

Grim and unanswerable recognitions such as those of Eunice Brown and Mrs. John Colyer continue to appear but much less frequently than they once did. Euphemism and avoidance were settling upon the land. James J. Farrell has identified two key intellectual factors that helped "to speed the dying of death in America." The first, "scientific naturalism," figured as the "crucial catalyst" in Farrell's depiction, but when we move the focus to unelevated people that seems not to be the case. Civil War soldiers exhibited a certain callousness that might vaguely resemble the naturalistic outlook, but the tone sometimes assumed by those soldiers came from a dreadful inuring, not from books. As a Mississippi soldier concluded after conveying some unsettling details to his wife, "this war is calculated to harden the softest heart." He put in succinct form what must have been a significant reality.[3]

One wonders also about the propensity, mostly southern, to employ the expression *according to nature*. That terminology might be taken as unthinking acquiescence in what Darwin and others were starkly depicting as man's lot, but the expression had a different resonance. J. W. Forbes, a photographer in a small town in Iowa, came out of a southern setting, and in 1870 he wrote to "Affectionate

Relatives (if living)" to determine who was where and who was no more. The former Tarheel asked particularly about Aunt Jane, from whom he had not heard since 1859. Was she alive, and, if dead, "how long since or when did she die according to nature?" Nature's sway could hardly be ignored, but Forbes's way of putting it involved hardly more than a delimitation upon nature. *According to nature* meant the inexorable decree that life should depart the body, but there was vastly more to the story. A few months later, having learned that Aunt Jane yet lived, photographer Forbes told her of his mother's death in 1865. Though suffering "extreemly," she had "exorted us all to prepare to meet death & follow her." He betrayed no doubt that so following would lead to a hereafter and a judgment of the "quick and dead." For this former southerner, the "*Grand Assembly*," mentioned in both letters, meant that setting where he would rejoin his mother and others "widely scatered by Death." What happened according to nature served merely as prelude.[4]

In 1887, when she told of the death of her husband, a Michigan woman did so in a way that might distantly echo scientific naturalism. Widow Lettie Pennoyer wrote, "Hard as it seems it is natures ways and we must submit." Death happened according to nature, but Lettie Pennoyer went well beyond that recognition: "Nature is wiser and better than *we*. *We* should not fear her." Whatever inspired Pennoyer to that uncommon thought, it comes as close to scientific naturalism in a deathly context as anything found in this research. Religion probably played a smaller part in this woman's life than it did in those of most of her contemporaries, but, even though religion yet showed more vigor than she allowed it, death was waning. "Liberal Christianity," the other of Farrell's two central ingredients in the "dying of death," surfaces much more often than does scientific naturalism in the writings of common people. Rarely does it assume clarity, but leaders of Liberal Christianity often skirted clarity themselves.[5]

At Christmas of 1863 an Iowa woman wrote to a brother in the army telling of the seasonal activities that were becoming a feature of humble life as well as of refined life. She told that one man, perhaps elderly, had ventured into the woods near Ottumwa for evergreen decorations and for his efforts suffered what appeared to be a fatal attack of pleurisy. "Thus; pain, death & sorrow seem to be mingled with everything earthly I often wonder that we are not always sad &

never cheerful." This woman expressed the general tone of much that was afoot religiously as Americans sought escape from the dour views of their ancestors. A few years later in Iowa City another woman had the comfort of hearing a genuinely liberal sermon "on the religion we need to live by—what a grand thing life is & the proper thing is to live right & not to be *always* thinking how we will die." Adaline Jones's predecessors may not have *"always"* thought of death, but it could seem as though they did. People now urged one another to shift the emphasis to living far more than they previously had, even when someone died. "We must turn our attention to the living," a Nebraska man wrote at the death of a family member in 1887, "trying to make it . . . plsant [pleasant] for those around us and allso for ourselves." Liberal Christianity spread the comforting word that life was meant for living, and death received ever less attention.[6]

People found a variety of ways to shift the focus. When Llewellyn Gushee of Osceola, Nebraska, dutifully wrote to a brother who had lost a child, he made short work of it, professing to be "a poor hand" at it. Some were literally poor hands, a description fitting Canan and Mary Duitt, who struggled to convey the following: "i was ~~sorow~~ sory to here that uncle ~~ritcharg~~ ritchard chesman was ded." One could hardly expect flourishes or elaborations from the Duitts, but others, in whom it cannot be so readily explained or excused, showed a growing perfunctoriness. In Warsaw, Indiana, a woman named Aggie reflected changing times in a letter to a friend in Missouri. Aggie moved briskly from a brief mention of the well-attended "burrial" of a child to a topic with which the dawning age would feel more comfortable: "Well now Lem I must tell you something about *Warsaw*." The dead child got uncommonly short shrift as the scene shifted to marriages and the like.[7]

Californian N. B. Booth wrote dolorously to a sister in the East in 1874, both reflecting the emergent alteration and offering a regional explanation for it. His letter lacks religious couching. He bemoaned, for example, that one man had been deranged throughout his last illness, but not for the spiritual reason so highly regarded by an earlier age. Booth felt regret for the reason put in sardonic terms by his fellow Californian Ambrose Bierce: "Death is not the end; there remains the litigation over the estate." Likewise, when the man in El Monte referred to another dead man as being now " 'infintly better off,' " he seems to have had in mind the condition left rather than the condition lying ahead. In summary, Booth extended a previous comment about neglect of Sundays in the West. In this country, he noted, sickness and death came with such infrequency that "we hardly realize death may be near as you do east."[8]

John Hunt of Indiana had California on his mind a year earlier, but he had now to write to a niece about the death of her sister. He, too, neglected religious idiom, as he assured the living that the deceased was "out of troubles now." As did N. B. Booth of El Monte, California, the man in Florida, Indiana, had learned the use of quotation marks, and here he employed them in a fully modern way. He did not refer to his niece's sister Hannah as being dead; she was " 'no more.' " Those quotation marks played the tendential role of veiling and euphemizing, qualities almost totally ignored in deathly matters by the previous generation.[9]

Beyond these somewhat mechanical matters people were more and more reticent in handling a subject the previous generation had deemed worthy of the fullest recording possible. The deathbed had loomed so large in fiction and drama because it had loomed so large in life. But in the late nineteenth century the curtain begins to fall, and we can see the emergence of what Geoffrey Gorer has termed the "pornography of death." In early 1881 Mary, the wife of James E. Glazier, fell ill in The Dalles, Oregon, to which the family had moved from California a few months earlier. Whatever the pulmonary ailment, it brought Mary Glazier down fast, and on March 5 at 4:00 A.M. "she breathed her last. *Dear Dear Wife!*" Wandering carpenter Glazier had retained some of his New England ways; he kept diaries and committed many thoughts to them. Now, however, the obligation to record fully failed him: "How shall I forget this day—I need not write of it." Two days later, he altered the form: "Oh I can remember all. I need not write." Carpentry work in the Columbia River town was scarce, and this newcomer had difficulty staying busy, something he dearly wished not only for his brood of small children but for peace of mind as well. He forced himself to find things to do, including writing at night to "keep my mind busy." What he wrote about is not clear, but those diary exclamations suggest that Mary's death, the details of which would have made great claim upon an earlier age, did not receive further mention.[10]

As with other moves to modernity, the older forms yet occurred now and again, and a woman in frontier Arizona Territory dutifully conveyed the word she had received of her sister's death. That woman had died among strangers, but she had risen to the occasion. She remained alert to the end and asked those who gathered at the deathbed to sing "while she was dying, O sing to me of heaven when I am called to die." One word more was needed to make the account fully gratifying by previous standards—a descriptive that figured ever less in these dolorous descriptions. *Triumphant* had put the semantic seal on deaths that came in spiritual fullness, and that term, too, was withdrawing from the scene. A rare instance in this later period comes in the diary of a Minneapolis woman in early 1885. When her mother died, Abbie Griffin wrote that she "went triumphly." At some point in the sad unfolding, Abbie collapsed in exhaustion, so it is not entirely clear whether she observed her mother's death. Whatever the case, those left behind were more often settling for less than Abbie Griffin noted. A decided shift was taking place in deathbed expectations, from triumph to ease, from final defiant and ecstatic demonstration of Christian faith to a passing unsullied by agony.[11]

The religious aura surrounding death was assuming a less intense, more mellow form. It remained pleasing, of course, that the stricken should be aware of their condition and resigned to their fate. In 1890 Susannah Scott wrote in the painful and unsteady hand that betokened the many years she had had to reflect on such matters, describing a deathly ill woman she had visited: "I talked to her of her condision she seamed to be [a]ware and was very much resined just as the will of the Lord will hav it." Being aware and thereby perhaps prepared and resigned yet had importance but not the crucial importance it once had.[12]

The move from ecstasy to ease must have involved the war to a fairly large degree. In war as in the West, dying among strangers became often enough the order of the day. To be sure, very many Civil War soldiers left their home areas in units made up of relatives, friends, and neighbors, and many who died did so with such people around them. Still, the vagaries of conflict assured that many others would depart in the presence of strangers or untended. That situation violated the formula whereby the vaunted family circle and friends could act as participants with the departing in an emotional and sacred drama of the first magnitude, a drama eliciting hardly more than unbelief and uneasiness from those who now encounter it in, say, *Uncle Tom's Cabin* or Charles Dickens's novels.

Those strangers in war or elsewhere, acting as surrogates for family and friends, must often have attended the death perfunctorily, not knowing and perhaps not caring what devotional ritual would be appropriate. With the war almost two years past, an Ohio woman fulfilled the promise she had made to a dying Confederate at Camp Dennison near Cincinnati. At Shiloh a shot through the lung brought Texan Darwin Seeley down and into Yankee captivity. After his arrival at Camp Dennison, the Ohio woman and her husband somehow came to care for him in his last two weeks. Now, almost five years after Shiloh, the Ohio woman wrote to Darwin Seeley's sister, reporting the demise. His mind, she wrote, had been "very clear at times" and generally "*peaceful.*" When her husband first spoke with him about dying, the Texan appeared " 'greatly shocked,' " but soon he came to view it as " 'alright.' " "This will be comforting truly," the Ohioan urged, "for you to know that death had no terror for him." Mr. and Mrs. A. B. Wambaugh of Ohio probably did their best for the dying Texan, but they went about their task with the comparative guardedness all but inevitable with strangers.[13]

Many of the men who perished in the traumatizing experience of war did so without any aspect of consecration. Protestants mostly, they needed little. But the lore and tradition of holy dying had some expectations if not prescriptions. In many cases these men perished starkly bereft of any comforting context. They died, by and large, without family and friends, especially without the old, whose experience fitted them to register and administer the code of death. The fear of "anonymous death," as Gerald F. Linderman styles it, did indeed feed "Disillusionment."[14]

These common soldiers had to make do with the resort to manly resolve and to the hope and prayer that death would come easily. Thus Frank Wilkeson, once a private soldier, recalled twenty years later "How Men Die in Battle," emphasizing stoic composure and lack of display. Near Spotsylvania his unit marched past a group of seriously wounded men gathered under an oak tree: "None of these soldiers cried aloud, none called on wife, or mother, or father. They lay on the ground, pale-faced, and with set jaws, waiting for their end." Wilkeson asked one of them what he was doing; " 'Having my last smoke, young fellow,' he replied." That vignette illustrated the spirit Wilkeson sought to convey; it revealed men who knew they would die and who set about doing it with composure and with whatever ease they could secure. These men suffered and they showed it, but, as Wilkeson put it, "none of them flunked." Here we have, in this 1880s recollection, a telling intimation of, on one hand, the late nineteenth-century onset of the image of steadfast manliness, which so many have since foisted upon so much of our history. We have, on the other hand and more important for the matter at hand, the grim reality of death reduced to the least common denominator, of dying divorced from the appurtenances of the death-bed.[15]

Wilkeson's arresting chapter contains just one word that suggests religion. Fighting in a strange unit, he came to know the "Christian" names of some of his comrades. Consciously or otherwise, he must have exaggerated the absence of the spiritual category, but that has some congruence with the spirit of the war generally. It has some congruence as well with what people wrote about death in the war setting. In September 1862 a "Home Visitor" for the Home of the Friendless in Chicago conveyed the sad word to John Black of Edina, Missouri, that his son George had expired in service. The Home Visitor, who had visited George in camp, told of the soldier's coffin he occupied and that he had died "very easy and gently." Leroy Streetman wrote back to Georgia telling that another John Black, this one of the Sixteeth Regiment of Georgia Volunteer Infantry, had died. Shortly before he expired, this John Black regained his "rite mind," but his comrade wrote nothing about the religious significance of that. Rather, he told that the dying man asked to have his remains returned to Georgia. It was comforting to suppose, as Leroy Streetman did, that John Black had gone to a "better world," but it seemed fully as significant to specifiy that "he died verry easy." If dying easy had not yet become the order of the day, it had at least assumed priority for Civil War deaths.[16]

Still neglecting to mention religion, Frank Wilkeson maintained that only in final delirium did the wandering minds and babbling tongues of dying soldiers hearken back to home, wife, or whatever. People other than Frank Wilkeson seemed to be making lessened claims for the spiritual, whether in life or in death. That appears in changes of language and tone. Language that once had specificity in the writings of common people was trailing off into the vague and the noncommittal. To get happy had involved transportation or ecstasy, which, if it came on the deathbed, figured as triumph. Now that word *happy* appears in more equivocal ways, ways less readily translatable. Levi Sowers, for example, used the word in writing to Emily Huckaby about the death of her brother Leander from wounds suffered in Pickett's charge. Sowers had not witnessed the death, but he talked with someone who had: "O my god I am glad to hear that he died hapy." Couched in such locutions, the word probably connoted little more than peaceful or, in military terms, at ease. People who once had hoped for charisma were now settling for contentment.[17]

They were claiming less and encountering ever greater challenges. Harriet Eaton did medical work among Maine troops, and that took her to the Harpers Ferry area, where she was soon tending a stricken young officer. She tried, but she could not prevail, either physically or spiritually: "Poor Lindley M. Coleman Capt of Comp. B. is no more. . . . Delirious with fever, neither any effort of mine, or earnest pleading and groaning from his brother could draw aught from him, but ravings like these 'march on my men, march on' . . . I tried to point him to Jesus but to earthly appearances such efforts were vain. I was permitted to close the dying eyes, and attend the last offices and there we must leave him." The brief vis-à-vis of Lindley M. Coleman and Harriet Eaton may tell us a good deal about the frustrations encountered in pointing people to Jesus during the frenzy of the Civil War.[18]

Finally, one might surmise, though hardly document or even illustrate in the written words of these unwordy people, that some imponderable quotient of horror and agony had rendered death altogether less palatable as object of instruction, although that instruction had once been of a crucially spiritual nature. Death may well have become for them, as George Fredrickson depicts Walt Whitman's coming to see it, a matter of "merciful release," pure and simple. In September 1861, Smith and Sally Lipscomb of Calhoun County, Alabama, wrote dolefully to their surviving son who had so recently gone to war. Of trouble, surely the Lipscombs were now encountering "a greate Eale," an arresting usage appearing frequently in southern sources. They pleaded with son William to seek a discharge or at least a furlough. As it had often done in the past, the following injunction figured centrally in their letter: "I wante you to be shure & let us know all that Joshua said to you on his death bed." William obliged them regarding Joshua, but he did so in a way that may have seemed unsatisfactory to Smith and Sally Lipscomb. The Civil War, so prolific in rendering people dead, had peculiarly little place for the deathbed, and the passing years left that once hallowed spot ever less the observed of all observers.[19]

In *Specimen Days in America* Whitman made the often-noted observation that "the real war will never get in the books." Most directly, "the seething hell and the black infernal background" of a myriad of horrors would never be recounted, and "it is best they should not," leaving a later age that fancies itself more realistic to bemoan Whitman's own failure to tell even more. Whitman's remarks admit of another reading. To him "the latent personal character" of those hundreds of thousands of men who fought in the war, especially those "stricken by wounds or disease," had "more significance even than the political interests involved." Immediately after that remark he offered a parenthetical observation: "As so much of a race depends on how it faces death, and how it stands personal anguish and sickness." What Whitman considered the real war would not get in the books in part because a people that had previously been fastidious about recording the real conflict were writing less about the particulars of it.[20]

When Mrs. Wambaugh of Ohio wrote to Darwin Seeley's sister, she did so to convey "the particulars of your brother's death." She wrote in time-honored terms. She was dealing, of course, with strangers, and her letter does not have the fullness one often finds in prewar family correspondence. Still, she took for granted the significance of at least some of the physical detail, and, more important, whatever spiritual intimations one might glean from the comportment of the dying. Here again, it was falling the lot of the aged to tend these fine points. In Bellota, California, Lucy Dawson moved a cramped and feeble hand to comfort a younger woman who had lost a child. Most likely, Lucy meant it when she wrote that she regretted that she had not been there when the child died. Such people sought not only to lend assistance but to attend a potentially inspiring spiritual display. Lucy echoed an old refrain now falling into disuse when she asked that the other woman write her "all the particulars."[21]

The particulars were losing a noteworthy particular application.

Closely viewed, almost anything had particulars, but in the previous generation the word had been employed so frequently in regard to death and, especially, its spiritual implications that it seemed to have some peculiar relation to that subject. The particulars had a mordant association, but the word was losing that special resonance as people grew more perfunctory in relating the matters of the deathbed. One fancies that Francis Squires's father had the last word in the matter when he died in upstate New York in January 1861. Francis followed the ways of the past in providing a fairly ample diary description of his father's demise, even to the last words: "'keep still.'" If not yet prepared to do that, people were at least showing a decided reticence on a subject that had previously inspired some of their finest efforts.[22]

Twenty-five years after they served together in the Union army, Henry Ruechel appealed to Jonathan Labrant to recall some particulars, and he stated the case as follows: "i wish you would state that i was a sound & healthy Person, wich is nothing but the thrut, & then all the Particklers that you know, that scrach with Ramrod was so littel at first & [I] had no idia that it would turn out to be so bad." Securing a pension, especially with Grover Cleveland in office, would require some compelling "Particklers." When Levi Powell died on the North Laramie River in 1872, his brother conveyed the "particulars" to a sister, but he offered those not in spiritual categories but to make a case against the "Red Devils" instrumental in Levi's demise. In these and countless other cases, particulars were escaping from a particular association that had amounted to a semantic pall.[23]

People wrote less about death, and that meant fewer particulars. That involves, primarily, a spiritual gravitation; religious considerations no longer compelled them to scrutinize such matters so closely. Jane Freeland, wife of a canalboater, told of her daughter's death in 1869 in a way that reflects older persuasions. She unburdened herself to a sister in a way that might seem callous to those unfamiliar with the setting. She summarized as follows: "if ever there [was] a poor sufferer she was the one." That qualifier *poor* had both descriptive and judgmental meaning. In the archaic terms of prewar America, a "great sufferer" not only bore a high quotient of pain but did so uncomplainingly and with rational awareness. A "poor sufferer" would not or could not meet such a standard of composure. Heartlessness did not prompt the grieving mother to describe her partially paralyzed daughter as lying "stupid." Supremely important things had gone unsaid and unintimated while the young woman lay "stupid," "not in her right mind," or talking "at random." The dread of deathbed derangement weighed heavily upon people of Jane Freeland's generation. "O I think what a consolation it would have been to us," she repined, "if she could of had her right mind and could have talked to us as much as bid us good bye but that was not to be."[24]

This account of the death of Maria, married daughter of a canalboat couple in New York State, has no mention of a medical doctor, but medical doctors and medical developments were entering such pictures in ever greater frequency, appearing vastly more in these humble writings. One can surmise that the contempt held during the Civil War by the United States Sanitary Commission and its medical and organizational functionaries for the Christian Commission and its "spiritual" role would be reflected in the ways that doctors handled patients in civilian life after the war. "Sanitary professionalism," as George Fredrickson has shown, could have little patience for the encumbrances of "devotion, piety, and zeal."[25]

Yellow fever struck Memphis in 1878, and Charles G. Fisher, a prominent Memphian active in the campaign against the disease, fell victim to it. Henry B. Williams attended the ill-fated cotton factor in some capacity, and to that black man fell the obligation of sending dolorous word to the family, which had apparently fled the city. He told that Fisher was "out of his head" nearly all of his last night alive, often calling the names of his wife and children. But Williams found more reason than that final delirium to explain why the dying man had done so little to offer hope or inspiration to those he left behind. According to Williams, Fisher "Did knot have much to Say While he Was Sick A Bout eny one for the Docturs Would knot Let enyone Talk to him." Four days later, the black man wrote again, "for fer that Some mis Stake" might be made or that Sue Fisher might have been unable to read his "Scribling." He repeated and rephrased a good deal, returning emphatically to Fisher's failure to say much; "But he wanted to Talk and the Doctors Did not Let him he New he was going to Die the Last eving he Live he Wanted to Talk But they never Let him Talk." Last words, from time immemorial seen as having unutterable significance, now suffered suppression. Black man Henry Williams may not have perceived those doctors as intruders upon holy ground, as suppressors of a crucial rite of passage; but there can be little doubt that doctors were elbowing family and circle away from the deathbed.[26]

Another agency, one that extended prodigiously in the war and related closely to the medical doctor's role, was doing even more to render the deathbed quiet and sterile of interesting particulars. A few days before old Susannah Scott made a visit to a dying woman to talk with her about "her condision," another visitor described the same situation. According to Rena Steadman, one doctor had diagnosed consumption, leaving nothing to be done. Two other doctors then pronounced the problem dropsy and gave the stricken woman medicine, which helped "write away." Rena Steadman's letter has no spiritual content, nor does it specify what medicine was given. Morphine is as good a surmise as any. That powerful opium derivative had replaced, apparently in medical usage and certainly in common awareness, both mercurous chloride or calomel and the gentler opiate laudanum. Morphine did wonders to lull the afflicted, as well as to render ancient spiritual considerations moot.[27]

In Manor, Texas, J. T. Gregg wrote to his mother about his sister's death of stomach cancer. "I never saw anyone suffer more," he noted, adding that only morphine allowed her to rest. A few months earlier in Cairo, New York, a woman told one sister of the imminent demise of another. The dying woman had encountered much agony, and then morphine was given. Now, "she is real comfertabel," but she "does not say much." Emma considered it a "blessed thing" that she could be there to assist, but she would not likely see anything triumphant in Eliza's departure. In 1884 an aged Michigan couple sent word of a daughter's death to a son and his family in Nebraska. Here again, nothing overtly spiritual intruded upon the account of the sad unfolding. The forty-one-year-old woman suffered "great distress," and the doctor gave morphine. "She did not talk any, only, occasionally ask for a drink of water." Much was gained in the mercy of morphine, but it did take a spiritual toll.[28]

That old couple in Forest Grove, Michigan, tended daughter Rachel until she died, and then "Mr. Hollis took charge of the funeral." Here in rural Ottawa County things were changing, as they were elsewhere. Mr. Hollis represents yet another degree of withdrawal made by common people from the excruciating aspects of death. Even before the funeral itself the "laying out" of the corpse— the washing, the shaving of men, the dressing in burial clothes— might yet remain in the hands of family and friends. That function,

along with sitting at night with the dead, appears in prewar documents with great frequency. It appears almost not at all in the later
period. More and more, as humble Americans made their way to
modernity, Mr. Hollis and his counterparts assumed such functions.
"The business of an undertaker," as Harriet Beecher Stowe wrote in
Oldtown Folks, "is a refinement of modern civilization. In simple old
days neighbors fell into one another's hands for all the last wants of
our poor mortality; and there were men and women of note who
took a particular and solemn pride in these mournful offices."[29]

The setting of death was yielding some of its bleakness. Thus in
Oldtown Folks none other than the "village do-nothing," Sam Lawson, stood "more than ready to render those final offices from which
the more nervous and fastidious shrink." In Stowe's fictive world no
one had greater capacity to soothe and sympathize than did Sam
Lawson, and he was there to lay out the father of Horace Holyoke,
the supposed narrator of the story, and to cajole that child into
peace of mind. In *Poganuc People* Stowe did not neglect death and
the deathbed, but she cast the light of mellowing didactic upon the
sternness of the older ways. A chapter titled "The Victory" treats
the death of Zephaniah Higgins's wife, a victory because it bore out
the import of "the phrase 'a triumphant death.'" The next chapter
portrays the funeral, an event in the prewar past that appeared in
the author's recollection as bereft of "soothing accessories":

> People had not then learned to fill their houses with flowers, and
> soften by every outward appliance the deadly severity of the hard
> central fact of utter separation.
>
> The only leaves ever used about the dead in those days were the
> tansy and rosemary—bitter herbs of affliction.[30]

In *Seth's Brother's Wife*, Harold Frederic shifted the focus to upstate
New York and intensified the starkness: "The American farm-house
funeral is surely, of all the observances with which civilized man
marks the ending of this earthly pilgrimage, the most pathetic."
Frederic considered farm life itself to be "a sad and sterile enough
thing," but when death came to rural America it brought "a desolat-
ing gloom, a cruel sense of the hopelessness of existence, which one
realizes nowhere else . . . the melancholy isolation and vanity of it
all, oppress the soul here with an intolerable weight."[31]

When Frederic was growing up in and around Utica, Truman
Pierce and his son, some seventy or eighty miles away in Broome

and Tioga counties, were making the move from farming and carpentry to dealing in furniture and undertaking. They were, of course, pursuing the main chance, but they were as well assisting their fellows to lighten death's sad severity. James J. Farrell has analyzed and interpreted the larger dimensions of changing funerary practices, focusing on Vermilion County, Illinois. It may not prove amiss, however, to get at least an intimation of how two men made the gravitation into some facsimile of modern undertaking.[32]

The 1870 census still designated Truman Pierce a farmer, forty-five years old with a wife of the same age and an epileptic daughter of ten. In that same year nineteen-year-old Clifford Pierce resided with another family, working as a farm laborer. As early as 1865, however, the elder Pierce had been getting involved in the tidying demanded by death's visitations, as on October 1 of that year, when Court Van der Lyn died: "Helped Fraser put him in coffin." By the early 1870s Pierce and his son became more fully engaged in that line of work. On a hot Saturday in August 1873, Clifford attended a Sunday school picnic while his father was selling and trimming a coffin for the wife of a neighbor. A year later the two made a trip twenty miles to Ithaca, where they "Bot Hearse." By the end of the decade the son had followed his calling to nearby Richford, where we find him characteristically engaged on January 6: "trimmed coffin for Phil Lacy tuck coffin to the house and put him in." Pierce completed the job the next day: "Attended Phil Lacy funeral Burried at Berkshire." His diarykeeping seems to have petered out in mid–1879, but rubber-stamped at the back of this handsome diary, which his wife had given him the previous Christmas, appears an indication of new-found substance and comparative specialization:

W. C. Pierce
Undertaker
And Dealer In
All Kinds of Furniture
Picture Framing a Specialty
Richford N.Y.[33]

Undertaker Pierce took the mortal remains of Phil Lacy to a grave in Berkshire, some three or four miles south of Richford. Those close to Phil Lacy perhaps revered that spot, but the grave and graveyard were slipping from their highly favored places as focal points for reflection and sightseeing. As James Russell Lowell's 1876 acerbity had it, a ride through Mount Auburn Cemetery after a joyless dinner remained a fixture of Boston hospitality: "Your memory of the dinner is expected to reconcile you to the prospect of the graveyard." Whatever Bostonians were doing, others were showing neglect. Previously we observed Mary Jacacks as she stopped in Brooklyn to hear a sermon by Henry Ward Beecher. The woman from upstate New York also went to Woods Museum to see the religious representations, and she attended a "Fulton St prayer meeting," leaving a "request for prayers" for her husband. But she made no mention of visiting a spot that had previously been all but obligatory for those of religious disposition, Greenwood Cemetery. Of course, people still visited and tended the graves of loved ones, and graveyards must have received ever greater physical care with the passage of time. But physical care did not translate into active interest. The graveyard no longer had the magnetic attraction it once had had. Perhaps people simply had other, better things to do such as attending a Fulton Street prayer meeting or hearing Henry Ward Beecher.[34]

A visit to a graveyard, any graveyard, had lost much of its fascination, and what appears at first glance as a good instance to the contrary was probably not to the contrary at all. Abbie Griffin of Minneapolis had a full Fourth of July in 1882. The man she would in time marry in a hastily arranged ceremony at her mother's deathbed, machinist Samuel Dike, took thirty-year-old Abbie on the cars to Lake Calhoun, where they went for a boat ride and stayed to watch the fireworks. They also visited a cemetery, and one might suppose that that represents the old propensity to gain spiritual enhancement from a burying ground, here perhaps carried to an extreme in impinging on the nation's birthday. In fact, this graveyard visit probably ended at a specific grave, that of her father. The old and indiscriminate inclination was distinctly waning. People still visited graves. People far less frequently visited graveyards.[35]

These common Americans were also losing their taste for composing poetry or doggerel, and that meant, perhaps fortunately, less deathbed and graveyard verse. A woman who had traveled far from her Maine home returned there to the Penobscot Bay area in 1866, and her musings provide at least a shadow of the old persuasion and some fairly supportable stanzas:

These precious mounds where mother, sister lie,
Here where the Atlantic makes ceaseless moan,
Suggests two kindred graves far far apart
Near the Pacific shore on hill sides lone.

In California, to which she alluded, Obadiah Ethelbert Baker farmed, sold farm equipment, and wrote much poetry, including "Lines in the Graveyard" done at Millville, Shasta County, on May 1, 1884:

Treading around in the graveyard,
    On this the first of May,
Treading around in this graveyard,
    No *wonder* that I stay.

No wonder because eight years before, the Bakers buried their "own sweet Grace" there.[36]

Baker did much in rhymed recollection of his war experiences, and the war itself may have, at least for that moment, quickened the poetic impulse, if for no other reason than Caroline Norton's "Bingen on the Rhine," with that soldier of the legion who "lay dying in Algiers." The Hutchinson family singers had rendered that piece into song, and it is not surprising that a common soldier appropriated something of its meter as he awkwardly transcribed a Will S. Hays song:

on Shilohs Dark and Bloudy grounds
the Dead and wounded lay
A moungst them was a Drummer Boy
Who beat the Drum that Day.

Each of the half-dozen verses return to the refrain depicting that wounded drummer boy "Who Prayed Before he Died." The scene if not the cadence had been removed from "dying in Algiers."[37]

Apparently late in the war an Indiana soldier wrote some reflections in verse about a detail to which he had been assigned, perhaps in the wake of action at Stones River:

On gard too night tis a lonly beat
And with heavey hart and wery feet
Amid the gloom and the dark i tred
for i am watching ore the unburried dead.

It is not clear if he composed this himself or remembered or tran-scribed it. Also late in the war, one of his enemies looked out upon an old battle site where many men, northern and southern, had been buried. This man used his own words, and they betrayed neither rapture nor poetry. Evidently, the invaders who had been killed at that site had been interred hastily, and Yankee bones and clothes had been "scratched up" and scattered about. That burying ground provided, the Tarheel noted, "a great place for reflection." One gathers that it did not inspire him to poetry.[38]

In fact, it was less the young—soldiers or otherwise—than the old who mordantly versified. They had done so with almost stun-ning frequency in the prewar period, indulging their propensity, to use the imagery of Abraham Lincoln, who absorbed much of the spirit, "Till every sound appears a knell, / And every spot a grave." When he wrote to his son in May 1879, William Van Scyoc of Hen-drysburg, Ohio, showed in his writing some of the infirmity of his eighty years, but he had full certainty about the authorship of the appended "sperital song a bout you mother": "i have not Stole it nor bored it i compose it." The first verse of five reads as follows:

Mary my dear is gone
to Swell the world a bove
Jesus stands redy to received
unworthy toungs of to praise.
"Composed and written by William Van Scyoc."[39]

Narcisa Johnson of Tishomingo County, Mississippi, came into the world a decade after William Van Scyoc, and she had reached seventy-two in 1882 when she set down a lengthy "song" that ended with this passage:

Young Ladys all in Blooming years
Think on these solum dying prayers
young gentlemen may you likewise
Remember that you have to dye.

Immediately after that last line she wrote that this "song" was "com-posed after the Death and conversion of Miss Anny Raws." But if one did not press on to a later annotation, one would miss a vital element of chronology: "the coppy of this song was drawn off the 2^d day of June 1837 and this the 2^d of June 1882. I have had it forty five years." Truly, the song of Anny Raws came from the past, a past even some nine years before Abraham Lincoln's deathly tropes. It echoed forty-five years after its creation, but its resonance and that of other deathly things like it were ever decreasing.[40]

At war's end soldier Henry Colyer wrote to his sister from George-town near the nation's capitol, opening with remarks on nearby Oak-wood Cemetery. Colyer failed to improve an opportunity, as the old expression had it; he neglected to grow pensive about that graveyard, a cultural and religious obligation readily assumed even by the youthful of an earlier age. Instead of the elegaic, he resorted to the flippant and the sportive: "Well, you probably think I have com-menced my letter with a grave subject." Whether or not this soldier from upstate New York consciously sought the effect of double entendre in the reference to a "grave subject," he was writing in a way theretofore largely confined to people of some elevation. Fare that had previously been seen only in gentlemanly publications such as *Spirit of the Times* now was insinuating itself into general use and awareness. This subject too will receive further treatment, but a di-gression here may show how parody of the funereal, previously quite untoward, was now assuming at least some pertinence to unelevated views. The religion of common people no longer had sufficient intensity to render them immune to the acids of waggishness.[41]

When the Gitchels in Forest Grove, Michigan, buried their daughter, they did so against the doctrinal backdrop of the ninetieth Psalm, which teaches us to number our days, and with the tuneful accompaniment of "Sweet By and By." The Gitchels combined an ancient text with a new song, one whose enormous popularity since its composition shortly after the war perhaps ensured that it would receive frivolous treatment. Della Moses of Minneapolis did just that on August 9, 1879, when she wrote in a friend's autograph book a "Burlesque of Sweet by and by." She had little space, and it may be as well that her contribution to comic verse is only partly legible. But modernity might wonder how else one could react to, for example, the following passage in that previously mentioned "song" about the death of Anny Raws:

A while before this damsel died
her toungue was speechless bound & tied
at length she opened wide her eyes
and said her tongue was liberisd.[42]

Here we have ventured into the milieu of Emmeline Grangerford, Mark Twain's virtuoso in deathly poetics such as "Ode to Stephen Dowling Bots, Dec'd." She "hung fire" on a rhyme for a dead person named Whistler and "pined away and did not live long." Here, we should keep firmly in mind that Mark Twain's *Adventures of Huckleberry Finn* caricatured some aspects of *prewar* America: "Time: Forty to Fifty Years Ago." Whether or not they "hung fire" on a rhyme and expired, the Emmeline Grangerfords of America did not prosper after the war nearly as much as they once had. Insofar as they lived on, they did so more in parodic fiction than in reality.[43]

That a genuinely popular literature could depict the previously sacred aspects of death in the way that Mark Twain did indicates much about the degree to which American religion was relaxing in the postwar period. *The Adventures of Huckleberry Finn* has more of the deathly than the story of Emmeline Grangerford. Later, the king makes repeated references to "funeral orgies," and he compounds that outrageousness with etymological rationale for rendering it orgies rather than obsequies. The funeral itself features an undertaker whom Huck Finn describes as "the softest, glidingest, stealthiest man I ever see; and there warn't no more smile to him than there is to a ham." Comic commotion then enters the picture with the dog in the cellar creating "a most outrageous row" that brought the ceremonies and the preacher to an awkward halt until the undertaker could get to the cellar to deal with that dog.[44]

Funerals provided even more fun when Mark Twain, and others, went west. "Buck Fanshaw's Funeral" in *Roughing It* presents the spirit of the West in contretemps with the spirit of "a fragile, gentle, spirituel [sic] new fledgling from an Eastern theological seminary." He appears as "the duck that runs the gospel mill" and "the head clerk of the doxology-works," now residing in the land of "You bet" and "No Irish need apply." This "gospel-sharp" fails to understand what "Scotty" Briggs has in mind in approaching him about Buck's funeral, so "Scotty" tries again: "You see, one of the boys has passed in his checks and we want to give him a good send-off, and so the thing I'm on now is to roust out somebody to jerk a little chin-music for us and waltz him through handsome."[45]

Mark Twain had many imitators, and intimations of those humorists, whatever their level of distinction, surface in common writings far more than in the prewar period. To a great extent, that involves technological change, but the upshot of the transformation, for purposes of treating the comic depiction of death and the grave, illustrates a notion formulated into a rule by Max Eastman: "Humor is of all things most unlike religion." Journalist and humorist Stanley Huntley appears about as "unlike religion" as one can get, as his tales of Dakota Territory gained popularity in the 1880s. He concocted a wide variety of witty devices for parodying religion, not the most offensive of which was the report of a sermon as done by a sports reporter.[46]

Near the outset of perhaps his best-known comic poem, "The First Woman of Bismarck," he struck a sentimental chord by using a couple of lines that many readers would have recognized. Before that first woman arrived,

> There was lack of woman's nursing,
>> And a dearth of woman's tears.

Those lines came, slightly altered, from Norton's "Bingen on the Rhine." Huntley wrenched them from the aura of that soldier of the legion who "lay dying in Algiers" to the aura of that first woman of Bismarck, her of unspecified calling who got off the boat from Fort Benton and luxuriated in the sobriquet "Short and Dirty," "from her longitude and looks."[47]

Profanation lay not far beyond the sardonic, as in the "hymn play" uttered by one of Huntley's characters in opening the "game" that featured the planting of Pete Mullins in "A Frontier Funeral," obsequies far more bibulous and unrestrained than Buck Fanshaw's. That character spoke as follows: "Dearest Pety, thou hast left us, and thy loss is deeply feel'd, but no bean eater could bereaft us if thou hadst have just been heeled." The narrator reckoned that the speaker of the "hymn play" had heard it "somewhere in the States," as well he might though not quite as it appears here. Though Sallie Rike of Alamance, North Carolina, grieved in 1868 over the loss of her mother and sister, she had comfort: "but I know that [it] is God that hath bereaft us and he can all our sorrows heel." Humorist Huntley had corrupted the sacred doggerel of a stylized address to the departed, which took fuller form in a printed funeral memento in 1873:

> Dearest sister thou hast left us,
> Here thy loss we deeply feel,
> But 'tis God who has bereft us.
> He will all our sorrows heal.[48]

Under the mocking touch of this scapegrace humorist a bean eater usurps God's place, and the healing balm becomes the vain wish that Pete Mullins had had money when he encountered that fatal "trouble with seven or eight soldiers" from Fort Abraham Lincoln. Huntley had an outré and exotic quality, but he wrote widely noted columns for one of the foremost newspapers in the country. Those columns appeared more than once in book-length compilations. If Huntley seems too outlandish, we can go to the gentler fare of Mark Twain's characters or Stowe's much-remarked Sam Lawson. They provide firmer indication that lesser people of this war and postwar period were being exposed to the inroads that wit worked upon earnestness. Our more distant ancestors guarded even more sternly than we often suppose against levity and the dangers they perceived its posing to mental and spiritual stability. Levity waxed, and other things waned accordingly. People were not, of course, laughing death away, but the almost inveterate attention to painful particulars was lessening, as was the solemn hush triggered by any death, any funeral, any grave.

To one who has spent much time in pre–Civil War writings of common people, some other subjects seem apparent by their absence. Expressions regarding sanctification in the setting of death figure far less prominently than they previously did. In a collection of papers relating mostly to some people in rural Oneida County, New York, there resides an undated and anonymous item consisting of several aged and badly mouse-eaten pages from a diary or commonplace book. Religious reflection was the order of that far-removed day, and a passage treating that demise toward which we all move contains an attenuated hope and prayer: "and sanctify your woes. " This document smacks doubly of the prewar years, a time with an all but ubiquitous prayer that the death of a loved one would do somewhat for the spiritual purification of the bereaved. This writer, probably Sarah Boody, born in 1810, compressed the traditional form that prayed that woes would help sanctify one.[49]

July 1865 seems part of a different spiritual age, and a soldier of occupation in Alabama showed the erosion of the language of sanctification. He had received some bad news from home, and here he was expressing his sympathy to a brother. He did so in a way that has only some echoes of the dying language of sanctification: "I feel very sorry for the great loss you have had which can sertainly never be replaced in this world. But I hop[e] its tri[a]ls will be of good service not only to you but to us all." Had Sarah Boody read this, she might well have wondered why soldier Alexander Borthwick put things in such spiritually unsatisfying ways. She might have been even more puzzled to find the language of service shouldering aside the language of sanctification.[50]

The Sarah Boodys of the land encountered a good many erosions of old ways and adoptions of newfangled ones regarding death. They also heard far less than they had the injunction to survivors to mourn but not murmur. That urging had taken on formulaic proportions, but now it was falling into disuse. The word *murmur* was losing its association with grumbling, a grumbling especially to be avoided when God willed the death of a loved one. Probably familiar with their elders' frequent use of the term, soldiers occasionally employed it to indicate a salutary avoidance. Thus a Georgia Confederate, who spent much time brooding about his inability to make sense of the campaigning, noted, not long after the victory at Fredericksburg, that he and the others marched along to their leaders' directions "without a murmur." That was sound doctrine, but it involved an avoidance that proved too much for many, soldiers or not. Soon the word *murmur* had gone its poetic way, leaving hardly an echo of the old acceptation previously resorted to so frequently at someone's death—mourn but do not murmur.[51]

As have others, these Protestant Christians had long sought to bear their difficulties uncomplainingly, and a tavern keeper in Pleasanton, Texas, urged the traditional posture in an 1877 letter. He wrote on learning of a "grate bereavement": "most cincerly do I sympathise with you, in this your grate loss, all meets with such loses at some time or other and we must submit to it with as much resignation as possible." That qualifier—"as much . . . as possible"— intimated that that posture was not as readily assumed as it once was. Born in 1796, Mason Arrowsmith of Champagne County, Ohio, knew full well that "it is our duty to be submissive," and thus he counseled the wife of his recently deceased brother. A Georgia woman who had once known comfort endured penury after the war, and she brooded about her inability to confront her many hardships as she had been taught. "I don't believe that I murmur," she agonized on one occasion, then came to a contrary conclusion and later resorted to hymnal plea: " 'O for a heart submissive, meek.' "[52]

Resignation—the desideratum of earlier reflections on death—was slipping from the pinnacle of priorities. Death did some visiting in the Marengo–Genoa Bluff area of Iowa in 1868, leaving in its wake bickering over small estates much as Ambrose Bierce held inevitable. Of one of those deaths James E. Morse wrote as follows: "He could not see why he suffered so much. He wanted the 14th of Job read at his funeral, but no remarks to be made." Though he had suffered much, this man had not been, as in an expression one finds far less frequently than before the war, a "great sufferer," that is, a resigned sufferer. "Man *that is* born of a woman *is* of few days, and full of trouble." Verse one and what followed admitted of no commentary, as far as Mr. Whittling, who died of dropsy on July 3, 1868, in Marengo, Iowa, was concerned.[53]

This dying man could not summon resignation, nor could a Georgia woman when her daughter died: "I could not then and can not yet say 'The Lord gave and the Lord has taken away blessed be the name of the Lord.'" With the child three months in the grave, its mother continued to mourn and to murmur: "O! I can not be reconciled to the death of my lovely little one." Such language had theretofore marked the otherwiseminded; such a view was perceived, by those who held it and by those who beheld it, as unchristian. Amelia Lines of Georgia and Mr. Whittling of Marengo, Iowa, seem not to have seen themselves as being beyond the pale. In general, resignation was ceasing to serve as sine qua non of the Christian view of death. Suffering in silence was going out of fashion, and the religion that common people espoused did not so fully equip them to acquiesce as once it had.[54]

In the summer of 1886 a young Kansas woman prefigured fuller modernity when her sister died. Mattie VanOrsdol was nineteen when she took a job in Medicine Lodge, over a hundred miles west of her home in Floral. In her absence her sixteen-year-old sister, Belle, fell ill of typhoid fever and died without Mattie's having been summoned. Her parents—father and stepmother—probably miscalculated the direness of Belle's condition, but Mattie would not see it that way. She assumed a headstrong posture far more in keeping with the twentieth century than with the faith of her fathers. To be sure, she addressed the Lord in time-honored fashion, "*Thy* will, *not* mine, be done"; but that did not suffice. Though she directed her discontent at her parents, she showed neither resignation nor reconciliation. A decided self-centeredness was entering the picture, and, though it will command our attention more fully later, this funereal instance is worth noting now.[55]

Thinking of how her dying sister had summoned each available member of the family for a final kiss and good-bye, Mattie then told of her sister in the coffin: "I gave my darling, the *very last kiss* of all, for she always wanted my last kiss, when going anywhere and *so my lips must be the last to touch hers*, and were." Five days later, Mattie concluded to return to Medicine Lodge, "where my friends think the world of me." "I must go away," she noted, "untill I get a little over dear Belle's death. I feel the folks have wronged us both, and so must go away awhile until I can reconcile myself a little." "Mattie Van," as she liked to be styled, grieved genuinely, but she also kept in mind the effect of her own postures. She grieved for her sister, but she did not lose sight of herself while she did it.[56]

By and large, common people evinced very little of the spirit that Ann Douglas portrayed in *The Feminization of American Culture*, but, as we have seen elsewhere, some intimations were starting to appear. They illustrate the general cultural drift whereby these lesser mortals were appropriating or aping the ways and attitudes of their social superiors. Here Mattie Van might be viewed in the terms Douglas used when she pronounced her inescapable feeling that grief had ceased to be "discipline" per se and was becoming instead "therapeutic self-indulgence." Mattie Van was neither mother nor minister, the archetypal figures in Douglas's account. Douglas made room, however, for a "possible stand-in" for mother or minister, and, surely, Mattie was that to her sister Belle. It may not overstate the case to see in her performance what Douglas called that "curious exhibitionism" that seemed to be doing "the work formerly expected of self-scrutiny."[57]

Though Mattie Van professed to be ready to die and rejoin her sister and mother, she did not give herself an endlessly repeated urging of the prewar period. She did not arm herself by pronouncing, "be ye also ready." (Being " 'smothered' " with Mac Reed's kisses on her return to Medicine Bow may have obviated that.) But in Red Creek, New York, Clara Madan recalled the litany in describing dolorous unfoldings there in 1874: "The events of the week remind us that in the midst of life, when all bids fair for a long life we are liable to die. let me entreat of you to prepar for death while life and reason hold sway." She intoned the old injunction, but so many others were neglecting it. This generation far less relentlessly burdened itself with that urging to "be ye also ready," in part because, as we shall see, the urging had become superfluous.[58]

As indicated earlier, there was a growing relaxation about the dying person's awareness of his or her condition. As a corollary of that relaxation, people no longer expressed such an intense dread of sudden death that might leave one spiritually unprepared. Occasionally, a Civil War soldier would pronounce concern when a comrade was so taken, but that worry atrophied. Generally, that change remained unremarked, but Aileen Fentriss of Pleasant Garden, North Carolina, moved inexorably into the subject when writing about the death of an uncle. "Oh! it is dreadful!" That exclamation came when at last the prolonged misery ended: "I have often prayed to be delivered from a sudden death, but after looking at Uncle Milton wasting away, I think it would be better to die from a sudden bursting of a bold [sic] from heaven, than to waste away."[59]

Common people were getting around to an occasional expression of the modern view in that regard, and that lessening of worry about preparation surely involves, at least to some degree, changes in perception of heaven and hell. Doctrines had softened, and these untheoretical people were more generously incorporating heavenly notions. References to heaven appear more frequently than in prewar writings, and they do so without the circumspectness of the earlier period. A literary instance of that circumspectness appears in Hawthorne's *Blithedale Romance* during the search for the body of Zenobia. As Coverdale, Hollingsworth, and farmer Silas Foster do that work on the river at midnight, the thought occurs that the "evil one" might also be in search of Zenobia. " 'He shall never get her!' " observed Coverdale. " 'That's not for you to say, my boy,' retorted the yeoman." The spirit of that cold 1852 retort, as rendered by Hawthorne's fictive yeoman Silas Foster, grew ever feebler in the decades that followed.[60]

By the same token, prewar references almost always confined themselves to the figure of speech regarding that place where parting is no more, a place given almost no specific feature other than the presence of singing children, especially when the occasion of grief was the death of a child. Now, heaven was losing some of its vagueness and some of the limits placed on its availability. Twelve-year-old

Barsina Rogers of Prescott, Arizona Territory, made explicit what remained implicit in most places. She did writing exercises in a book that had once served as a journal of the overland trip from Indiana. She did nicely with such homilies as "Honesty is the best policy" and "The beginning of wisdom is the fear of God." At the bottom of a page she added special emphasis in offering, "*Heaven* is a PLACE where ALL good people go after death."[61]

One must not make too much of such an observation without knowing the family's particular religious persuasions. Still, the readiness with which heaven, that "Sweet By and By," appears in such writings suggests the further abandonment of the doctrines of Reformed Christianity. A photographer and his wife in Manchester, Ohio, lost their "Dear little Johnnie" to consumption in April 1868, and Mrs. Cruson wrote a lengthy letter describing the death in ways that resemble previous practice. There were such gratifying details as that the child "kept his mind" until the end and that he died in his father's arms with friends standing about weeping. "Well dear friends," she concluded, "it was a hard trial for us to give up our darling boy & say 'O father thy will be done,' yet we feel reckonciled." But this sentiment fell short of an unconditional reconciliation to God's ways, however severe. A condition of reconciliation was entering where none had been thinkable before: "yet we feel reckonciled in the hope of meeting him again when done with earth & earthly things." A sunnier version of the most fundamental matters colored the outlook of this postwar generation.[62]

One might contend that, if heaven were waxing, religion could hardly be waning. But to follow the logic of James Turner, the Henry Ward Beechers of the world were making telling demands upon God, as was Mrs. Cruson of Manchester, Ohio: "Thus, for example, God had to be a humanitarian. . . . In many of the major denominations, it became acceptable to preach nearly universal salvation or some kind of probation after death; by the 1870s, the theological flight from hell was in full swing. And, increasingly, people simply assumed that dead folk they cared about had gone to heaven."[63]

Among the wags in the West who did so much to undermine reverence, the "flight from hell" rarely took on a "theological" cast. In 1878, however, the *Sentinel* of Santa Cruz, California, carried a jewelry ad that opened with the information that Henry Ward Beecher had thrown the "theological world" into a tizzy over the existence of hell. Perhaps to comfort those who might feel unwanted without hell, the ad insisted that there was "no occasion for worry, however, as EFFEY is still among us with his IMMENSE stock of ELEGANT JEWELRY!" In Colorado Territory a mining westerner grumbled when men in his party got drunk: "*Hell yawns* for Such & if there is none tis a pity." It might be a concern to some in Santa Cruz, or a pity, or even a threat to moral economy; but the demise of hell and the corresponding inflation of heaven did a good deal to ease the Argus-eyed scrutiny of death and the things surrounding it.[64]

Once again a qualifier regarding the South must be entered. "In many (if not most) aspects of the dying of death," as James J. Farrell put it, "the South lagged behind other areas of the country by twenty or thirty years." Reducing such generalizations to a matter of years may be risky, but the proposition strikes me as generally sound. Southerners kept death more firmly in mind, and they, far more than northerners, closed letters with the words "until death."[65]

For another example, the disinclination to name children until they had survived at least a few months seems to have all but disappeared in the North but is still found in the postwar South. A woman in Genoa, Indiana, found it surprising in 1882 that the child of some acquaintances had "no name yet," but that would not have surprised people in the South. The awed recognition of death's dominion remained more intense there, and in that same year of 1882 Callie Coble of North Carolina wrote an even month after her child's birth telling that it had no name yet. Farther south a father in Laurinburg used an old but now unusual designation in referring to the baby girl for whom he and his wife were choosing a name, considering foremost a name previously given to a child now dead. He referred to the child as "the strainger," what had often appeared in such writings before as "the little stranger," a term starkly betokening life's fragility and the emotional hazards of cementing ties prematurely. To move from the outset of life to its conclusion, with death skulking along at every step, we can go to Aileen Fentriss, whom we saw soliloquizing about sudden death. Fifteen months later, she came down victim of a fever epidemic, and Callie Coble was there to describe the end: "She did not have the dying grace she wanted to die with but we trust she was not lost as she seemed to have faith."[66]

Aileen Fentriss had not managed to go triumphantly, and the

concern with the particulars of dying now characterized the South a good deal more than the North. In a similar vein, Michael Barton concluded from his analysis of soldiers' correspondence that southerners more frequently wrote letters of condolence than did northerners. Condolence and obituary did indeed seem to lay greater claim upon the spirit of the South, whether or not we wish to explain that in the terms that Barton employed: "Southerners seem to have *felt* more strongly: they seem to have been more romantic, sentimental, and consoling."[67]

We can conclude this comparison with the "Obituary of W. B. Powell" written by H. C. Kendrick, a Georgia soldier who was one of his "comrads." At Second Manassas Powell "was shotten throug the arm, and while indeavouring to get to the rear another bullet struck him in the leg." Powell met death, "that terrific agent . . . which rejects every bribe which fair promises can offer, and heeds not the entreaties, or claims of doing right." He had been an unprepossessing man, "little known" beyond his "immediate friends," and he had been a man, as well, who "had not professed religion." He had, however, prized the religion of his "kind sisters and good mother." The humble soldier who eulogized Powell knew full well that that man had achieved nothing noteworthy, but "any one who has gone to number among the dead" has it "due" to him to have his "virtues" recorded. Kendrick brought that theme to a fairly impressive conclusion: "There is in the life of an independent and honest man something so worthy of imitation, something that so commends itself to the approbation of others, that his name should not be left in oblivion." Kendrick fulfilled an obligation that lived on in the South. If Ralph Waldo Emerson saw men dying without being mentioned, it amounted to little more than the sad commentary that this Georgian might have expected of Yankees.[68]

When Lewis Atherton reconstructed the life of small-town Midwest in *Main Street on the Middle Border*, he placed death and funeral practice in a chapter titled "Belonging to the Community" and in a subsection titled "Recognition for the Common Man." Though well removed from Georgia, those words suggest some of the spirit in which H. C. Kendrick wrote. Atherton did not explore the religious implications of things surrounding death, but he did stay entirely clear of the sort of sensationalizing that has been done regarding the observances of death in the late nineteenth century. Writing of burial and mourning customs, one author pronounced as follows:

While some were comforted, others, overcome by forboding, killed themselves and their children so that they might at least master the time and conditions of a death that seemed inevitable. . . .

If a man didn't kill himself or if a woman didn't murder her own children, the countryside had other things to offer them to pass the time.

This arresting venture—this "death trip"—betrays little if any conversance with the religious views of that era, relying instead on modern psychological theories, which have however much pertinence to the late nineteenth century as individual beholders will have to decide.[69]

Death and the growing evasion and denial of it involved religion foremost and changes in religion. Of course, the evasion and the denial were only partial, even if one shifts the focus a bit and thinks of the "domestication of death" as presented by Ann Douglas. Nicely done letters edged in black, for example, went on betokening the ineffable, as did one sent by Julia Keyes from Wilmington, California, in 1877. Carpenter John K. Baldwin of Bladen County, North Carolina, probably could not afford such stationery, but he could neatly blacken the top margin of the diary page containing the latter half of June 1873. On June 20 his father died. The son spent the next day helping tend a very sick baby and making and trimming a coffin for his father. Four days later, on June 25, the fifteen-month-old baby died, perhaps yet unnamed. Having blackened the top margin of the page, Baldwin went on to provide black borders around the entries for June 20 and 25, and he might have found it puzzling that people a hundred and more years later should be writing about the denial of death in his time. That denial had not gone so far in carpenter Baldwin's area as it had elsewhere, but it went forward nonetheless. More and more, death was becoming a natural phenomenon, plain and simply. Whether or not heaven and hell remained, death was retaining ever less of the exquisitely significant spiritual considerations it previously had had. And Emerson had not been entirely wrong, only premature.[70]

5. *Society and Self*

An essay that Ralph Waldo Emerson published in the *Atlantic Monthly* in 1857 bore the title "Solitude and Society." When that same piece appeared as the title essay of a book in 1870, it bore the title "Society and Solitude." One feels the urge to view that small change as a reflection of a larger alteration of priorities, as an item in the deflation of individualism ascribed by some to the later period. To cite scholars who have been mentioned before, George Fredrickson depicted the war as having an almost inevitably negative effect on Emersonian individualism, with the aging philosopher himself acquiescing in the transformation. In a roughly parallel fashion James J. Farrell portrays the diminution of the individual as an important ingredient in the scientific naturalism that helped alter America's perception of death. That gravitation of emphasis from self to society has some congruence with humble views, but some important complexities or cultural lags require attention.

In that essay of 1857, reprinted in 1870, Emerson still employed a premodern notion of society. Masses had not yet entered his picture. He dealt with the individual on one hand and the approach of another person on the other: "we sit and muse, and are serene and complete; but the moment we meet with anybody, each becomes a fraction." Society meant hardly more than company, and that is the way common people had employed the word in the prewar period.

Raymond Williams points out in *Keywords* that *society* entered the English language in the fourteenth century from the Latin root word *socius*, companion. The gravitation to the more general and abstract meaning accelerated from the sixteenth to the nineteenth centuries, but humble Americans stayed doggedly with the ancient acceptation. Given the terms of the tension—the individual juxtaposed with those immediately around him—the unsophisticated were making a slight but interesting change. They were losing their steadfast suspicion of individualism. They were lessening their once intensely high regard for society and all it entailed. They were making at least a start, slowly and perhaps unwittingly, toward the realization of the untrammeled self in modernity.[1]

Early in 1860 Andrew Jackson Stone wrote to his brother from a "hydraulic diggins" in California after "Eight long ——— long ——— years," with wealth and even comfort as fugitive as ever. His situation prompted him to bemoan the absence of what his brother could enjoy, "the society of kind friends." A decade later young Nettie Snow went for a visit away from the Stafford Springs, Connecticut, area, and word followed her surmising that she must be "almost perfectly happy in the Society" of her grandparents. Usages wherein society meant hardly more than company appeared very frequently before the war but much less so in the next generation.[2]

The word was assuming somewhat different connotations, none involving the massiveness of scale of, say, the Great Society. In one variation *society* meant, not company or the approach of another person, but the social tenor of a particular setting. In the same year that the Emerson essay lent its title to a book, Charles Carver sent happy word home urging that others in the family sell in New York and join him near Spencer, Iowa. "And then we have," he concluded the glowing description, "such nice society here too," meaning among other things that church membership was high and there were no saloons in the county. In the previous year Jacob and Eliza Beth Hufford had had a different story to tell the folks back home in Indiana. The Huffords had "ruined" themselves "forever" by the move to California, where Jacob was cutting wood for three dollars per cord in Contra Costa County. "Society," they explained, "is knot very good Drink whiskey play cards fiddle and Dance." As a character pronounced at the end of "The First Woman of Bismarck" after "Short and Dirty" died heroically,

> "I believe that Short and Dirty
>   Has found a better place
> Than Bismarck for society
>   Put that blue stack on the ace."[3]

A meaning that does not rest entirely comfortably with some of
the general contentions of this chapter had *society* acting as designation for a group more or less formally organized. Thus on November
12, 1873, a Connecticut woman recorded in her diary that "the
society was over to Mrs Converses." Uses such as this and the one of
the preceding paragraph were largely replacing the most basic use of
the previous decades, that rudimentary sense involving no more
than the entry of a second person into the picture. The most significant second person was husband or wife, and discussions of marriage reflect the changes in language and the change in attitude.[4]

On the last day of 1868 a North Carolina carpenter, whom we saw
in funerary setting in the last chapter, took stock of the expiring year.
In so doing, John K. Baldwin was falling behind the times, as end-of-
year reflections became ever rarer. "And so closes the long and
dreary year," this unfashionable man soliloquized, and by the aid of
the "divine ruler I am yet alive to Slate my life for another year."
Then he focused on an event that had occurred just twenty-five days
before: "I als[o] marrid the past year I have a very good quiate and
peaceble and industros Companion."[5]

One has no reason to doubt that description of Susan Cain Baldwin, and the capitalization of *Companion* suggests the prominence
that word previously had. In prewar writings *companion* figured
centrally in the discussion of marriage and of marriage construed as
society. Now, in the postwar years, a scattered few such as this
North Carolina carpenter employed that designation for spouse, for
him or her who had the crucial role of dispelling solitude. Somehow,
companion was getting dropped. It would not do to suggest that
common people had embraced Thoreau's view: "I never found the
companion that was so companionable as solitude." Whatever
caused it, that alteration in terminology betokens other changes
taking place in vernacular treatments of marriage.[6]

The general lessening of the religious dimension meant that the
religious tone no longer so fully permeated discussions of the union
of man and woman. For example, one no longer encounters so many

uses of the term *better half*, which was the attenuated version of the better half of self, whether male or female. That had previously appeared as a parallel or extension of the spiritual category designated by the term *the better part*, that "good" part of life or reality chosen by Mary and not by her sister Martha. The things of the world, which, in the account in Luke 10:39–42 so engaged Martha, would prove transient. Mary had chosen that "good part," the word of Jesus, "which shall not be taken away from her."

The more intensely religious people of the prewar generation could hardly think of marriage in any other than religious terms. That was changing. Writing from the Hassayampa country of Arizona Territory, where she and her husband engaged in the hazardous frontier trade, a woman offered the following advice to the newly married daughter of a friend: "tell her to try to prove a worthy wife, & conduct herself in such a way as to become a great blessing to her husband. May their hearts be united in mutual love for each other is my strong desire." Apache trials notwithstanding, this woman had not lost her religion. But here, addressing sober words to a loved one just entering married life, she neglected, as did many others now that which had previously figured almost obligatorily as the one thing needful for any condition or any undertaking.[7]

In the marital sphere also, in what might first appear as contradiction, as religion receded heaven became all the more evident. Heavenly metaphor and talk of union or reunion in heaven came forth far more readily than before the war. Reticence characterized the heavenly projections of humble people in that earlier period, but now some certainty and detail were entering the discussion. Difficulties beset the Lipscombs of the Spartanburg District of South Carolina in the years after the war, and in 1875 Edward wrote to his brother on learning that the brother's wife had died. He specified to his aggrieved brother his hope that it would be "only during this life that you will be seperated" from Sally. Though not very audacious, that went beyond what had previously been customary.[8]

Using more elevated sources, Ann Douglas depicts sentiments that far outstrip what was written by the Edward Lipscombs of the land. Employing an imperialistic analogy, she tells of people who were "sighting and colonizing territory theoretically of infinitely greater importance than the Southwest: heaven itself." Humble people seem to have harbored almost no such "aggression" as that; but when the focus is altered to such imagery as "Heaven Our Home," at least some aptness obtains. On May 18, 1879, Lizzie Scaper of Memphis addressed some poetic lines to a brother who had recently married or who was nearing marriage. Bearing the title "Married," those lines contained some "simple Precepts" for making "Your Future Home a Heaven" or "A Sweet Foretaste of Heaven." These heavenly invocations fall far short of conquering and colonizing. But they do reveal a familiarity and a boldness that were new to the likes of Lizzie Scaper.[9]

Lizzie Scaper began her poem in a way resembling a more comprehensive theme of Ann Douglas's book. "Well Johnny," Lizzie addressed her brother, "you are caught at last / The Hook by Cupid Bated." Cupid had had little place in the thought of such people, and the transformation—what Douglas calls the "sentimentalization"— that left an opening for Santa Claus and for St. Valentine allowed this figure to squeeze in also. As the language of religious and spiritual dedication waned, the language of romantic love waxed. The transitive verb form of the word *love* now came far more fully into play, crowding aside the more staid nominal form of that word and, of course, those locutions wherein reverence and dedication had been expressed without resort to that word *love*.[10]

At Greenville, Texas, in 1867 a former Confederate soldier who had been captured at Chickamauga composed or, possibly, transcribed "Poetry To Annie Sampson
From Her Devoted Husband James P. Sampson."
Directed to the woman he had married a year before, this two-part effort projects to such things as separations and griefs which may await them, and it artfully returns in both segments to this refrain:

Think all our loving oer again
And whisper softly, softly then
He loved me.[11]

Three years later an Indiana couple, Jesse and Ella Sears, wrote to Ella's parents, closing with a blessing that betokens the changing times. They invoked "the greatest blessing which children can bestow on parents, that being "'Our Love.'" Here, adorned with creeping quotation marks, appears the gospel of love which, as it did here, was superseding the gospel. This sentimentalization often assumed less palatable forms, as when Jesse, a small-town singing teacher, had courted Ella. He could become downright effusive about his "darling 'One,' " for whom he was composing a song to be sung by them at their wedding, "We are made one." Jesse Sears made heavy use of the word *darling* and other unaccustomed items: "How sweet and affectionate will be our honeymoon, darling wont it last forever?" Theretofore an alien abstraction to unprepossessing people, *honeymoon* also was now occasionally entering their language and their practice.[12]

This Hoosier singing schoolmaster had growing company, for example, a Hoosier barber and the woman he married. Delbert Boston figured as "darling" in the language of Ella Furney of Harlan, Indiana, and he made an effort to oblige poetry, if not common sense, by signing his letters, "Della." That, it almost grieves one to point out, rhymed with Ella. Treacle was reaching common people, leaving the forthright ways of the past in disarray. In fact, this romantic barber could plummet almost all the way into that "Gospel of Love" which the *New York Times* reviled in the wake of the Beecher scandal. In one letter, not far above the subscription "Your Devoted Della," Boston offered what would have been to people of the preceding generation a shockingly inadmissible expression of love: "Now my dear little angel, or should I say little Goddess, for I worship you, (forgive me please) more than I do my God." He recognized his impropriety, as that parenthetical construction attests, but the offense of idolatry appears all the greater for the admission. His ancestors had been Argus-eyed in their avoidance of that sin.[13]

Writing from Findlay, Ohio, where he worked for a few months, the young barber closed an 1889 letter to Ella with "Your own boy. Della." At other times they exchanged such ascriptions as "your own little boy" and "your own little girl." Infantilization came hard on the heels of sentimentalization. Such untoward usages came at least in part from the war experience, when many of the "soldier boys" were indeed no more than boys. Thus a Vermont mother importuned a son to behave properly, reminding him of his promise of "what a good *boy* you would be if only you could go to war." That "*boy*" had been either seventeen or eighteen when he went to war in early 1862, and many others were even younger. Henry Clay Work's war song "Pictures on the Wall" moved the nexus from the parental to the romantic in the plaintive wonderment of a young woman longing to see her "boy" once more. Soldiers acquiesced, and Sylvester Smith of upstate New York, for example, often ended letters to his wife with "your soldier Boy."[14]

Perhaps one should not add such usages to the list of the war's regrettable consequences, but that conflict certainly had something to do with their emergence. Henry Wight was born in the Bandera-Fredericksburg area of Texas in 1869, son of a Confederate veteran, and he almost certainly had reached his twentieth birthday when he wrote home from West Texas in late 1889. He had been in the Big Spring–Sweetwater area for months, and success had evaded him. His parents' recent expression of concern about him pleased young Wight because, as he put it, "I am a Boy that loves sympathy." Then he compounded his wretchedness by chastising himself for staying away from home so long: "I am a hard hearted Boy." A few weeks before this "hard hearted Boy" wrote from Big Spring, Texas, back in Harlan, Indiana, Ella Furney married her "little boy" and Delbert Boston married his "little girl." Perhaps they all were preparing for the extension of childhood in the century ahead, in what Ellen Key heralded in 1900 as "the century of the child."[15]

With some of the marks of the sentimentalized and the infantilized emerging, a place can be found for what Ann Douglas sees as the urge to establish "a perpetual Mother's Day." Dwight Bartlett of Connecticut fits the northeastern focus that Douglas maintains, and in 1870 and 1871 he wrote home from places in Nevada and Utah Territory agonizing over the sorrow he had worked upon his mother. Writing from Winnemucca, Bartlett resorted to the ever-waxing language of luck and concluded that he had brought ill fortune upon himself by his disregard for his mother: "I often think my leaving you is the cause of my bad luck." Another sign of changing times involves swatches of cloth cut from garments and sent with letters. In the prewar period those generally came from burial clothes, and they are occasionally still attached to the sad letters that carried them. In the later period such clippings nearly always came from a new garment that someone would wear in life rather than in death. In October 1871 Dwight Bartlett told his sister that his mother had sent him a cut from her new dress, and this Connecticut Yankee was carrying it in his pocket "for luck."[16]

A sound emotional attachment to a mother probably defies precise description, and one would need to know far more about 125-

pound Dwight Bartlett and his mother to generalize confidently. But an emotional inflation did seem to be occurring, and not just in the Northeast. At the end-of-school exhibition in Jefferson County, Tennessee, in 1868 some humor entered by way of a performance of "A colloquy in which 8 sciences are explained to Hezekiah Stubbins, a genuine Yankee, but as green as a gourd." The tone was altogether different, one assumes, at the reading of a composition titled "*Mother, Home and Heaven.*"[17]

A perpetual Mother's Day and a colonization of heaven seem apt ways of designating such developments as these. In the previously mentioned "Drummer Boy of Shiloh," as crudely transcribed by a soldier, that dying youngster turns from addressing God in the second stanza to addressing mother in the third: "Oh mother Sa[i]d the D[y]ing Boy look down from / heaven on mee oh take mee home to the[e]." One of the composer's lines was dropped, but the gist remained intact. The formulation—mother, home, and heaven—may have been approaching currency if not triteness among humble Americans.[18]

"Rock Me to Sleep, Mother" appeared in 1860, just in time for the war, and the echo of its opening lines, done "with feeling," endured: "Backward, turn backward, oh, time in your flight, Make me a child again just for to night!" Apparently first published in Boston, it went far afield, and one manuscript repository contains a carefully done transcription of an enlarged version of the song. Probably the transcriber was a Confederate soldier, likely from the Memphis area. That writer felt the urge to specify time and place: "Written in Lake Station Miss in 1863." "Mother come back from the echoless shore, Take me again to your heart as of yore." These words have an ineluctable poignance about which it would be mean-spirited to cavil: "Toil without recompense tears all in vain . . . Rock me to sleep, mother, rock me to sleep." Perhaps one can see in items such as this a move toward the fulsomeness Ann Douglas has in mind.[19]

In St. Paul, Minnesota, in 1883 George Crosby became enmeshed in the sort of impulses considered in the past few pages. He worked in a store in Hudson, Wisconsin, and he had frequent occasions to make the twenty-mile trip to St. Paul, especially as he developed a greater acquaintance with Sarah Reynolds. That young widow had a daughter, and just how the twenty-five-year-old Crosby fit into the picture is unclear. Nevertheless, some of the modes of expression have pertinence. Possibly at her mother's direction, young Mamie Reynolds quickly took to addressing Crosby as "Dear Big Brother," and when he neglected to write to Mamie she referred to him, according to her mother, as a "Bad Bad Boy," fighting back tears while she made that assessment. That suggests a mother's efforts to contrive a big-brotherly association for a child suddenly rendered fatherless, and that becomes perhaps painfully clear when widow Reynolds urged George to let her know should difficulties overtake him: "Let me know & you will always find a Mother with a Big warm Heart."[20]

Five weeks later, addressing "My Dear Big Boy," the widow moved into a different tone as she discerned more fully that George had in mind something more than being a surrogate brother to Mamie. Now she urged patience, and she employed the trope of casting bread upon the waters and awaiting the returns: "Let us Hope that it will be all the Sweeter for haveing to wait for it." Nothing came of this. Widow Reynolds went on advising patience and addressing George Crosby as "My Dear Big Boy," as she did some nine months after the line about casting bread on the waters. In the later letter, written in early 1884, she urged George to come to see them on a certain day, and she envisioned visiting with him "like two Sisters or Like a Lonley Mother & a Big Son."[21]

Confusion besets the reader of this feminized and infantilized language, and in this same letter widow Reynolds indicated that some confusion or tension beset her, too. Talk of "two Sisters" or "a Lonley Mother & a Big Son" simply did not fit the situation. Little wonder Sarah Reynolds suffered "Conflicting thoughts and immotions" and that "Evry thing is so strange to me & I am allmost a stranger to Myself." In 1885 she was working in the City and County Hospital in St. Paul, and George Crosby was getting out of the Hudson, Wisconsin, store to go on to work as, among other things, photographer and sheet-music salesman, one who never married.[22]

Marriage, the most fundamental dimension of society, was coming to be seen in somewhat different ways. The heavy reliance on the word *companion* and the spiritual and godly overtones of the idea of companionship were slipping away, in part to be replaced by sentimentality. Also, rejection of marriage as an institution appears more frequently and more openly than it had in the previous generation, and that rejection was not confined to individuals who had had difficult experiences with it. Now one finds an occasional deliberate, even principled rejection.

Among the Nutting sisters of Decatur, Michigan, two expressed views on marriage that would have been seen as worrisomely eccentric in previous years, unless, of course, pronounced by someone who had suffered a bad marriage. Shortly after Christmas of 1869, unmarried Lucy wrote to a married sister to tell what had transpired in that growing festival, mentioning a sign of the time, Dickens's *A Christmas Carol*. Lucy also reported that on the day after Christmas she had attended a wedding, an event she never enjoyed. She considered "crape" an apt decoration for such affairs, but then she cheered herself by recalling the fine sleigh ride she had had with her beau on Christmas day—"a good looking young man with a fast horse would bring a smile to my lips in my most down hearted moments." It seems unlikely that married sister Lois would have found that "shocking," as Lucy thought she might, but Lois might have wondered if young Lucy's disdain for marriage would endure.[23]

Lois had an older sister, as well as a younger one, who could raise doubts about marriage. Ada Nutting had married a doctor, and there is little if anything to suggest that she was not fairly content. Indeed, she could brood because her husband, Charles, bore a disproportionate share of the burden of caring for members of the Nutting family, appearing to her as "pack horse for the whole Nutting crew." She apparently had a good husband, and she recognized that fact. Possibly, that very condition might have prompted or allowed some heterodox notions about family and marriage.[24]

People often passed letters around, in some cases reading them aloud to others; but some content was not to be treated in that way. So a wartime letter from Ada Nutting Baker to Lois Nutting Dane had, following a remark about someone's little boy, a passage marked "Private—I never have seen the day since we were married I wanted such a boy—nor Charlie I think for I never heard him say he did, and if he wanted one very bad I think I should hear of it—nor girl either—" This letter, like others, escaped the flames to which its writer directed it. Ada told Lois to burn the letter after reading it, but not because of the passage just quoted, nor because of some thoughts more directly pertinent to the matter of marriage: "We are so glad you have a good girl don't let her get married." Ada wanted the letter destroyed because she had unburdened herself of some uncharitable thoughts about another of the sisters, and she invoked the emergent gospel of love by bemoaning her view that there had never been "*love* enough in our Family." Instructions to burn were not always followed. And the grousing of Lucy and Ada notwithstanding, Lois went on delighting in marriage and motherhood.[25]

Two of the Nutting sisters had not had bad marriages, but they dissented anyway. The marriage of James and Emily Gillespie of Manchester, Iowa, degenerated into the pathological, and discouraging words are understandable. Emily came to consider James insane, and she once recorded his accusing her of intending to murder him. Physical disabilities compounded mental ones, making Emily's account one of the saddest one will encounter. Supposing her own perceptions to have been sound, one might expect something even more emphatic than she wrote when her twenty-two-year-old daughter, who had previously been dedicated to never marrying, became engaged to a sixty-year-old pawnbroker in a nearby town. "Ah," she repined, "*marriage is a lottery*," and she embroidered a bit on how "full of deceit" men were.[26]

Emily Gillespie's complaint about marriage seems eminently explicable by her circumstances, but that embittered context was not always there. Stella Atkins of Massachusetts made the move to Minnesota in some subordinate association with another couple, and in April 1872, she received word of warning from her home area regarding a certain man. That specific warning then enlarged into a general one about the hazards of marriage:

On the north lies the empire of jealousy
on the east lies the region of care
On the south lies the state of discontent
on the west a world of unhappiness.

Stella may have appreciated the urging to "look before you leap," but the quadrants were all taken. Stella had nowhere to leap.

I never will marry
Nor be no man's wife.

Though those lines probably had far more aptness for the 1970s, when Linda Ronstadt revived them, they were assuming a modicum of believability in the late nineteenth-century setting from which they apparently sprang.[27]

In that constricted view of society with which this chapter opened, marriage occupied a crucial position; but perceptions of marriage were undergoing changes, often quite salutary to a modern eye. For example, when Adaline Jones of Iowa City, Iowa, heard a sermon by a liberal minister on "marriage and the home, the woman's part," she hardly needed to specify what made it "just as good as it could be." But the large, historic alterations in marriage doctrine which this sermon may well have illustrated had not informed the attitudes of lesser mortals. To them, marriage had appeared as a straightforward shield that a permanent companion provided against a dreaded, isolated existence. Their persistence in that view was lessening. Themes suggested by titles of scholarly works treating women's assertion with words such as *Disorderly Conduct* and *At Odds* have direct aptness for very few of such people as, for example, Stella Atkins; but one can, far more than in the prewar sources, discern in the writings of her kind an undercurrent of otherwisemindedness about marriage.[28]

Unelevated people more and more appropriated the language of social classes above them to sentimentalize marriage and to wreathe it in the heavenly qualities that must have all but invited disappointment. However toweringly important it had seemed to the previous generation, marriage had not been asked to serve as transport to ecstasy, or as ticket to heaven, or even as earthly surrogate for heaven. One feels tempted to press on and associate these emerging notions with the great expectations regarding marriage examined by Elaine T. May, those inflated expectations that helped pave the roads to divorce courts. But instances pertaining fairly directly to divorce in sources such as these are too few and too thin to sustain such a venture. One perhaps can say that, insofar as marriage was being romanticized, it was, at the same time, being trivialized, or at least being exposed to new challenges. Marriage—the linchpin in the common man's perception of society—was undergoing some redefinition, and to some degree that entailed questionings and erosions.[29]

Education figured as another major dimension in the common people's microcosmic view of society. Notions regarding education were also undergoing changes, ones that roughly parallel those affecting marriage. Here, too, one can see an inflation of expectation, not quite a sentimentalizing but rather a start to idealizing. At the most, the gospel of education had been only incipient in the writings of common people of the earlier period. Now it was emerging. As it did so, it affected the perception of society in the same corrosive way that changing views of marriage did. Education was becoming less the comforting and sanative matrix for the young and exposed self. It was becoming more the springboard for individual success.

Late in the war, when Albina Wilson wrote to a brother-in-law serving in an Illinois regiment, she invoked time-honored apologies for the quality of her letter. "I am sutch a poor scribe and bad spellar," she noted, adding that she had gone to school enough but had been "so dumb that I never tuck learning to do eny good." Then Albina shifted the focus somewhat. She allowed that, should she have another chance to go to school, she would take fuller advantage of it. What she said next typifies the period after 1860 far more than the period before 1860—"education is the greatest thing to posses in the world." Here, she ventured onto unfamiliar ground.[30]

Such people as Albina Wilson had, one supposes, always valued education, but in previous years they almost never spoke of it in absolute or superlative terms. Education had not loomed so large as preparation for life, and surely in part that involved its comparative inaccessibility. To be sure, most people learned to read, write, add, and subtract, all of which were nearly necessary and certainly prized. Far more than is generally recognized, however, education had previously had value in and of itself and for its own moment, more than for some moment ahead. Along with family and church it served in that cushioning way until replaced by marriage, by one's own family, by church, by fraternal organization, debating society, and whatever. Now, a projective view of education was emerging, one that involved a payoff after education had been completed. That some ordinary individuals had risen to success in America needs no illustration. That ordinary people had supposed that success was within easy reach or that a common education assured success would require a great deal of illustration. If they believed that, they did not set it down in writing, at least not until the late nineteenth century. Then we begin to see indications of why Albina Wilson could refer to education as "the greatest thing to posses in the world."

A year after Albina's letter, Americus Buck of upstate New York wrote to his mother and brother from an army camp. In urging younger brother Marco to diligence and study, he pointed out that

he wanted him to "succeed and you will not unless you are edu-
cated." To modernity, that line seems dismally threadbare, but, for
unsophisticated people, it was not when Americus offered it to his
brother Marco. It incorporated the somewhat novel language of
success, and it offered that notion of success predicated upon something that had rarely borne such a heavy burden before, education.[31]

Americus Buck went on in this letter to intimate the necessary
condition for the primacy that Albina Wilson and others were coming to ascribe to education. Supposing that his brother would have
attended a certain camp meeting, he drew an invidious comparison.
Though he wrote on stationery provided by the United States Christian Commission, he saw fit to belittle that religious camp that Marco
would be attending: "that is not half as pretty a sight as this camp."
He then offered some particulars of the matter. Soldier Buck probably wished religion no harm, but he was internalizing more secular
ways of viewing things. The educational improvement he urged
upon his brother had previously had a socializing purpose that
connected with and was subordinated to the religious desideratum.
Nothing could assume the role of "greatest thing" until religion
surrendered it. That surrender was under way, and that which
cannot be taken from one was being expressed in the language of
education rather than the language of Luke's account of the sisters
Martha and Mary.

Once arrived here in the war and postwar period one readily finds
that fulsomeness regarding the value of education that one might
well suppose had been there all along and may well have been there
all along among people of more attainment. Once embarked upon it,
however, our essentially humble people learned the lesson of education's value quickly. Thus a young man from Connecticut who was
trying his luck in Minnesota counseled the family at home about his
younger sister. She should have, Leonard Dibble pointed out, "an
excellent education something more than a common school, and
teach her why she should have it." He stopped short of calling it the
one thing needful, but he did say that education "together with a
good character is what makes the difference in the position occupied
by men or women."[32]

Dibble offered abstract advice to people afar, but others duly
assumed the burdens and sacrifices involved in getting an education, especially for their children. While poetically inclined Obadiah

Ethelbert Baker worked as a traveling salesman in California in the 1880s, his wife struggled in San Jose to provide at least some education for their children. About 1881 the Bakers left their small farm farther north in California, and they labored both to maintain ownership of it and to expose the children to the comparative advantages of San Jose. Melissa Baker fought homesickness and fatigue while earning an undependable dollar a day sewing, plus a pittance gained by taking boarders at their rented house. The winter of 1882–83 proved especially bleak, leaving them unable to spare even enough for Obadiah's fare home for Christmas. Still, much as she suffered, Melissa Baker did not succumb to sorrow or regret because the education "is going to be such an advantage" to the children.[33]

Two months later, this indomitable woman renewed her resolve; whatever the deprivations she could take comfort in knowing she had done "some good for the children—at least in this life." The meaning of that last phrase depends on inflection, and so it does not lend itself to certainty of construction. One can state confidently, however, that, insofar as her letters reveal her, Melissa Baker kept her eye and her often troubled mind on the affairs of this world. In this world son Milo proved a success; the sacrifices of Melissa and Obadiah paid off. Writing to his mother from Modoc County, where he may well have been teaching school, twenty-year-old Milo responded in 1889 to his mother's mention of some money she owed him. She must forget it: "What you gave me in those five[?] years at San Jose, by so much hard work and self-sacrifice, can never be counted in dollars and cents. . . . I have much to be thankful for." In time, Milo gained even more education, and he went on to become a faculty member at a junior college, as well as a nice illustration of the American dream, modestly construed.[34]

In the mid–1870s George Loring left Massachusetts because, as he put it, "there is no prospect in the east to get a head." It troubled him sorely to leave his wife and infant son, but, as he explained to his mother, he must go where there was opportunity so as "to cloth feed *educate* and fetch up" that child. His young wife would die shortly after reaching frontier Arizona Territory, but the competence needed to "*educate*" her child was forthcoming. Loring's emphasis of underlining fits the emerging mood. Of course, New Englanders had rarely been neglectful of education. As Ada Nutting Baker, another migrant from Massachusetts, put it when praising the letters written by a young relative: "he got the ground work of his Education down where the *Puritans grow*." Educate as they might, however, those Puritans had been careful to keep first things first. The likes of Leonard Dibble and George Loring were becoming vague, circumspect, and unsatisfactory about what their predecessors had deemed the one thing needful.[35]

The tendency for common people to lodge an almost inordinate faith in education grew dramatically, perhaps roughly in proportion to the growth of the education system, and it grew not only among New Englanders and among those such as Milo Baker of San Jose, who needed only an opportunity. Many others joined the chorus, often lending to it an overtone of poignance. Sometime in the 1860s a crippling accident befell Columbus Furnas of Benton County, Iowa. Early in the 1870s this now impoverished man wrote to a sister in the home area of Ohio to tell of various challenges, especially his daughter Delia. Her father remarked sadly that she would make "a Smart Girl if I was able to move to town & educate hir as I ought to." Life was bleak for a woman in Bennington, Vermont, in the summer of 1888. She brooded over the recent death of a sister and the inability of her and her husband to make ends meet. Also, the sister to whom she wrote had had to remove one of her daughters from some educational program. If only young Bertha could have been kept in school until the coming June, "she could of ben one"—a graduate— "& ben fitted for eney posision." Such hopes and concerns took on an even humbler cast in the South, where common people were becoming aware of and much interested in "free schools," publicly supported, rather than subscription schools. Thus a Rienzi, Mississippi, man considering a move to Arkansas asked a brother who had preceded him there if "ther is eney frew chooles out ther or not."[36]

The poignance thickened when those who had been deprived of education themselves attested to what the deprivation meant to them. Carter Page of Kentucky may have had a distant connection with consequential Pages of Virginia, but, if so, it meant nothing as he sought work in St. Joseph, Missouri, in the mid–1870s. Book-keeping held the most promise, and the town had a school that taught only that subject. But when a rare place in it became "vay-cate," the professor selected a personal acquaintance to fill it. Of course, "if you have the Gift of Gab yow mite Get to Clerkin in a dry

Goods stor or some other buisness." When Carter wrote to his mother in July 1876 he made no mention of the centennial, but he did say that he would send her enough money for a new dress when next he wrote. "I hope you can see a better day some time," he noted, and you "must not dispair for we are all young yet." Still, with "no Education" one must "fight at a disadvantage . . . and when one goes out in the world he sees the need of it." People were indeed going out in the world, ever more seeing the need of education.[37]

Stephen Barron grew up on a small farm near Ellsworth in Hancock County, Maine, with, as indicated by the 1850 census, an apparently widowed mother and six siblings. Aside from farming, he worked in the woods, got married, and served in the Civil War before going west. Probably in 1870 he wrote from the Hell Gate area west of Missoula, Montana Territory, urging that his daughter Mary learn "to kep school" and not be allowed to go to the "facters" (factories). He could elaborate from personal experience: "If I had good lerning I wood not be so hard up all the time. I wos oferd the sherff ofes but I dasent take it for I did not know a nof to do the bissness." That he had signed on as a civilian packer for a military operation came to his family in Maine as the last word from Stephen Barron.[38]

Nellie Kittredge's parents brought her as a small child from Massachusetts to the Glyndon, Minnesota, area, and in time she would have an interesting career as a teacher in Alaska. For a while, as she was making her way out of Glyndon and on to better things such as Carleton College, Nellie corresponded with childhood acquaintances whose circumstances held less promise. When "lizzie morr" responded to a letter from Nellie in the harvest season of 1883, she told that she had had "thrishers" and could do no "ritting" when she had wanted to answer Nellie's letter. Three months later, another friend who had left Glyndon addressed the matter of education and the separations it worked: "so you and Minnie are out of the corner are you but I ant I am further back than when I was in Glyndon."[39]

Nellie's friend Mabel Johnson described the situation best of all on learning that Nellie had more school before her. Farm work dictated a different course for Mabel. She supposed that Nellie would soon be qualified to teach, but the best she could hope for herself was work as a seamstress. The whimsical projections Mabel then offered must have exacted at least some small price in pain: "I shall have to hurry and learn my trade so as to make your dresses, you know that was the bargain, but then when you get back from collage you will be so tony that I won't dare look at you." Mabel had "almost dispared of going to school any more," but she managed some bittersweet musing about a surrogate scholar to go in her place: "I have a real cunning little kitten have promised it a good education if you see it at Carlton College some day don't be surprised."[40]

What lay in store for "lizzie morr" and Mabel Johnson would be very difficult to determine, but, in one of these cases, a happy unfolding came in time. Stephen Barron's strictures against it notwithstanding, his daughter Mary went to the "facters." There she met the grandfather of the man who, over a hundred years later, edited her father's primitive letters from the West. Mary's grandson—Stephen Barron's great-grandson—served as curator of manuscripts and archives at Baker Library, Harvard Business School, before turning a hand to that editing task. On a modest scale, this too represents a success story, but not the one through the educational channel that Stephen Barron had had in mind.

Perhaps curiously, as education's reputation rose, education itself, as it had previously been construed, encountered jarrings and frustrations. Like virtue, it had been its own reward in large part. Though it had a role as preparation for life, it figured crucially in its own moment by guarding the unformed self against the onslaughts of the world. Now, education had assumed a far greater burden, bringing success to those who negotiated its course. Realities intruded. As with romanticized marriage, stifled by the prodigalities of its own claims, education ran afoul of overgrown expectations. A hard-pressed Arkansas farmer-teacher could have warned the world of the dangers in claiming too much for the educative process. Along with his own litany of burdens, William B. Bradley entered thumbnail diary assessments of students. Of Mary Swarz, for example, he said, "Poor Mary was constitutionally opposed to studying and learning." Nathaniel Palmerton could learn, but it would require a "hickory thicket" to make him. More gently, he observed that Sarah Newbury "Will never learn enough to hurt her." Probably gallantry more than phrenology lurks in the remark that Margaret Hayes's "head is not shaped for learning." One ought not to marvel that "W B Bradley accidentally fell from grace on Wednesday 23rd Oct and got drunk."[41]

Whatever the reason for Bradley's accidental fall, dissatisfaction with the schoolmaster's lot may have been increasing. Certainly, that sentiment abounded. Newly arrived in Bexar County, Texas, in the 1870s, David Perrin wrote home to tell of the conditions there and to give an indication of what his nine children were doing. His oldest, a woman of twenty-one, labored in the "low-business" of keeping school. One of the Nutting girls of Michigan spoke for herself at the close of a school term through which she suffered in early 1862. She had had no intention of becoming a teacher, and the brief experience only hardened the dedication to avoid "that detested name School Marm." Young Nellie Nutting avoided it by becoming a seamstress, or, apparently the preferred term, milliner, until she married a foreman of a stove factory in Kalamazoo and took up housekeeping. She had followed a common path from schoolteaching to millinery to marriage and housekeeping.[42]

In that same winter of Nellie Nutting's discontent, Charles Ross labored as unhappily in his school at Lyndon in northeast Vermont. Even before diphtheria began a devastating visit on Christmas Day, things had gone very badly, and two days before Christmas Ross wrote asking a cousin to send him a " 'rawhide.' " The local functionary who had hired Ross advised him to "break the will" of troublemakers by "thrashing" them, and young Ross prepared to do just that. "School teaching," he concluded on December 20, "is hard business." Nellie Nutting escaped to millinery; in the same year Charles Ross had another avenue of departure, soldiering in the Civil War. The vexations besetting them may have been no greater than those encountered by teachers from the dawn of time, but an added ingredient of disgruntlement had entered the picture. So much more was being expected of the educator, even leaving aside the case of Theron Ireland, who entered an agreement with a school district in Lucas County, Iowa, to report "all Scholars who may be guilty of gross immortality." Conceivably, these teachers entertained the thought that education, if it had all the fine consequences people were coming to ascribe to it, ought to confer rather greater rewards upon those who superintended it.[43]

Dimensions of society such as marriage, family, and education encountered these challenges because now common people were resorting, at least to some degree, to the language of the self and of the individual, categories that Emerson and many others saw as contrary to society. "The determination of each," Emerson wrote, "is *from* all the others, like that of each tree up into space. 'Tis no wonder, when each has his whole head, our societies should be so small." Among ordinary people these impulses came slowly and not yet at all imperiously; but they were coming. As will be discussed in the next chapter, these people were launching forth into society construed as macrocosm rather than microcosm. They were doing so far more nearly as individuals than they had been before.[44]

Once again, the Civil War's involvement in this development bears some examination. A seeming irony that we considered before again confronts us. That lesson in organization that the war apparently provided for some seems curiously absent from the writing of humble combatants. One supposes that they must have internalized the value of discipline and coordination, but they often expressed themselves in ways quite foreign to such qualities. At one level they simply rebelled, often attitudinally and sometimes physically. A man from Maine, for example, served briefly in the Union army and left it without standing on formalities. Then, for whatever reasons, he enlisted under an assumed name in the navy, which he found little better: "I long to be my own master again to go whare I like and to do as I like I dont like to be a slave nor I never will be a gain." One has no reason to suppose that he neglected his intention to go "on a regular tare" when he got out of the navy. His rebelliousness has a perfectly understandable quality, and many others followed a like course. He had declared independence from the army, and he wished to do the same with the navy. He did not command the eloquence that Emerson showed in "Self-Reliance," but he did show some of the same spirit.[45]

The war taught lessons of independence in ways less negative than was the case with this man from Maine. For all that military operations supposedly partook of order and precision, ordinary soldiers often could not perceive that. Instead of coherence they saw chaos. Combat—their reason for being—especially struck them that way, and even in Sherman's triumphant march, as presented by one scholar, "pure chance" and "randomness" informed the soldiers' perceptions. Coordination must have been necessary, and Edwin M. Stanton, Grant, and others seemed to have masterful control of things. But private soldiers said little about such things as teamwork. Indeed, they often expressed themselves in contrary terms. Often they arrived at a sour self-reliance through the conviction that no one would care for a soldier but himself. In large frustration, Henry Bailey of Indiana used characteristic language to tell his sister the simple reality: "i must doe the best i can for my Self."[46]

Very frequently, that theme appeared in discussions of rations and resourcefulness. Henry I. Colyer of New York arrived at a standard generalization after telling of a two-day march before which he had taken pains to pack extra supplies. "The boys laughed at me," he noted, but they changed their tune when hungrily watching him enjoying the fruits of his care. "A soldier does not," Colyer explained, "give away his rations or water from his canteen. They all have their haversacks and canteens—they ought to look after themselves."[47]

Possibly, this outlook permeated the more loosely organized and less well-equipped Confederate armies more than it did the Union ones. Missouri Confederate Tom Colman wrote to his parents from Tennessee in December 1862, and he mentioned the dread of illness—"if a person gets unable to care for No one he is in a bad row of stumps." "No one" is, of course, Number one, not a new expression but one that was gaining currency among such people. A Georgian put the matter in a less folksy but more emphatic way: "when a man gets any thing here he eats or wears it himself, and the rest may go without. . . . I tell you that every man is for himself here, you may be assured." A month before at the first Battle of Manassas, the writer and his comrades demonstrated that they could fight for each other, as this writer contended. But "necessity has brought us to care for self and no one else."[48]

Necessity also impinged on those who were far removed from such settings. Self-reliance became the order of the day for people far less prepared for it than that army deserter from Maine whose otherwisemindedness can be seen in his willingness to "cut every nigers throt in the united states." No sanguinary thoughts appeared in the letter written by a member of the Twelfth Texas Cavalry to his wife in February 1864. His own suffering aside, he dwelt on his concern for his wife and baby. "I want you to take no thought about me," he urged. "Take care of yourself and the baby and I will take care of myself." The words have just a bit of that flinty tone that often surfaces in the language of self-reliance, Emerson's or anyone else's. But John Truss of Pinoaks, Texas, meant nothing callous. In fact, this letter has, overall, a tender quality, and religious sentiments inform much of it. This Texan simply set down unblinkable realities. With no one to take care of him, he might well have been approaching, as his fellow cavalryman from Missouri put it, "a bad row of stumps." Nor could he help his wife. She would have to do that herself.[49]

Independence imposed upon women by the war has such legendary quality as hardly to need mention, except to put it in a general context and to indicate that it has more than one facet. At one level, this untoward self-reliance appears in the wife of a South Carolina farmer as she struggled to handle the family, the farm, and the few slaves: "I shall never get used to being left as the head of affairs at home. . . . I am constituted so as to crave a guide and protector. I am not an independent woman nor ever shall be." Emily Harris hated what had fallen her lot and feared for her sanity before the war ended. Others responded more positively to the challenges, perhaps in part because theirs were less severe than those of Emily Harris.[50]

Soldiers' letters home contain many comments and suggestions about livestock, crops, and the like. No, Hezekiah Mowers informed his wife on the New York farm, he could not recall exactly when the cow Polly "comes in." He thought it should be this month, February 1863, and if his wife would send him the June and July pages from his last year's almanac he could tell her within a week when to expect that calf. Hezekiah's wife was probably no stranger to these matters of animal husbandry, but now she became immersed in details she had previously been spared.[51]

Beyond details such as when Polly "comes in," men often wrote to their wives and others in a spirit far beyond the conveyance of information and directions. Recognizing that the best of such efforts could not suffice, these soldiers were telling the women at home to think and act for themselves. To us, that seems as natural as it does self-evident, but to men and women far less versed in self-reliance than we commonly suppose, the message had an unfamiliar ring. In November 1864 a North Carolina soldier had specific suggestions about some debts, but he urged his wife to "do as you pleas" in that regard and "do as you like about the yearlings." Louisa Phifer ran the farm in Fayette County, Illinois, while her husband served in the Union army, and a line he wrote her in January 1865 illustrates the general tone of many of these exchanges. After expressing concern for his family and some thoughts on planting oats, George ended the discussion as follows: "But you know best how to farm and what to do for you are there and I ant so do the best you can under the circumstances and it will be right." A Georgia soldier adopted language theretofore almost entirely confined to those of means or education. His sister had lost her teacher, probably to military service; but this Georgian in Virginia told her that "self-reliance and [self]-dependence are productive of much" that is good.[52]

Women could hardly do other than heed the advice to be self-reliant and to do the best they could. Mary Labrant meant to do that when she wrote to her husband from De Kalb County, Illinois, in the summer of 1862 telling of a report that all men between the ages of eighteen and forty-five would be drafted: "i for 1 wil help to til the land perhaps you men would say women would make prety work with land but if they haf to go we wil sho you that we can do some thing." As did many others, Jonathan Labrant told Mary to do what seemed best, but she may not have needed the injunction. Almost a year after her determination to "til the land," her husband wearily answered a question she had posed "by simply saying. do as you please." He said it more than once. Mary needed to decide if she should live for a while with her mother and father-in-law, an arrangement Jonathan viewed coolly: "I will close the subject by saying the third time do as you please." A bit of testiness had entered between the first and third offerings of that advice, and Jonathan allowed that she would "do as you choosed" even if he did offer his advice. With her husband hundreds of miles down the Mississippi, Mary may have been all the quicker to heed his advice.[53]

The antagonisms involved in such matters did not always have the modulation the Labrants brought to them, and we can move over to Missouri to see things put more bluntly. In the fall of 1864 Confederate General Sterling Price yet again brought an invading army into his home state. As that force made a swing toward St. Louis, a contingent of it passed the farm of Willard Frissell near Hillsboro. A native of Massachusetts, Frissell joined the "stampead" to get out of the rebels' way, leaving his twenty-three-year-old daughter Caroline at the farm. With the crisis past and things again going as "yousual," she wrote a sister expressing the resentment of an untutored daughter of a fairly prosperous man: "well I had 2 weeks of pleasure and freedom while the rebs had dad run off if I never do again I tell you there is nothing like being your own master men can be so hateful."

Willard Frissell had spent handsomely for the education of another daughter, but the 1870 census suggests that Caroline remained a worker for her father six years after Price's army had provided at least a brief interval of "pleasure and freedom."[54]

Jennie Spencer of New York felt put upon by a husband, not a father, and the troubles reflected in Edward Spencer's letters to Jennie illustrate a source of tension that has received little comment, the fact that so many Civil War soldiers left home voluntarily. These volunteers had not been compelled to leave, though many would have been drafted in time. These early or unnecessary departures did not always set well with those left behind to hone their self-reliance. Jennie was expressing herself in ways marked by sullen-ness, and Edward did treacly compensation in such emergent forms as "Darling," "Pet," "Baby," "little 'Girl,'" and the like, as well as conveying kisses, a communication development just now entering the letters of common people. Soldier Spencer sometimes allowed 450,000 to suffice at the end of a letter, but he once threw "400,000,000,000,000,000,000,000,000" into a particularly salient situa-tion.[55]

Still, Jennie had dark thoughts about a report that he had spent a month's pay *Whoreing and drinking Whiskey* and that letters he mentioned having sent to her bearing money had a suspicious way of never arriving. She hit upon an appropriate response. She in-tended, she told Edward, "to go on the stage to dance" and to travel with a theatrical troupe, an egregiously self-reliant course in a small town northwest of Syracuse. Fairly early in this exchange Edward diagnosed the situation in a way that, in one form or another, frequently lurks in family correspondence of the war. A letter that he wrote to a friend in Syracuse had a passage marked as follows: "dont read this to any One. be sure." "I had my way about coming to war," he noted, "and she will have hers now." If men were going to summon the independence to follow where patriotism—or what-ever—led, women might well do a bit by way of reciprocity.[56]

The West, too, did its part in this exfoliation of self-sufficiency. That theme has been worried almost to death, but common people remarked about it, so it seems apt to consider it briefly. Brevity is in order because things related to it have appeared in another context. A young man in the Bath, New York, area had spent time in the West but had returned home, where he worked as a farm laborer in the fall of 1873. In describing his situation to a friend he told that, when at work, he could be content, but a day of rest brought dissatisfaction: "when sunday comes and i am setting around my mind runs back to when i was west and no one to care for but my self."[57]

For women, the similarity between war and West looms large, though their contact with the former was indirect in most cases. Like the war, the West enticed their men away, leaving them to worry and to assume some manly and unfamiliar functions. Thus two "women in waiting"—waiting for husbands to get things ready for them in Montana Territory—"experienced almost instant autonomy" and an "increase in self-reliance and in independence of speech and action." The modern scholars who used those terms may have gone a bit far, but it could hardly have been much different.[58]

These two women and hosts of others went west, and to some people, especially men, that move made a difference in them. For example, when writing to his mother in Baltimore, a man in San Francisco resorted to hyperbole in depicting westering women: "They become self-reliant, shrewd and energetic at the expense of their more womanly endowments." Truth and fiction, playfulness and earnestness probably blended in his account of one of these "self-reliant" types putting to him the question, " 'who do you like best in California?' " His answer proved unsatisfactory, and his interlocutor kept at the questioning, next? who next? and so on. Finally, after his responses had gone down the list past " 'Rare beefstake' " and " 'Apple dumplings' " he obliged this assertive creature by blurting out "disparingly," " 'Yourself.' " In Prescott, Arizona Territory, a new arrival playfully described one of the local characters as "a strong womens rights woman she has taken upon herself pants and flannel shirt and high top boots and works out to one of the mines, comes in with the boys once in a while spends her time with them drinking smoking and swearing. . . . She will pat one of them on the shoulder and address him in this style, how are you *old hoss*, come up and take a drink that is my style you bet your life."[59]

These letters involved some effort to amuse the folks at home, and they involved male depictions of what were probably isolated or eccentric individuals, though one encounters an occasional and striking deviation from decorum in some western women. Thus a young California woman divulged to her sister that a certain man had become angry with her because she went to the theater with another man, "but he can go to hell I dont give a damn." This same letter contains some material yet more arresting than that, but even in the Far West women very rarely wrote such forceful expressions of independence.[60]

More commonly, that emergent independence took some such form as Hattie Kingman betrayed in a letter to her native locale in Erie County, New York, from the Nebraska home where she and her family had located sometime between 1850 and 1860. The war caused a labor shortage at planting time of 1863, and Hattie saw the following consequence: "I suppose we girls will have to do what we can toward planting." Then twenty-three-year-old Hattie recalled that she would not be involved in that activity because her school term was soon to commence: "I am sorry, I had rather *plough* than teach." On an assertiveness scale, this ranks nowhere near "he can go to hell I dont give a damn," but modernity came slowly, with planting the crops and preferring ploughing to teaching being small steps along the way.[61]

Whether explained by the war, by the West, by the delayed arrival of Emersonian individualism, or by something else, women were employing appreciably more assertive language than before. Neither drama nor rebellion was entering the picture, but a decided gravitation was under way. While Melissa Baker scrimped and toiled in San Jose she concluded some thoughts she conveyed to her husband about their situation by saying, "I cant advise but I must manage to get the daily Mercury & look for farms for sale." That passage "I cant advise" represents vestige or unthinking formality, certainly not reality. It squarely defies the purpose in the second clause regarding the San Jose newspaper, a purpose that comes as capstone of a long passage in which she had indeed advised, and in a way that was realized. Daughter Carrie wrote a section of this letter, informing her father that she and her mother had heard a temperance lecturer that day: "She was a splendid speaker. It was Miss Willard." In 1884, Cornelia Perrigo of Gowen, Michigan, expressed near election time some disappointment that a son preferred Grover Cleveland: "i thought he was too good a temperance Boy for that." She, too, offered a ritual line about there being some who might view it as "wrong for a woman to say any thing," but that did not deter her. Indeed, her male cousin learned by this letter that Cornelia foresaw the day when the death penalty would be imposed on those making or selling strong drink.[62]

To those younger than Melissa Baker and Cornelia Perrigo, the emergent ways came easier and more emphatically. Maggie Sepper was doing common housework in De Witt, Iowa, when she wrote a letter to a friend named Willie. Her unpretentious calling did not prevent her assuming tones that were breezier and more vigorous than her kind had previously managed. She delighted in being, she informed Willie, as "wild" as an "untamed colt." The move toward a positive appreciation of the "wild" and "untamed" will engage our attention more fully later. Now, to keep the focus directly on women and their growing assertiveness, we can go some eighty miles across the eastern Iowa landscape to the area around Mount Pleasant. There, on the day after Maggie Sepper wrote that letter at De Witt, Martha VanOrsdol was born.[63]

The VanOrsdols moved to Kansas when Martha was five, and at age fifteen she began a diary, one that soon revealed a rebellious turn. A stepmother had replaced a mother, and that stand-in could not always take a fond view of Martha's ways. On one occasion threats of having to go to bed early fell on worse than deaf ears: "*she can't put me to bed, anyhow.*" The difficulty had arisen over her allowing boys to walk her home, but she assumed as much assertiveness with them as with her stepmother. She was delighted that her girls' baseball " '9' " took on the boys' " '9' " and "beat them every time." What Maggie Sepper had kept largely in the abstract—being as wild as a colt—Martha almost translated into reality: "I *Dearly love daring,* am a good rider . . . and have rode nearly every kind of animal, from a Jack-(Jass-ack), Burro, Cows, Hogs, Young Steers, Stallions and all, but for *solid fun* give me a colt to *break.*"[64]

Colts were not the only thing she could break with relish. Her diary teems with her flirtations, her "mashes," in the language she had adopted. When a new telegraph operator came to town, Martha decided to " 'mash' him, to see what he's made of." The makeup of Oren Kettlewell included a bit of the flirt, and Martha, then twenty, recognized a challenge. She "vowed" to show him who could do better in that arena, showing an initiative that approaches aggressiveness. She made her vow in mid-June. Three months and three days later she exulted in total victory: "He *cried* almost the whole night, but I would not give up, and now *I have him at my feet,* where I *vowed three months ago I would have him,* and I think it shows me to be the best *Flirt.*" A year earlier Martha ended her description of a similar situation with a single word standing in thorny isolation. In time, Martha married, first unhappily and then happily. But that single word breathed much of the spirit that she and others were assuming. Martha may have stolen a march on most of her peers, but that word has far-flung pertinence: *"Independence."*[65]

Had there been more Martha VanOrsdols and had they been even more rambunctious than she was, one might credit the great self-assurance that Elizabeth Hampsten perceives in the women whose writing she studied. She tells of "their inevitable self-assurance," and she depicts them as appearing "solid in their own eyes" and "sure of themselves." "Such letters display not only self-assurance," she goes on, "but also confidence in the person being written to." These qualities appear far more clearly to Elizabeth Hampsten than they do to me. Rudimentary reality resides in the contention about writing itself that "forming the event into sentences is a way of gaining control." But that does not justify presenting the details people wrote about death not as callousness but as "a way of gaining control." Callousness does not enter the picture, except to squeamish modernity. Religion does enter the picture of those nineteenth-century people, profoundly; but it hardly enters Hampsten's picture of this womanly self-assurance. Nor does that effort to gain control justify one, to cite another example, in working this interesting exegesis of a dolorous letter written by a New Hampshire woman after the Fourth of July in 1884. Foremost among the sad unfoldings, "grandpa" got run over by a wagon and seriously injured. Still, we find this assessment: "what might be a listing of dreary calamities she turns to an exuberant joke." Some may wonder what the exuberant joke is.[66]

Also, those separate spheres of which Hampsten and others have made a good deal seem a bit more congruent with postwar than with prewar writings. The growth of self-reliance all but necessitated that, but among common people the move was hardly hasty or headlong. On a Sunday in March 1885, Kansas farmer Peter Conron encountered a "new turn," but it had little of the revolutionary about it. In the afternoon his wife, Luisa, went visiting, probably with some neighbor woman, and nineteen-year-old daughter Clara wrote in her diary: "Pa thought that was a new turn, I guess, for he thinks Ma ought to be at home always and *especially* if he is here." "New turns" for pedestrian people such as these are perceptible but not dramatic.[67]

Those new ways of discussing things were beginning to appear. In September 1890 Mrs. Delbert Boston, whom we earlier saw in courtship, gave birth to her first child. Delbert had disappointed Ella by not being with her in Harlan, Indiana, when the baby came, feeling obliged to stay at his barbershop in Findlay, Ohio, because workers were receiving their pay and he was squaring accounts. In mid-October she wrote acknowledging "that I received ~~your~~ the money all right," then explaining that correction as caused by trying to write and converse at the same time. No corrections came in a passage wherein she said that they would be together in about two weeks and that he probably felt eager to see "what you did make," the baby. "You know," she continued, " 'it takes a *man* to make a boy, but *anybody* can make a girl.' Don't you feel rather small when you think how many times you said those words? Do you like our baby, Dell? I'm afraid you don't because it's a girl." However proverbial the barber's flippancy, it never came to my attention in such sources starting in 1830 until his reported use of it in 1890, and that after reading all but countless discussions—sober, playful, and other-wise—of babies born, to be born, and so forth. Perhaps with our vaunted individualism we were learning distinctions of a less salu-tary kind.[68]

Willard Frissell, whom we saw scampering out of the way of "Pap" Price's army, wrote to a daughter in April 1862 noting some improvements she should make. He was almost sixty years old and could instruct her in the ways of the past. Unlike Caroline, her sister at work on the farm, Eliza was receiving an education, but she had lessons yet to learn. In noting a death in the neighborhood, her father reminded Eliza that "every step we take is one step nearer the grave." People were calling that to one another's attention with ever less frequency, but Frissell met his obligation. Then he turned to a particular matter of writing style: "use the pronoun I only when necessary." He then quoted and corrected a passage from a letter she had written to him: " 'I guess you think I have forgotten you all but I have not' I will render it thus—Perhaps you may think that you are all forgotten by me but not so." Whether Frissell succeeded in teach-ing his daughter a proper avoidance of the first-person singular lies beyond determination, but it surely would have kept him busy had he decided to set up in business to subdue self in postwar America.[69]

Emerson had been altogether premature in heralding the age of the first-person singular long before, but humble Americans were at last catching on. In 1880 Edward Rust of Brattleboro, Vermont, wrote to some relatives whom he had finally located. He told them of a very difficult life begun as an orphan and continued in a "hard time of it," bound out to a farmer for a pittance. In her part of the letter, Edward's wife, Fannie, wrote that her husband had had "a rather hard life. He has worked hard and has never had a chance to assert himself." The typical prewar American resembled Edward Rust in being too hard-pressed in a "hard" life to be able to "assert himself." Moreover, because of the almost unquestioned primacy of society he avoided doing it. Now typical Americans, men and women, were learning to assert self, or to bemoan their failure to do so.[70]

In her late forties, Iowa farm wife Emily Gillespie settled into declining health and bitterness, but she could take some satisfaction from what a phrenologist had long before told her: " 'I had the most remarkable head he ever examined . . . I could be one of the finest poets—best author—artist.' " As a young woman in Morenci, Michigan, she had been urged in 1858 to go to art school in New York City, but her mother effectively opposed that. As she neared death she regretted having burned some stories she once had written, and her last request was for pen and paper, which she proved too weak to use. At about the time Gillespie slipped into bedridden paralysis in eastern Iowa, Willard Clendenen, who was working in Kansas, addressed a question to Mary Cowan, who was working in Missouri: "Which is better, a man who depends on self or one that depends on rich parents." Soon they married. Years later Willard received a letter from a brother, who apparently had had little contact with him. Willard now lived in Denver, working as a car oiler for the Union Pacific Rail Road; his brother Amos lived in Dalhart, Texas. Both were far removed from the Ohio town from which their father had gone to war but did not return. "You married," Amos began a long, sad discussion, "something near 20 years ago as you know without a dollar, You asked no one nor consulted neither mother nor I. Many things were said that hurt at the time but I overlooked them and do not hold any malice now." Things were lost and things were gained as the Willard Clendenens and Mary Cowans set about doing what Emily Gillespie had failed to do, assert themselves.[71]

Society suffered somewhat, as it did for the Clendenens, but we can close this chapter with a couple of things that were gained or enhanced. Common people had been, by and large, too inured to grim realities to entertain heady aspirations associated with ideas of the self-made man, but now they occasionally employed language that partakes of the success ethos, done in a rather low key. Uriah Oblinger of Indiana went to Nebraska in 1872 to ready a place in Fillmore County for his wife and child. In the winter of 1872–73 he worked in Lincoln hauling ice for a bit more money. He had asked his father for a loan, without success. Now Uriah told his wife that his father could keep his money, "for I have got a will to steer my own boat and have a good sound body to help me steer it." Along the way he invoked the emergent language of luck, noting that bad luck might get in his way. Otherwise, he would secure that home in Fillmore County, "and no thanks to no one." If he sought God's assistance he made no mention of it. He had faith in his own sufficiency, unless bad luck should trip him up. Or, as the message came from another young man, this one near Saint Peter, Minnesota, "I set out to run my own machine and am bound to do it."[72]

Civil War veteran Alonzo Choate of Michigan meant to better himself by attending business school in Chicago. Writing to a former comrade in arms he recognized the "good many difficulties" to be encountered. Still, the tyrannical circumstances were giving way to Alonzo Choate as they had once given way to Ralph Waldo Emerson. As the former soldier put it, "it all depends upon the student whether he will be successful . . . if a man will but try he will succeed." Now, too, small children may have been occasionally learning one of the tritest pieces of encouragement. In an 1878 diary I finally found an instance overheard spoken by a seven-year-old: "If at first you don't succeed, try, try again." Here the impulse of self-assertion may have interacted with the growing faith in education, as it seems to have done in an 1876 poem in the "Hebdomidal Thunderbolt" emanating from the Spring Hill school near Kansas City, Kansas: "And a blessing failing us once or twice / May come if we try again." Irvin G. Wyllie referred to the "doctrine" he studied in *The Self-Made Man in America* as "simple and unsophisticated, more at home with ordinary men than with philosophers." At least to some degree, those ordinary men obliged us by leaving an occasional reflection of that flood of handbooks and manuals showing the way to success.[73]

The proposition that effort assures success involves a venture into the fanciful, and the fancy and the imagination were getting free of the fetters that had formerly bound them. In 1867 Martha Lane of Greeneville, Tennessee, wrote an old-fashioned stricture against reverie in a letter to a cousin. "I am trying," she wrote, "to crush out evrey dreamy power—know I will be happier in after life, if I succeed." The damnation of Theron Ware, Harold Frederic's upstate New York Methodist preacher, came, most centrally, from his venture into the imaginative and the beautiful. Scientific naturalism played only a small part. The elegance and mystery of Catholicism were far more important, especially those of a beautiful and rich woman who espouses the view that " 'beauty is the only thing in life that is worth while,' " particularly insofar as " 'it expresses *me.*' " Celia Madden's playing Chopin on the piano for the enchanted preacher serves centrally in his plummet from grace, the " 'Helenizing' " of him, as Celia Madden puts it. Common folk were not, by and large, encountering the allurements of Celia Madden; nor were they reading Ernst Renan or listening to Chopin's piano music. The precocious and fictive Reverend Theron Ware and the precocious and real Reverend Henry Ward Beecher had stolen a long march on their more pedestrian fellows, but those less sophisticated people were also showing signs of movement.[74]

Previously, both mental and spiritual considerations kept people from castle-building, and frequent warnings against that waywardness appear in prewar sources. Now, people were letting down their guard. Even in places tailor-made for moralizing about its dangers, it went unnamed. Chauncey Stearns had made his way from Vermont to California, and in April 1866, he obliged a brother at home in Swanton with a brief summary of his past few years. Writing from San Francisco, he told a story of general failure. He had arrived in the West years before, "filled with dreams which I never realized." The situation all but begged for some heated words directed at castle-building, but none came.[75]

Off a Caribbean harbor a very young sailor admired the view from a United States vessel in December 1863. Perhaps unwittingly, he employed some of the key terms in the tension surrounding the imagination and the proper checks upon it. "To a person of romantic temperament," he noted, "this place would afford food for the imagination to almost any extent. . . . But to a sailor the romance is gone, the moment the Boatswains pipe calls him from reverie to the stern duties of a sailors life. There is one word in the Navy that speaks as with a thousand tongues that is 'Discipline.' " Theretofore, imagination, romance, and reverie had all surrendered to discipline, though not quite the variety of discipline that this Philadelphia sailor had in mind. Now, discipline—the mental discipline of, say Isaac Watts's *Improvement of the Mind*—grew lax.[76]

Before long, castle-building would lose all of its ominous acceptation, and almost all would come to applaud fantasy and imagination. Sometime in the 1870s a Connecticut schoolgirl prepared a composition that nicely reflects the drift. Nettie Snow's essay titled "A Voyage to the Mediterranean" told of fulfilling the "long cherished dream of my life," travel in France and Italy. The 1870 census reveals that Nettie Snow was the eleven-year-old daughter of a single parent, Jane C. Snow. That "dress maker" of Stafford Township, Tolland County, had no real property and little personal property. That trip from which daughter Nettie returned with "treasures of memory" surely took place in her imagination, and the school in which she prepared that composition had come a long way in not only allowing but encouraging such ventures into castle-building.[77]

At the outset of *The Hoosier School-Master*, Edward Eggleston's central figure in that 1871 work reflected the new dispensations in his choice of methods to win over the family with whom he boarded. He told stories, any stories, even Baron Munchausen. "Ralph had caught his fish," as Eggleston put it, "The hungry minds of these backwoods people, sick and dying of their own commonplace, were refreshed with the new life that came to their imaginations in these stories." Storytelling has always been with us; but we had kept some constraints upon that activity until the time of Eggleston's resourceful teacher, and of Harriet Beecher Stowe's redoubtable storyteller Sam Lawson, and of Mark Twain and the rest. While common people ventured ever more indiscriminately into make-believe, they withdrew from other areas. They debated less, and they wrote less poetry. The founders of a debating society in Mount Hope Township, Orange County, New York, in 1856 gave among their reasons the desire to "cultivate the social faculties of the mind." That meant imposing order upon discussion, just as the appetite for rhyming showed a desire to impose order upon language. Even for ordinary people, order was now ceasing to be heaven's first law.[78]

When Chauncey Stearns died in Somersville, California, he left behind some photographs, very likely of family members, and when that sailor aboard ship off Aux Cayes ended his discussion of the imagination he went on to depict crewmen at leisure perusing "New York pictorals." In a roundabout way that betokens one last aspect to consider in the enlargement of the self, that being the change from a generally negative to a generally positive view of the natural. A drift that had been under way for a long time gained speed among common people in the late nineteenth century, and it involved the self quite centrally. Simply, to express the self means being natural rather than following some form or discipline. Forms and disciplines remained, but they, like some figurative boatswain's pipe, no longer spoke with a thousand tongues. Common Americans probably knew little or nothing about Emerson, but they now had a good start at appropriating his urging to eschew models and be themselves.

Improvements in printing did much to make fiction far more available and, to some degree, more acceptable. Photography had a parallel influence in domesticating for ordinary people such categories as the self and the natural. At compelling moments in the lives of prewar Americans locks of hair and neatly cut swatches of cloth from garments made their way from one to another as mementos, however sad or pleasant. Photography changed that. When Dwight Bartlett received a clipping of cloth from his mother's new dress, he carried it for luck. In the same letter in which he told of receiving that piece of cloth he mentioned what was replacing it: "I will certainly send my likeness next time."[79]

Of course, not all people yet had ready access to photography. For example, in early 1861 Nancy Williams of Oregon, Illinois, sent relatives some "peaces" from her dresses, saying that she would like to send a photograph but feared it might be lost in the mail. Given her financial situation, loss in the mail may not have been the foremost concern. Still, photography became increasingly available, and its spread must have been hastened by the separations worked by the westward movement and, more dramatically, by the onset of war. In the latter regard, Harold Frederic in his story of photographer Marsena Pulford wrote of the "universal notion of being photographed" that came with the war.[80]

Now the pleas and instructions about photographs in humble correspondence almost weary one. Matters of terminology need some attention. The word *artist* often designated a photographer, probably an attenuation of *Daguerrian Artist* and other such terms. The names of the artist's products posed other problems for many unlettered people. Nancy Williams once thanked relatives for a "~~Pategh~~ Potegraph." A man in North Carolina simplified things by referring to a "type" he was sending, thus avoiding daguerreo-, ambro-, ferro-, or whatever. The word *likeness* served well enough, except that it could get entangled, perhaps because of photographic flash, with "lightness," as one man put it. Interestingly, the word *picture* appeared rarely, thus sparing us the corruption into pitcher.[81]

These and other usages were simply the verbal awkwardnesses involved as unaccustomed things started to look, as it were, natural and real. Thus Ben Maddow, a modern practitioner of the cinematographic arts and of American history, wrote of the change wrought by the photographic process, a change not in "the matter of the nineteenth century, but its consciousness. The photographic image became a new and original and highly forceful mode of art—not of books and museums, but the art of daily life." That change of "consciousness" has greatest import for common people in that it involved an enticement into the realm of the natural. Those who recall how stiffly posed those people in the photographs of that era generally appear will, of course, rightly insist that it is only a comparative matter. Still, the word *natural* had never escaped the incubus of its identification with that category that stood in stubborn antinomy with grace. It had, literally, a damned lineage, as Marjorie Hope Nicolson urged us to see in considering the old idea "Curséd is the earth." Among common people redemption of the natural came, at least in part, in an unthinking adjustment to the powerful impact of the photographic image.[82]

"Well Lou," Benjamin Mabrey angrily addressed his wife in September 1863 from the Chattanooga area, "i must tell you somthing about you and Alis the rebes sons of bitches got you both and my nap sack and all my close." One surmises that those "rebes" of questionable ancestry somehow got, among other things, the photographs of his wife, Louisa, and daughter, Alice. The heat of his language suggests the degree of his loss, but, thankfully, he received replacements before long: "I think Alis lookes vary nateral and your picture lookes vary nateral to." Little if anything suggests that Private Mabrey had a voguish streak, but he was appropriating a telling alteration in usage. Others were going even beyond him.[83]

"Nateral" here pertained to the quality of the work some Indiana photographer had done; the images of Louisa and Alice firmly resembled them. At this same level, a north Texas woman described a photograph she was sending by noting that it was too dark and that her hair needed rearranging. The photographer was "not a good artist." Almost naturally, the word *natural* crept past this meaning and on to figure as a normative indication, not of the image or of the maker of the image but of the object of the image. When an Iowa woman remarked that a photograph "looked as natural as life," she had not quite made that transition. But her abundant use of quotation marks and her reference to " 'cunning little babies' " assures us that she would not be left far behind.[84]

A woman in Massachusetts went a bit farther when she thanked her niece for the picture of "Darling Little Nellie," who looked so "cunning and natural." A year or so earlier, Malinda Burton of Mount Pleasant, Iowa, sent a doleful letter which contained an apology for not sending a photograph. The loss of her upper teeth figured in the list of distresses, and that and her general condition caused her to avoid having a photograph made: "my helth not very good yet and I think that I would not look natural." A Mississippian who had relocated in Texas let the folks at home know that the family members were all "fat and sacy," then employing a wonderfully flexible qualifier common in the South and the border states to indicate the degree of someone's natural condition. A man whom the relatives at home knew had recently visited, and, though he may not have been "fat and sacy," he did nonetheless look "tolerable natural."[85]

Natural was swiftly becoming a synonym for *good*, a change that borders on transmogrification. In May 1890 a Texas family made its way into New Mexico to visit the wife's parents, and the wife kept a diary of the trip. As they neared her parents' home she noted seeing things clearly at great distances. At a surprising remove she saw her mother working in the yard and could discern both her dress and bonnet moving in the wind. They looked, she noted, "as nacherl as though we had jest saw them." Without some context, the meaning of this could evade us; but whatever her difficulties, Lydia Dorian was registering approval, as she did in recording that her parents' horses, Rollie and Flake, also "looked nachael."[86]

As in life, so in death, natural was becoming a byword of approbation. In the fictive realm Stowe's Sam Lawson, who often uttered perhaps ironic lines in which nature stood as dark counterpart to grace, nonetheless comforted the grieving Horace Holyoke by assuring him that he had laid out his father so that he looked " 'jest as nateral as if he'd only jest gone to sleep.' " In August 1884 Nettie Comins of Connecticut attended the funeral of an acquaintance, and the dead man "looked very natural." In that same month Rachel and Fannie Ross in North Carolina wrote of the death and burial of someone very close to them. The dead young woman, Sarah Ross, as was so frequently the positive case, "looked very natural"; indeed, another relative judged her as "the sweetest corpse I ever saw."[87]

There were, of course, photographs of the dead, but, by and large, people considered in this study probably could not afford that luxury. Whatever the case in that regard, photographs gave them a greater appreciation of reality, of nature, and of themselves. Photographs helped to ease them into more natural modes and to show greater interest in themselves. Not all took a fond view of that. Sour observer Herman Melville had made the invidious comparison between the age of the portrait and the age of the daguerreotype: "how natural then the inference, that instead, as in old times, immortalizing a genius, a portrait now only *dayalized* a dunce." Modern scholar Richard Rudisill arrived at a kinder conclusion in his study of what the daguerreotypists of America had done: "They taught Americans to be American more completely; they confronted Americans with themselves and sought to help them recognize their own significance."[88]

They were indeed coming to recognize their own significance. These people of the years 1860 to 1890 talked the language of self-awareness and self-assurance appreciably more than their immediate predecessors. As always, when some things waxed, others waned. The self emerged not at the expense of society in the modern sense, the sense of masses, nation, or whatever. As we shall see, the mansions in that realm grew statelier in the eyes of ordinary beholders. Rather, insofar as the self emerged, it did so at the expense of society in the old and confined sense, the sense that that generation abandoned. *Society* had meant *companion* and things partaking directly of companionship. Perhaps with little conscious intent, common people loosened the ties that society in that constricted sense involved. They became freer. They had covered at least some of the course in what has been styled "the odyssey of the self-centered self." They had a long way to go to become Tom Wolfe's comfortable, assertive, self-indulgent "dreary little bastards," but perhaps the pace quickened in the twentieth century.[89]

6. *Politics and the Nation*

Politics and the affairs of state have appeared frequently in the foregoing pages in various ancillary ways. Now we can turn more directly to such matters for yet another appreciable gravitation in common values and expressions. Ordinary people now wrote far more openly and lengthily about the political arena, for which, it has often been assumed, they had long had an addiction. That addiction was not so pronounced as has been commonly supposed. In comparison with what emerged in the war and postwar years, what had gone before appears tepid and halfhearted. Because of the war, it could hardly have been otherwise, but the details of the emergence of the ordinary man as far more nearly political man has both interest and significance. In 1838 in the "Divinity School Address" Ralph Waldo Emerson bemoaned the drift that he saw being described by the nation's "genius," the nation's spirit and interest. "Genius leaves the temple," he noted, "to haunt the senate, or the market." One can see common people making something of the move he indicated, not when Emerson pronounced the above but a generation later.[1]

Though an ever more secular people were heading in that direction anyway, they received the most intense schooling in the use of political language and categories during the calamity of war. Whatever personal, racial, or other considerations may have entered the picture, the logic of the two party traditions became manifest more than ever. Those traditions may not have been the bone of the contention, but they provided two somewhat differing responses to the impasse in the winter of 1860–61 and to so much that came thereafter. And in a blurred and impressionistic way they informed much of what common people said about what was afoot in their troubled land.

Twenty years earlier Emerson made his often-cited remark about one party having the better men, the other having the better principles. Those better principles involved a cluster of notions often distilled into something of a motto of the Democratic party: The world is governed too much. The party with the better men—say, Daniel Webster and Henry Clay—remained unconvinced of the wisdom of that Democratic motto. When the government confronted the secession crisis, it had to determine what, if anything, it would do. However agonizing the decisions may have been, the logic of the situation was fairly clear. By and large, one party felt substantially more prepared to do something than did the other.[2]

Of course, the simple logic sometimes took on complications, as it did for a member of the Third Texas Cavalry as he served in the Memphis area early in the war. While strolling in the city he came upon a statue of Andrew Jackson, an archetypal Democrat but one who could, in certain situations, deviate from that central precept of his party. The cavalryman saw among the "principal preciptions" engraved on that statue a message from Old Hickory: "The Federal Union it must be preserved." That sent him walking out along Poplar Avenue toward camp, "studying about" Jackson's words. He found a way out of the quandary. Seeing two attractive women in a yard, he stopped and spoke pleasantly. After some conversation they gave him a "pretty Bouquet." He tipped his hat, stuck the bouquet in the muzzle of his rifle, and went on his way more cheerily: "says I the mystery is solved . . . what are we fighting for[,] why 'By George' we are fighting for the women."[3]

That cavalryman circumvented the political problem with a resort to a blend of gallantry and playfulness that others could not summon. Hugh Scott of Prairie City, Iowa, showed a more common quality when he wrote to a nephew back in Indiana just after the war. The 1866 midterm elections lay a few months away, and now he fumed about disfranchising "evry rebble, north & south." That led to the sad state of affairs he described: "I have four brothers living, have written to each of them since the commencement of the National calamity, received no reply as yet,—the cause I am left to conjecture,———I know that as a *general* thing I differ from them in a religious point of view, and more generally in a political point." The Scott brothers apparently came out of the Ohio-Indiana setting, but that did not render them impervious to the political tensions now coming to rival or surpass, as they did for this family, religious tensions as a source of disagreement.[4]

Inflammatory language in a turbulent time would surely lack precision, but one can recognize in it points on a spectrum that evidently had sufficient meaning to the people who employed them. As Hugh Scott's letter indicates, there was much more involved than a simple North-South division. That fact has properly become legend, but it is also a reality susceptible of illustration in the lives of common people, almost none of whom ever went onto a battlefield burdened by worries of having to shoot at a brother, a cousin, or another relative. A young Hoosier, who was casting his lot with the Confederacy, wrote home to the young woman who could have altered his course, conveying his regard for her and his solicitude for her brother Henry, who might appear in the ranks of a North that "wages on us a ware we do not want." "I promis," he continued, "my gun shall never shoot Henery." Hugh Scott encountered vexing reality. Young James Caseley, as he assumed Confederate identity, entertained an exquisitely unlikely possibility.[5]

Fully identifiable enemies were there, of course, in the Confederate, the rebel, the secessionist, the traitor, on one hand, and the Yankee, the northern tyrant, the abolitionist, even the Tory, on the other. Beyond that, however, especially in the North, the labels became political; they became embattled indicators of policy preferences within the society. Once past *Confederate* and *Yankee* almost none of the terms had clear usage as epithetic identification of a genuine outsider, some redcoat, redskin, Hun, or Jap. However great the exaggeration, the terms identified people of one's own community, and they firmly applied to those who had, on one hand, long contended that the world was governed too much and to those who had, on the other, long disagreed with that appraisal.[6]

The party of Thomas Jefferson and Andrew Jackson yielded not only War Democrats but Peace Democrats as well, also known as Conservatives, Copperheads, Butternuts, and various local usages such as Yellow Hammers. From the party of Alexander Hamilton, Daniel Webster, and Henry Clay came not only Republicans but also Black Republicans, Radicals, Woollies, and Abolitionists. The two lists contain, in part, synonyms and, in part, gradations, all carrying much opprobrium. Party battles of the preceding generation, however much publicists and politicians may have harangued, seem to have had nowhere near as much reflection in the writing of common people as these labels did. Again, it could hardly have been otherwise. Parturition years or whatever, these times possessed a deadly intensity, and politics came to be, in the eyes of humble beholders, a good deal more than mildly deplorable, periodic diversions.

Abner Beech, the title figure of Harold Frederic's novella *The Copperhead*, explains in a rather self-evident way: "people've been a good deal worked up about the war—havin' them that's close to 'em right down in the thick of it—an' I dessay it was natural enough they should git hot in the collar about it." New York farmer Beech has had his house burned by people who had gotten "hot in the collar" over his political views. Politics now translated into prosecution of the war, and, whatever the stakes in terms of Union, slavery, and so forth, common people had no difficulty remembering that their sons and husbands would be called upon to do the fighting.[7]

Operating in the fictive realm, Frederic could take time at least to illustrate that prosperous farmer's views. An orphan boy living with the Beech family narrates the story, and he tells of Abner's appetite for reading such things as George Bancroft's *History*, Thomas Hart Benton's *Thirty Years' View*, campaign biographies of Lewis Cass and Franklin Pierce, and more substantial treatments of Jefferson and Jackson. In fact, that orphan boy shares his benefactor's fondness for reading, and he too comes to see Hamilton and John Marshall as having been "among the most infamous characters in history." Abner Beech and that boy had full preparation for understanding the crisis of the Union when it came. With real farmers and others like them we have to make do with far less. Though their writings have much more political content than before, they almost never give anything more than intimations of how those beliefs came to be formed.[8]

At election time of 1860 Andrew Jackson Stone wrote from California to a brother in the East, saying much about politics. He clarified a matter regarding his namesake, "the Hero of New Orleans," and, after that, he broached something even closer to hand: "Now brother Wesley I hope there is one thing you will indulge me in saying; you wrote in your last letter that Politics is a trade, and you and I had nothing to do with it; Brother I am sorry to hear that from you; It was for that very same thing that *Our* Grandfathers shouldered their muskets in the Revolutionary War—" "It is necessary," he insisted, "for all us hard fisted fellows to keep posted on these things." Many people such as Andrew Jackson Stone were now coming to do that. They were trying to keep posted, far more than they had previously. The Californian then informed his brother that he had, his namesake notwithstanding, ceased being a Democrat. He had become a "Black Republican," and here he turned to the infamous Broderick-Terry duel of a year earlier to post his brother as to how far the administration would go to "carry their points; Murder if need be."[9]

Wesley Stone's avoidance of politics, a posture far more widely assumed in prewar America than often supposed, was fast losing its tenability. A few months after Andrew Jackson Stone's letter and with that 1860 election now decided, Sarah Kenyon, wife of an Iowa tenant farmer, wrote to a brother and sister back in Rhode Island. A recent letter from them elicited reactions from the spirited Sarah on several points, the political situation especially: "You spoke of politics dont talk to me of that for I get enough of that here." But this seeming effort at avoidance involved hardly more than playful flourish. Sarah Kenyon could no more wish politics away than she could the dreadful winter—"cold as Greenland snow up to Johns, well, (where his legs start from)."[10]

For good or bad, politics had become the order of the day. "Oh dear the *tarnal lection* made awful work here brought produce flat and what you did sell and get the money for perhaps the money would be worthless before you were home." That "*tarnal lection*" of 1860 had, of course, implications beyond the price of produce and that banks were "suspending and smashing": "its all war here they are drilling companies for *sarvices* right smart." It may not have occurred to Sarah Kenyon that the word *service*—generally bereft of misspelling, of underlining, and of plural form—was making a speedy move from the spiritual realm of churchly functions to the secular realm of military and national functions. Whether or not that thought occurred to her, she went on to tell what a neighbor had said of a brother who joined the volunteers: "he would s . . t more than he would shoot." That statement, too, betokened the future a good deal more than the past.[11]

Months later, with war under way, Sarah Kenyon wanted nothing to do with "Secession" or with "rank abolitionism." It seems unlikely that Delaware County, Iowa, entirely spared her such tensions. Parallel tensions appear much less frequently in southern sources, and that may well be in part because the South quickly became an invaded country wherein comparative unity came from palpable threat. Also, those elements and areas in which otherwiseminded-ness appeared most markedly had least ability to leave written expression of it. Such a reality was not confined to slaves and free blacks. Thus a Confederate soldier from central Georgia wrote home from east Tennessee, "one of the dark corners of the world." Old men of that benighted area prided themselves on never having been thirty miles from home; young men were all gone serving in Yankee armies. The women were at home, but they did little but chew tobacco and "cuss the Rebbels." East Tennessee was, of course, a marginal part of the South, and Georgian Thomas Gurr would probably have concluded that it and the North deserved each other. That a former tailor from nearby Greeneville would soon become vice-president of the United States would only confirm such a dark assessment.[12]

At the North antagonisms abounded from the outset, and some sisters in Decatur, Michigan, serve well as illustrations. In September 1861, for example, strongly Unionist Nellie Nutting encountered vexation while trying to write a letter to an older sister who had just had a baby: "Lue keeps singing Dixie Land and I cant write no way." Thirteen-year-old Lue may have insisted that she sang to strengthen a throat rendered weak by illness, but that could hardly have comforted her fifteen-year-old sister. "Dixie Land" was not the only affront to Nellie's patriotism. Within a few months it became apparent that that married sister to whom she wrote did not share her zeal. Americans were becoming far more avid newspaper readers, and Nellie Nutting not only identified but defended what she read: "I read the Chicago Tribune almost every day that *paper* that *you* would not have in the house Lois I am surprised I want to know if you have got[ten] to be a *Democrat* I am an abolishnest and allways will be."[13]

Writing to a friend in Coloma, California, in December 1861,

Becky Baye recalled how, when they had been together there in their hometown, they had argued over the "*Union*." Now Becky was at Benicia, and arguments had assumed such different form that nearly all of the officers from nearby Benicia Barracks had gone east: "Isn't it a shame?" Over three years later Gustave Genthner painfully addressed his father back in Maine from Benicia Barracks. While his brother had stayed home to learn the blacksmith trade Gustave had sought his fortune in California. Little had come of his ventures, and in 1861 he enlisted as a private soldier in California's First Cavalry Regiment, a unit that went east to help meet the Confederate threat in New Mexico Territory. The fortunes of war had made Genthner a lieutenant, and perhaps that compounded his discomfiture in addressing "My Dear Father": "Your letters (I say this with due respect) would be far more pleasant did they not smell so coppery and it is almost impossible for me to answer them with the respect that a son should use in writing to his father."[14]

Such exchanges, whether in the frivolousness of Becky Baye or the earnestness of Gustave Genthner, appeared with great frequency; necessarily, they took expression in political terms. Politics and support of the war had profound interest for soldiers, perhaps more than has been presented. For example, Bell Irvin Wiley's *Life of Billy Yank* has no index entry for *politics*, nor for *Democrat* and *Republican*, though Wiley did, in some general comparisons of the northern and southern soldier, note that the former had "a far livelier interest in politics." And Wiley did devote two pages to what appears in the index under the entry "Copperheads." He provided some lively quotations and generalizations about that subject, but those two pages appear in a chapter titled "The Spirit Ebbs and Flows" sandwiched between the impact of defeat and the impact of simple hardship.[15]

That placement has some aptness, of course, and nothing could be more self-evident than that setbacks and frustrations can cool ardor for a cause. Thus an Indiana soldier, who with so many others was on the move northward in late June 1863 toward Gettysburg, told of struggling through mud with nothing to eat but crackers and water and of camping late in the evening on the south bank of the Potomac only to be roused from rest to spend most of the night crossing that river. "The boys were considerably demoralized," he noted, "and swore they would vote for Vallandigham Dan Voorhees & co."[16]

Understandable vexation does not explain all of the "coppery" remarks. Feelings other than total dedication to the continuation and extension of the war surfaced in innumerable shadings. Modern wonderment about, for example, conspiratorial Knights of the Golden Circle, or interest in desertion statistics, ought not to obscure the fact that legions in the North suffered mixed feelings about the war. More than half of the North's people were or had recently been Democrats. Untold thousands of them felt some degree of misgiving on witnessing a stupendous extension of government power. Concern for personal safety and the safety of others and doubts about massive killing done to free black slaves heightened such misgivings. Political ideas, however vague and flexible, now had consequences far greater than before, and common people registered their feelings accordingly.

The ambivalence and the misgivings surfaced time and again in wartime writings of common people. Vermont soldier George Mellish received a good deal of guidance from home, and he admitted to his mother that his enthusiasm for the war ebbed and flowed. He had experienced "rebellious feelings" and had seen moments when he would "as soon have been on one side as the other." In April 1863, he could laugh at his moments of disenchantment. "I am no Traitor," a comforting fact punctuated by his identifying with the spirit of a recent Ben Butler speech. George Mellish had many counterparts, and the words from home did not always carry the patriotic spirit of Mother Mellish. Private James Glazier of the Twenty-Third Massachusetts Infantry received no such encouragement from brother Ezra back in Worcester. James, a devout man, could hardly have found comfort in Ezra's deriding the "*Ministers of the Prince of Peace*" such as Henry Ward Beecher, who had done so much to precipitate the conflict. For forwarding the "work of the Devil" such clergymen would, Ezra opined, "have more to answer for than Jeff Davis."[17]

As Ezra Glazier's dim view suggests, soldiers had frequent occasion to question or admonish those at home. Thus an Indiana soldier followed a description of action at Gettysburg and the "ticklishest" situation he had encountered with some doubts about the relative to whom he wrote: "it is hard to tell whether you are a butternut or not." A year earlier another Hoosier wrote heatedly to a brother and sister regarding the views of "my most Devoted." What follows intimates lively times ahead for George Lambert and his "most

Devoted": "when I get home, I will teach her that the 'Republicans are *pretty* good *sort* of *fellers* after all' . . . and when the army is discharged I think we shall teach such men as my *Devoted's* Father that the Republican party is a little more popular than he perhaps thinks at present. They may tell you that there are as many Dem in the army as Rep, but tell all such that I say that it is a *lie*." The grumblings and the imputations went on throughout the war and long after, and the bone of contention raised in George Lambert's last sentence—whether Democrats were underrepresented in Union ranks—became nearly all-pervasive.[18]

When the war had hardly begun, a Minnesota soldier serving at Fort Abercrombie in far-removed Dakota Territory lay one evening on a top bunk in the barracks writing a letter, listening to others, and occasionally "putting in some 'lip' with the 'boys' who are talking at once some Politics some religion and some 'Old John Brown.' " Both the casual tone and the blend of subjects register the emerging era. With the war just over, a New York soldier whose name suited his intense patriotism lectured his mother about her "hatred for an abolitionist," later assuring her that he remained "as much of a Radical" as ever. Though Americus Buck did not make clear what they were, he believed that there had been "great principles involved in this struggle." Even as a hospital steward young Buck witnessed malingering, insubordination, and corruption around him, but his belief in those "great principles" did not diminish. The war had now ended, but the political refrains that had been all but pathologically intensified during that bloodiness lingered on. People went on "putting in some 'lip' " on such matters, though late in the war Mollie Wetherald of Thorntown, Indiana, asked Sallie Bradford, who was coming for a visit, if she were a "butternut," or perhaps even a "copper." Republican Mollie probably had an eye to arranging conversational guidelines.[19]

Mollie Wetherald assumed the burdens of civility more than others would in these tempestuous days. The river counties of central and western Missouri experienced extraordinary tensions, but the ugliness there appears as little more than violent extension of what took quieter form elsewhere. As hatreds intensified there during the war, Unionist A. J. McRoberts of Saline County sent his wife home to Ohio and then tried to play "secesh" so he could stay on his farm. That went "against the grain so mutch" that he abandoned both the ploy and Saline County. Learning that his wife, Mollie, had given birth to another child, the father obliged by not only suggesting a name but by doing some editorializing as well: "I shal call him Jim Lain and the first thing I shal teach him will be radicalism and to hate rebels." The name of Jayhawker General Jim Lane of Kansas would register more than ample wrath in western Missouri. Over in Clinton County Sarah Harlan had watched the coming and going of "bushwackers" in the Haynesville area late in the war, mentioning in one letter such border noteworthies as Ol Shepherd, Clell Miller, and the James brothers. So it seemed a relief to her that an election in the fall of 1865 "went off peacable," though "some of the drunken rips like to have had a fuss." At nearby Weston decorum faced even greater challenges some fourteen months later. Indeed, Henry Colman reported that things had been "turbulent" there, with five or six fights the previous day: "the Concervitives hurrahing for Jefferson Davis while drinking the Radicals taken exceptions to it. I think the Rads got the worst of the sport. (No fire arms used)." Henry Colman seems to have been a confidant of the Pool brothers, former Confederate guerrillas.[20]

West-central Missouri was extraordinary, and the line between politics and bushwacking was not clear. For the type of expression encountered in less turbulent locales, a Connecticut Yankee making his way west will serve. He illustrates that side of the tension which, in the North, was comparatively understated. Democrat Leonard Dibble wrote home from La Crosse, Wisconsin, in August 1865, and he took the opportunity of sending a specimen of that party's message done up in what was coming to be called the "red hot" style. Marcus Mills "Brick" Pomeroy had come to the nation's attention as editor of the *La Crosse Democrat*, one of the foremost purveyors of the intense version of the Democratic faith. "I sent you one of Brick's papers," Leonard informed his brother Willard, "He is what he seems[,] fearless[,] the opinions of others not biasing his own." Dibble then turned fond attention to the personal appearance of the redoubtable "Brick" Pomeroy.[21]

Soon Dibble located in southern Minnesota, and in the summer of 1867 he wrote enthusiastically about the efforts of the Democracy in the Le Sueur area, noting especially that former Ohio Congressman George Pendleton, a noted peace Democrat, had spoken at a rally nearby. He also learned that the "radicals" had met defeat in state elections in Connecticut: "May the Democracy triumph." Here he used the old designation for the party of Jefferson and Jackson: the Democracy. He most likely subscribed to the old articles of faith that many saw threatened and then all but destroyed by the northern war effort. Thus in treating the "politics of dissent" in wartime Connecticut, Joanna Cowden describes views such as those held by Leonard Dibble as "not confined to a small and vocal group of insiders." For those dissenters, prosecution of the war meant traducing "the principles upon which their party stood: individual liberties, states' rights, and a modest and unintrusive federal government."[22]

Zina W. Chase, another New Englander in Minnesota, made his way farther west in September 1866 for a stay in the Colorado mining reaches. Apparently in the excitement of the famed midterm election of that year, his wife, Lydia, back in Maine mentioned the possibility in a letter that war might return. Because of what he called the "Traitor Johnson Policy" (elsewhere "Tennissees Drunken Tailor") Zina Chase believed there was a "possible Chance" of that. If it came, it would involve, he surmised, a "war of extermination, and Valantighams of the North will be in the Number." Clement Vallandigham of Ohio apotheosized what people such as Zina Chase perceived as the traitorous impulses of the Democratic party, but that sanguinary business the man from Maine envisioned would extend to "Brick" Pomeroy, most likely to George Pendleton, conceivably to fellow Minnesotan Leonard Dibble.[23]

Very near the time that Democrat Dibble made a brief stop in La Crosse, Wisconsin, Union veteran Uriah Oblinger of Indiana passed through that Mississippi River town, also bound for Minnesota. His view of politics differed a good deal from that of Dibble, and his correspondence with Martha Thomas, the woman he would soon marry, provides additional touches to the notions he shared with fellow Republican Zina Chase. Writing from Rice County, Minnesota, some thirty miles from where Dibble first located at Le Sueur, Oblinger told of the boat ride on the *McClellan*, a vessel named for Union General George B. McClellan. President Lincoln had wearied of that leader's caution, and when others took command McClellan reasserted his Democratic principles to head that ticket in the 1864 election. At least the boat bore an apt name, Uriah grudgingly owned, "for we stopped twice on the way up the river for repairs; and it took us from wednesday morning to thursday evening to reach Hastings," a rate comparable to the general's early war advance on Richmond. Shortly, Oblinger was doing farm labor in Rice County and rankling because he was employed by a copperhead who had proved to be "a good slave driver."[24]

Between Uriah and Mattie, as between so many others, politics came far more readily and fully into consideration than it previously had. In October 1866 Mattie left off writing in an intimate vein to tell of the excitement at a "soldiers meeting" at Logansport. She had made the ten-mile trip and felt "double paid" for it, largely because she got double fare at that gathering—"our noble Gov Morton and Col Ingersoll of Ill." Oliver P. Morton had suffered a paralytic stroke, but that could not keep him entirely out of action in 1866 as he attacked Democrats with, as John D. Hicks once put it, "a ruthlessness and a ferocity that set the pace for Republican orators for many a year." At Logansport Governor Morton made brief remarks, and then Colonel Robert Ingersoll obliged Mattie Thomas fully: "He commenced his speech by say[ing] 'I do not believe that God has ever created the Copperhead that can answer Gov Mortons speech' and then went on I never heard or read such a speech He made the Butternuts look cross eyed and sickly." It may have troubled Mattie Thomas to learn that Colonel Ingersoll would come to be identified with endeavors other than making Copperheads look "cross eyed and sickly," but his Logansport effort had delighted her.[25]

Out in Rice County Uriah suffered troubling dreams about Mattie, as well as worries that she might weary of him. It did not improve his frame of mind to come home "mad" from a political gathering when Republican Congressman William Windom came through seeking reelection in the company of his opponent. Windom had given "hail columbia" to that "Rebel." Thankfully, only a few "copper-Johnsons" had appeared at the meeting, but one had had the audacity to approach Uriah after the speeches. That small Hoosier made bold to inform the "copper-Johnson" that it would provide more pleasure to shoot at him than at a real "jhonny" (sic).[26]

Time and again, distinctions fell by the way. Vehement Republicans such as Uriah Oblinger and Mattie Thomas simply divided the political spectrum of the North into Republicans and Copperheads. Thus in the summer of 1868, with a national election demanding attention, Uriah, still roving and now in Illinois, gave thought to when he and the woman he would marry would next see each other. Tellingly, that would not come "till election time this fall when I will be at home to kill some rebels vote for I want Grant and Colfax to rule our nation for the next four years and not traitors." Six days later Mattie reciprocated in a long letter replete with politics. She told Uriah that a Democratic picnic had been held nearby: "Old Milligan the unhung Rebel held forth nothing but secesh doctrine." That President Andrew Johnson had commuted Lambdin P. Milligan's death sentence, and that the United States Supreme Court, in that bulwark of civil liberties known as *Ex parte Milligan*, had worked his release in finding that he had been wrongly tried would probably have only vexed Mattie Thomas of Onward, Indiana.[27]

However imprecise and epithetic, the language of politics now came easily to humble people. Some three weeks after noting his resolve to get home for the election, Uriah Oblinger told Martha Thomas that he had been ill with the flux, what we would call diarrhea or, perhaps, dysentery. Doctors in the central Illinois area where he had been on a pump-selling tour besieged the stricken Hoosier with calomel, turpentine, and castor oil, through which ministrations his weight dropped to 133 pounds. Those doctors apparently feared for his life for a while, but, as Uriah put it, they did not know "how much constitution" he had: "I know the flux is unconstitutional but then I had a two thirds majority and voted it down." Nothing prayerful intruded upon this account of a serious illness described playfully and rather adroitly in the regnant language of the Fourteenth Amendment and the impasse between President Johnson and Congress.[28]

Of course, tense times were upon the land, and that may account fully for the heightened awareness of national and political issues. But the awareness continued. Having learned to talk politics in these troubled years, these humble people did not promptly forget. Needless to say, the war left a legacy of bitterness, and when, for example, H. P. Shumway, who was teaching a country school in or near Lyons, Nebraska, told of difficulties he encountered regarding his job in 1876, he explained the situation in eminently understandable terms: "It is the old war feeling breaking out again." It broke out times beyond reckoning, as surely it did in November 1884 for a Union veteran turned poetical implement salesman in California. He inscribed five stanzas of eight lines each "On hearing the news that Blaine was elected President."[29]

Two days after those lines of mistaken celebration were penned, Tobias Goodman reported the situation at Hornsboro, South Carolina, near which he had been running a backwoods, state-line groggery. Locally, all had gone Democratic, and he gathered that Cleveland had been elected president, though he had heard reports of "fiting" in New York over that outcome. On the previous day Goodman had gone to nearby Wadesboro, North Carolina, with the intention of taking one Nettie to the fair there: "but her pa wood not let her go becaus I was a Rep well I dont care for that she is all right and he may go wher the wood bine twinest for what I care." Whether Nettie's pa went there or not is unclear, but it seems likely that he had had a return of the "old war feeling." Tobias Goodman, the young grogshop keeper, however, seems not to have been so affected. Like others, he had become interested in politics, as well as in Nettie and in selling whiskey to the folk from the "terbentine" hills and the sand hills. Four years later, with the Democratic victory of 1884 having been overturned but with Republicans yet to take office, a young woman in Indiana told the man she would soon marry that she had been angry at not receiving a letter, then learned that the mail was somehow to blame: "come to find, it was all that old Democrat's fault. I am very glad to know that someone else, (some good Republican) will soon manage the post-office." "War feeling" probably had little to do with this impatience and playfulness and probably little to do with the delight felt by the young barber, who would soon become her husband, at the prospect of hearing a speech by Congressman William McKinley, "one of the best speakers in the U.S."[30]

That party not quite believing that the world is governed too much had vastly extended government, and the war effort itself was only the epicenter of the development. Government intruded and assisted in almost unheard-of ways. It had long carried the mail, and a few years after Ella Furney's eagerness for a Republican postmaster it extended that service to America's farms. Government, at one level or another, had assumed a far more visible posture than it had in those many years when the party of Jefferson and Jackson had run the nation. It may go too far to adduce an interesting case in Pontotoc, Mississippi. In writing to a sister in 1882, Nettie Rowzee responded to a question about cousin John Rowzee, and Nettie delightedly sent the good word. John was not only living there in Pontotoc, he had become mayor. "I suppose you know," Nettie continued, "that he drank himself ald most to death untill the people took him up and gave him the Mayor's office." All had gone beautifully since. Once he got the mayor's office, he got religion and joined the Methodist Episcopal church, making his wife one of the happiest "wimmin" in the world. It would seem almost mean-spirited to contend that the world is governed too much when there might well be other John Rowzees needing to be taken up and set on a proper course.[31]

The people of Pontotoc took up John Rowzee, but most Americans were being affected by other, larger government agencies. The war itself involved, as wars before it had, the combined actions of federal and state governments. A railroad trip to training camp at Burlington suffered delay when the engine hit some cows, and a recruit from Woodstock became excited: "In my haste to see what happened, I ran my head through a window in the car, which was charged to the state of Vermont." Not all blessings flowed from the government of Vermont, and a sailor from Philadelphia, pondering a Caribbean cruise, which struck him as peculiar if not capricious, wondered if Secretary of the Navy Gideon Welles knew of "our doings"—"but what is the difference Uncle Sam can bear the expenses." Whenever Uncle Sam entered the language, he now appears superabundantly.[32]

For enlisted men the impress of Uncle Sam could betoken both the niggardly and the munificent. That excitable soldier from Woodstock, Vermont, now with a year and a half of service behind him, offered sarcastic reference to the "'Grand Excursion Party'" on which the Army of the Potomac had recently been directed by General Ambrose E. Burnside to the disaster at Fredericksburg. An editorial flourish after the signature seems altogether understandable: "High private and Government mule in the service of old Abe and Ambrose E. & Co." Ten months later Woodstock's George Mellish altered his imagery in noting that at least he had been able to save some money "since I have been Uncle Sam's nigger (I mean soldier)." More positively, an Iowan signed himself "uncle sams boy," and a New Yorker referred to his pay as "$32 from my uncle Sam."[33]

It seems exceedingly difficult to determine the degree to which soldiers internalized these notions and expressions which they set down in mockery as well as in earnestness. Even a telling juxtaposition that an Ohioan incorporated in a letter defies one's efforts at construing. Myron Love wrote to his sister from Missouri to assure her that he enjoyed himself and he was not "unthankful to Him who bestows all blessings." From that bow in the direction of God he moved on to an assurance that he would be content to remain in Missouri, or return to Ohio, or go into the South, "just as Uncle Sam orders." What association might be drawn between "Him who bestows all blessings" and "Uncle Sam" will have to be left to others. Perhaps coincidence alone placed them cheek by jowl in this letter.[34]

One can move readily to the commonsense position that people of the Civil War era felt the strictures and the ministrations of government as never before. Of course, southerners had been less accustomed to having government intrude, and that seems to have been true of their armies. Two weeks before being killed at the Wilderness a South Carolinian noted the customary lack of food and supplies but concluded that he would "trust in R. E. Lee for all such." The far more numerous and far better-equipped invaders not only ate far better, they felt the solicitude of such agencies as the United States Sanitary Commission and the United States Christian Commission, on whose stationery they often wrote letters. As George Fredrickson has argued, the tender mercy of the Sanitary Commission admits of some qualifications, but a soldier at Andersonville, noting that there had been a distribution of blankets sent by that commission, probably would not have understood such caviling. Common men seem not to have worried about the philosophical foundations of that agency, though they readily perceived that it was involved in a bloody business. Thus when a convalescent soldier from New York wrote to an aunt from a hospital in Alexandria, Virginia, in early 1863, he informed her that such facilities were not crowded at the moment, then added sardonically that unless another " 'Great Union Victory' " occurred, the " 'Sanitary Commission' " would be " 'Bankrupt.' "[35]

Another New Yorker spending time in a Washington hospital had improved enough to pull some light duty in the bakery, and he was in fine enough fettle to write in archly general terms to his mother:"Dont you think Uncle Sam has done pretty well by me. He first called me out to fight for my country gave me a ride gave me Clothes another ride gave me money learned me to drill gave me another ride learned me to march and to remarch to shoot and to be shot brought me to this hospital & took care of me till I got pretty near well gave me permission to go home on a visit and is now learning me the Bakers trade." Such men occasionally fumed about red tape, something that was now preempting the ground of what had often been called preventing Providences. "What a vast amount of Red-tape there is in the army," a Vermonter remarked. They knew they were enmeshed in that red tape, and another man from Vermont, farmer Russell Silsby, awaited the end of his term of enlistment while convalescing. "The ball of red tape is not unwound yet," he told his wife, Marinda, "but I suppose it will be in the morning, and we shall know our destiny." As an Iowan wondered when he would be sent home, he recognized that "government runs the mashine and we have to let it."[36]

And as these men left the army they did so fully aware that Uncle Sam had not left their lives. Americus Buck still served in August 1865, and he brooded about what to do when discharged. In keeping with a theme discussed earlier, Buck recognized that his army days had changed him, that his father's ways no longer suited him. "All I have any doubts about," he told his mother, "is whether hard work and I have not had such a falling out that I could not work in a tannery." Father Buck would have to get along in the tannery without Americus. "Uncle Sam would give me a farm if I would take it," he continued, "but that is a *rough* job." The Homestead Act did indeed involve a "*rough* job," and Uncle Sam's new-found largesse took happier form in pensions.[37]

Before turning directly to that subject, we might pursue very briefly that allusion to the Homestead Act and the western setting it betokened. The war intensified political interests prodigiously, and, here again, it had a helpmeet in the West. The political liveliness and opportunity in that arena has received much comment, and Edward Eggleston left a nice literary illustration of the theme in the "old story" of a westering youngster who begged his father to join him "because 'mighty mean men got in office out here.' " Five years after that story appeared in *The Hoosier School-Master*, a new arrival in Phoenix, Arizona Territory, gave an indication of how things were going there in the early stretches of the 1876 campaign: "Politicks and a great deal of rum drinking is the order of the day here." In that midway world between fact and fancy occupied by scapegrace journalist Stanley Huntley the campaigning and the bibulousness got some artful elaboration. His Bismarck, Dakota Territory, experience equipped him to tell a tale of historic figure John McLean, demonstrating his oratorical prowess: "When John was elected mayor he gave a spread and made a speech that catched the boys. 'When I came here, by G——d! there wasn't a house here, by G——d! Now you look around, by G——d! What do you see, by G——d! Lots o'houses, by G——d!' That's his speech, and you bet she was a good 'un." Fact often gave way to legend, but politics ran high in such settings. But pensions came from the war, not the West.[38]

"I should like to be home this fall about lection," William Harper wrote to his wife from a New Orleans hospital in August 1864, "I dont like the idie of loosing my vote I would like to have my finger in the pi as the solgers are interested in goverment afairs." That Hoosier, who expected never "to be a sound man again," summed it up nicely, but "solgers" were not alone in wanting to have a "finger in the pi." In that same year of 1864 Mary Crapo wrote to her sister Sarah Mowers about the forthcoming funerals of their husbands, and that involved not only the deaths of two young men from upstate New York but also discussion of "bouny" and "back pay" and "penchion."[39]

William Harper lived on in infirmity, and twenty-one years after that stay in the Marine Hospital at New Orleans he received a letter from a former comrade who wrote to him from nearby "F.T. Wayn," Indiana, with a particular purpose: "Dear friend In anser to your pleas find In closed Afidavit With Signatur and seal as desired And my Wishes for your Success In obtaning Pention Which is Just and Right too all Min Hoo But [put] His life at Stake And lost His Helth too Defend our cuntry But I thin we as a union have lost at the Poles Whitch the soldier gained At the Baynut and sord But We will let the futier look out for itself And if it Bee nesarie We can sholdier the muscat Again." A. J. Adams of Fort Wayne sought to do for his old friend in the Forty-seventh Indiana what a great many sought to do around the country, though that reference to the loss at the "Poles," probably referring to Grover Cleveland's victory a year before, would do Harper no good at the moment. Across the state in Advance, M. M. Brinegar found comprehensively generous terms in which to express her feelings, as she wrote to a nephew who, twenty-three years after the war, had secured a pension: "Perry I was glad when I saw that you had got a Pension—I wish all honorable Discharged Soldiers was Pensioned." She took that position in 1888, a fine year for pensions, but Democrats sometimes prevailed, as they had in 1884. In east-central Ohio two-term Republican Congressman Joseph D. Taylor lost the election in that year of 1884, and John Henry Van Scyoc complained that Taylor was "bete by a rebel by 196 votes." In his anger Van Scyoc expressed the hope that any "solgers" who had voted against Taylor would fail to get pensions because Taylor had been a "grate pension man the best we had."[40]

James "Corporal" Tanner became, in historical recollection, the greatest pension man in this era when common people started to realize what government could do for them. In 1888 Tanner stumped Indiana for Republican Benjamin Harrison, and, whether or not he influenced the views of M. M. Brinegar of Advance, he received the office of commissioner of pensions. History remembers the avidity with which he set about spreading and raising pensions by anticipating his opponents' prayer: "God help the surplus!" "Corporal" Tanner meant to spend that surplus on pensions, but he went too far, even for a Republican administration. Shortly after he left his Interior Department post in the fall of 1889, a Bureau of Pensions functionary wrote to an old army friend about an application that made him uneasy. The bountiful ways of "Corporal" Tanner seem reflected in John Brewster's telling his former comrade in a Pennsylvania unit to let him know if he wanted his pension raised, noting that he had gotten his own raised to seventeen dollars per month. But now there were limits, and the furor over the "Corporal" may well have been involved. Anyway, the claim of Mrs. Nathan L. Brown regarding her husband's condition while a member of the 141st Pennsylvania simply would not do. "I was as much in the *dark* as you was," Brewster noted, "in regard to his cough while in the Co. and, like you, *could not make oath* to the fact that he contracted the disease while in the army."[41]

So went the applications and appeals, often carefully preserved in written form as legal evidence for monetary claim. Few things could enliven one's interest in politics and government the way a pension could. Of course, the situation differed in the South. As rebels, southerners deserved nothing; as pre–New Deal Democrats they may have harbored reservations about such programs. The pension theme has little place in southern sources except in rare and roundabout ways. In 1886 a letter writer in Flora, Mississippi, told various pieces of news, including the fact that a neighbor had made arrangements to sell her house to an "exyankee soldier," who would complete the deal when his pension money arrived. A year earlier a Texas woman told of an attempt at alternative entry to the pension arena. Mrs. Calvin Roberts recognized that her sister had a "craving" inclination: "a few years ago she got it in her head that she could draw our Grand Fathers pension from 1776 & it would be an indepandant fortune for us all. she set in writing & I dont doubt she wrote up a half quire of paper writing to Washington City & other places." The effort went for nought, but it was perfectly understandable in that period of pensions.[42]

That period also saw a series of economic reverses, and those reverses became ever more apparent in the writing of common Americans as they drifted, to one degree or another, away from subsistence agriculture. When Truman Bradway became a private soldier in the Forty-sixth Massachusetts Regiment, he appeared on the records as a young farmer from Monson. In 1878 he wrote to a wartime friend to report that he had taken a job as a night watchman, after growing "tyard" of better work in a boat manufactory in Ashland. Boatbuilding had "plaid out": "I had to loose so much time in the winter and they cut them down evry year and make one do the work better & better." As for many others assuming wage-earning roles, farm life lay far behind Truman Bradway, perhaps irretrievably. The house he had lost in Ashland also lay behind him.[43]

Financial difficulties confronted many, and a week before Bradway wrote that letter, a counterpart grumbled about having scoured much of the Kansas-Missouri area for work. From Buckner, Missouri, E. K. Lee told of finding only farm labor, and, "as times are now," that would "hardly keep starvation off." In the severe times earlier in the decade John Winsell informed a friend that he had managed to get work on a steam thrasher in Madison County, Illinois, and he stayed with it though it almost blinded him. And things were getting worse there in September 1874; "thar never was shuch a time lots of men ar loking for work and can not get it." In 1873–74, in 1877–78, and to a lesser degree in the mid-1880s such reports abounded.[44]

In the South conditions generally wore an even grimmer cast, but a couple of things did a bit to sustain the southern spirit in hard times. Hatred of the North probably helped some, and William Littlejohn of Union County, Mississippi, put it neatly in noting the dearth of money in mid-1876: "I think it is all gone north among the theavesh ginerration of man kine." The other ingredient appears even more fully in this letter—the need to give thanks to Him who works all things according to His pleasure. That austere Christian perseverance, even fatalism, was becoming, as noted earlier, more a feature of the southern persuasion than of the northern.[45]

The solemnly providential view may have been waning, but Robert Wiebe seems to have generalized too boldly in setting the backdrop for *The Search for Order*, which he depicts in the years from Rutherford B. Hayes to Warren G. Harding. Certainly, "dislocation and bewilderment" abounded. Even granting the vast enlargement of the category of chance as treated in the first two chapters of this study, however, it goes too far to write of a "precarious existence where only chance made sense." In the war and often in the West that was, for many, the simple fact of the matter; but in the more interconnected nation that was emerging, sense could be made in other ways. Whether it involved approval or disapproval, some modicum of sense could be made by the actions of government. The considerations that rarely if ever entered the writings of the members of those island communities of previous years now begin to receive frequent expression. In common American people we can now discern the emergence of the modern insistence described by Jacques Ellul as the "political illusion": "The motives, the processes, the mysteries that made man accept religion and expect God to accomplish what he was unable to do leads him nowadays into politics and makes him expect those things from the state."[46]

Writing from Springfield, Illinois, in the fall of 1867 S. H. Parsons assured a friend that he was doing his best to clear a debt he owed him. But money was scarce, and his efforts to sell a part of his land had failed: "everybody is afraid to do any thing and since the elections in Ohio & Pennsylvania it is worse than ever people say they had rather do no business at all for a year to come." He may have been delaying payment of a debt, but to a vastly greater degree people such as he assumed their vital interest in the political arena. Five years later, in the wake of the election of 1872, N. B. Booth wrote east from El Monte, California, telling that that area east of Los Angeles "went for Grant" even though it was strongly Democratic. That involved no mystery, only the Southern Pacific. Republicans, worrying less about governing too much, showed greater alacrity in supporting such things as railroads. Booth gathered that the line would run somewhat to the north of him, with a depot within three or four miles. Surely, that "will improve business . . . and better our prospects." That would be none too soon because a grasshopper plague had rendered the neighborhood all but "deserted," leaving only Booth, "another American family a mexican also and the store with two Jews within the circuit of a mile." Such slogans as "anything to defeat Grant" made no sense in El Monte. At El Monte or elsewhere, westerners, wanting the federal government to work its extensions as quickly as possible, often echoed the refrains of such figures as Henry Clay, once known as Harry of the West.[47]

Some details in the often sad odyssey of James Glazier reflect the theme in another way. He served in the war and then went west, thus getting spiritual certification in the most basic ways of his time. Misfortune overcame him in the Far West at the beginning of the 1880s, and he made his way back to Salem, Massachusetts, his home area. There he placed some of his motherless children and went south with his two oldest boys in search of carpentry and masonry work. Thus we find him in January 1883, seeking employment on the construction of the Leon County courthouse at Tallahassee and almost despairing: "At home gloomy day—no income—debts—darkness—O my God—what a *life!*" Four days later the darkness had worsened: "These are among the darkest days of my life—no work—cant compete with negros—expenses 1.25 a day." The worst lay ahead, and on November 4, 1884, Republican Glazier "voted entire Democratic ticket National Cleavland & Gov E. A. Perry," both winners. It would be futile to try to establish a relationship between Glazier's efforts to get work on government projects, such as the county courthouse and the state capitol, and his erratic vote of 1884, a vote cast, of course, before the days of the Australian ballot. Several miserable months yet separated Glazier from his return to California, where, back in Mendocino County, he wrote on November 6, 1888: "Presidential Election Voted straight Rep ticket Harrison & Morton."[48]

James Glazier probably cast an expedient vote for the Democratic party in 1884, not, of course, an unprecedented act. Others were showing awareness of and occasional involvement in even likelier means of improvement through social and political devices. The Grange movement, for example, appears now and then in these writings, and from far-off eastern Oregon Rachel Atteberry sent an encouraging assessment to a relative back in Indiana: "Mrs. Ireland I say hurraw for the grangers If I was there I would join them." Old Aaron Stryker of Brownstown, Indiana, who was probably in some way related to Rachel Atteberry, could not share her enthusiasm. Once postmaster at Brownstown during the Buchanan years and sufficiently staunch in the party faith to have deserved the label *Butternut* if not *Copperhead* during the war, he agreed that the Grange seemed to have some worthy goals "(But might there not be a negro in the wood Pile.)"[49]

Rachel Atteberry probably saw little if anything in the Grange movement other than a means to alleviate the loneliness of rural people, much as Oliver Kelley intended. The awareness of such quasi-political organizations certainly rose among common people, but little indicates that they had goals other than social enhancement. Mentions of the Grand Army of the Republic, for example, generally come in innocuous references to post meetings or encampments, though one must assume that members appreciated the organization's supposed political influence. Such people were being led gently into the larger involvements of a more interconnected society and nation.

One also encounters brief and occasional mentions of labor organizations, but, here again, one enjoys no certainty as to what was expected of those organizations, or, for that matter, what they were. A barber in Findlay, Ohio, decided to join a "union" in the fall of 1890, and he deemed it better to go to Toledo to do so: "We can't join here unless we join the 'niggers.'" He soon overcame those unseemly qualms and joined in Findlay, pronouncing firmly: "Yes I am a union man now and a good one too." Whatever his joining a union meant, it did nothing to curb his appetite for hearing speeches by Republicans such as John Sherman, whom he meant to hear in a few days. In Iowa City, Iowa, the wife of store clerk Hubert Jones recognized at least a part of what it meant when her husband became a member of some such organization. "Hubert joined the workmen this eve," she noted in her diary, "and now he will have to go to lodge once a week." As one who kept close account of her husband's extramural activities, Adaline Jones must have viewed this development with thinly veiled skepticism.[50]

Just what organization Hubert had joined is not clear, but it probably combined the fraternal features mentioned by Adaline with some form of insurance. Insurance was emerging not only as an important part of the economy but as something with which humble people showed an ever-growing conversance. Often an insurance arrangement came as an ancillary part of membership in an organization at least nominally social in character. Thus in the hard times of the early 1870s young farm worker Ossian Scott wrote from Lyon County, Kentucky, that he managed to stay at work, though averaging only $1.40 a day. Whatever the pay, he deemed it advisable to have some life insurance, and so he had gotten two thousand dollars worth by joining "the Society knowen as Knights of Honer One of the best insurance that is knowen."[51]

As these ordinary Americans became more aware politically, they almost necessarily showed more alertness to reformist causes than had their predecessors. Again, the Civil War does much to inform this matter, as many who had had abolitionist persuasions readily turned them into other channels. At war's end forty-five-year-old Mary Mellish of Vermont lectured her soldier son on his duties and various other things. Three weeks before Lee's surrender, this wife of a small-town shoe store operator anticipated the next struggle: "Intemperance is the monster they are to make war upon" next. She had readily accepted the story that Andrew Johnson had been "so drunk he could hardly take the oath of office" as vice-president, and, when the assassination came, she found at least some slight satisfaction to be derived from that "calamity"—"Andrew Johnson may be saved from intemperance."[52]

Mary Mellish had more capacity for fine didactic frenzy than the great majority of her contemporaries—"(I wont say anything about *Smoking* this time)," she mercifully ended one letter to her son. Still, she has aptness because, insofar as these lesser mortals entertained reform notions, they centered upon temperance and prohibition. In this, they showed continuity with the persuasions of the preceding generation. And here, too, the political party that did not instinctively suppose that the world was governed too much showed greater readiness to do something. In Iowa City, Iowa, in 1879 Mrs. Hubert Jones noted her satisfaction at the outcome of a local election in a way both direct and symbolic: "The brewery whistles did not blow and that is a sign that the democrats were beaten." Later that same year over in Hillsboro, Illinois, George King told of an acquaintance who was generally sound except for being a Democrat. It was true, King admitted, that many good Democrats lived there, then he caricatured the means whereby his area accommodated them: "we sort them as you do your corn." Some fill our poorhouses; others fill our jails; yet others fill our penitentiary; "and still we have enough left to run all our saloons." In the "humble a pinion" of old William Van Scyoc of Belmont County, Ohio, there would be no whiskey or tobacco in "the kingdom of heaven," leaving it unclear whether he also foresaw an absence of Democrats there.[53]

Temperance and prohibition loomed by far the largest in whatever concern such people had with reform, but now, unlike the prewar period, at least an occasional positive reference to other reform impulses can be found. Tariffs had long exercised people with political awareness, and now one finds some indications that others were finding that issue worth written comment. Thus at a "Society" meeting in Riley County, Kansas, in 1888 things proved "lively"—"discussed the tariff." In that same year a hundred miles to the northwest a young man near Butler, Nebraska, moved in his letter home from a recent blizzard to a national political issue: "Well, Father, we are going to have a discussion of the tariff tonight."[54]

Also there appear serious as well as sardonic references to woman suffrage, especially in Republican Kansas. In the summer of 1867 newcomer from Michigan Milton Townsend had the unusual experience in Topeka of hearing "a woman speak as a preacher." Moreover, woman suffrage was "all the rage out here." A couple of years later Theodore Wilkie, who had moved from a nursery in South Bend, Indiana, to one in Topeka, set down a more favorable reaction: "For in what manner can the vote of inteligent women be hurtful to public welfare." New Topekans Milton Townsend and Theodore Wilkie seem to have viewed woman suffrage in somewhat differing ways. They and others were providing themselves more things about which to disagree.[55]

Such people had come to lace their writings with far more political content than they previously had, and sometimes that content had a mildly reformist tone. This research uncovered almost nothing, however, other than the radicalism of abolition, going beyond that mildness. A Californian with a penchant for poetry set down lines dated February 1885 that register the standard revulsion against extreme postures:

Anarchists, and Socialists,
Just call them what you will;
They are ready any moment
To burn, to mob, and kill.

As this implement salesman understood it, those "Dynamiters" got their start "In Russia's vast domain," but they could now be found in his own home state, New York. The violence in Haymarket Square in Chicago fifteen months later must have sorely tried Obadiah Ethelbert Baker, born in New York, grown to manhood in Iowa from which he served in the Civil War, and living out his years in the Far West. That sanguinary affair must also have borne out fully Baker's conviction that those "Dynamiters" did indeed stand "ready any moment / To burn, to mob, and kill."[56]

Anarchists and socialists aside, common Americans were necessarily making attitudinal accommodation with alien elements. Matters of race and nationality intruded upon them with a bluntness most had not experienced in their island communities. Perhaps foremost for many northern people came a fuller acquaintance with blacks, of whom they had heard so much but, in most cases, had seen so little. Unfortunately, much of the process of introduction came against the ugly backdrop of war, and ungenerous predispositions quickly hardened into active dislike. Surely, a large and largely unappreciated aspect of the northern abandonment of the newly freed people in the years after the war and after Reconstruction involves negative reactions toward the blacks that Billy Yank formed during his southern sojourn and brought home with him. Bell Wiley long ago called attention to the "enormous amount of antipathy toward Negroes" in the writings of northern soldiers, but Wiley struggled in that chapter, "Along Freedom Road," to what almost seems some vague equipose in attitude. To be sure, one occasionally comes upon a sympathetic Yankee soldier, but the overwhelming preponderance runs the other way.[57]

Wiley provided ample illustration of the verbal marks of that antipathy, and some are necessary here. In remarking the filthiness of his southern experience, Ohio soldier Thomas Hawley judged "nineteen twentieths" of the "niggers" to be "to darn filthy to be allowed to go north." "I have seen enough niggers," he fumed, "and I am getting pretty sick at the sight of niggers." He had no fear of repetition on this score, nor did others. Though he wanted the preferment of a commission in a black unit, Sergeant George Jewett of the Seventeenth Massachusetts Regiment showed an equally sour and often repeated view—"monkeys aint a circumstance to them." He stated the comparison in unusual form but with unmistakable intent. Necessarily, these views had political implications. The Massachusetts sergeant wanted a commission in a "nigger regiment," and the Ohio soldier wanted blacks returned to Africa. An upstate New York soldier who used more decorous language and did everything he could to avoid blacks wrote from barracks near the national capitol early in 1865 telling that he often went to hear Senate sessions. When the galleries were cleared on February first for "Executive Business," he and his fellow soldiers surmised that the Senate meant to discuss the " 'Race' question that is causing considerable excitement here lately." That indicates emphatically that a political issue was involved, a fact that these soldiers could illustrate far more firmly. George R. Wheeler, born in Canada, apparently raised in New York, and living in Minnesota when the war came, summed it up for many as he awaited the 1864 election. He informed his mother and sister that he could not vote for Lincoln and the present administration: "They have got the Nigger on the brain rather too much They want to make the Nigger equal with us in every thing Voteing and all."[58]

In C. Vann Woodward's classic terms, a "capitulation to racism" occurred over the course of the late nineteenth century, North and South. Though it defies measurement, the sourness of former soldiers must have entered that "capitulation" quite generously. They had found themselves wheedled and dragooned into suffering, bleeding, and dying, not just for the Union, which nearly all supported, but more and more for the sake of a people upon whom they could look with pity at the very best. Disgust, loathing, and hatred usurped pity's place in many cases. The "Northern armey" did not "deavid" (divide) physically over the issue, as a Nebraska soldier predicted. But sullenness must have skulked on home with many, as perhaps it did with a Cheshire, Connecticut, veteran doing carpentry work in his native area. As the parties warmed up for state elections in 1870, Alonzo Smith told that an acquaintance had gone to New Haven for a Democratic gathering. The activities of the other party received this cryptic indication—"Nigger worshippers in Town Hall."[59]

A few months before Henry Colyer conjectured about the "Executive Business" in the Senate, he told his mother of the distractions he suffered while trying to write a letter in Sherburne Barracks in Washington, D.C. Animated conversation abounded, and that in "German, French, Irish and United States." As was so frequently the soldier's lot, Colyer was encountering an earnest of the polyglot ways that would be visited upon this land ever more fully as the postwar decades moved along. The Irishman especially emerged in common awareness, and for soldiers the common military acquiescence in St. Patrick's Day's observance assured that. "It being St. Patricks day to day," an upstate New York soldier noted, "we have a hollow day." Here again, there is no knowing if playfulness informed that misconstruction.[60]

When practicable, conviviality became the order of the day, and an 1863 diary entry for March 17 worked a fairly common conjunction; it remarked the day of note and reported that the captain returned to camp "rather tight." A few years later a farrier with a column pursuing hostiles in Indian Territory had an unusual perspective on March 17 as his unit awaited the arrival of George Armstrong Custer—still general in this Pennsylvanian's book—on the very ground where Custer had routed the Cheyennes at the Washita a few months earlier. "Plenty of fun in camp" prevailed, though there was "nothing to be seen but some old skull bones of dead Indians." Americans accepted Irish help in adding to the list of calendared good times, whether those days be hollow or holy.[61]

Inevitably, discordant notes sounded, and on the same day that Sergeant Winfield Scott Harvey made that entry while on the battle site at the Washita, a California woman also noted the occasion. After mentioning the saintly auspices, she matter-of-factly observed that all the "micks" had turned out in San Francisco. The mood of the San Francisco Irish may have been in that period not "pessimistic" but "excited and triumphant," as a recent book has contended, but censure often surfaced in the beholders of the "micks'" ways. Harold Frederic duly depicted beleaguered Abner Beech, "The Copperhead," befriended by an Irish laborer, a Catholic one at that. Thereby, he put in literary terms what many Americans believed or suspected. The Irish ran afoul of some unfortunate associations—real or imagined—in the war and postwar years. Thomas Nast's cartoons conveyed those perceived attachments with greatest artfulness and rancor, but many others partook of the spirit.[62]

At election time in 1865 a Union soldier still serving in a hospital unit showed some surprise at the vote of those immediately around him. The preference had gone Republican, five to four, but this Republican observer suspected that "the result would have been otherwise but an Irishman voted the Rep. ticket by mistake." A teenaged soldier from Wayne County, New York, followed another path—consciously or not—in making the almost ineluctable identification of Irish and rebel. On observing the hapless condition of Confederate prisoners in Virginia, he noted that they appeared no more like soldiers than "a gang of Irishmen that work on the canal in New York state." A gang of Irishmen assumed more ominous potential for a Vermont soldier who had been sent with his unit to New York City in the wake of the antidraft riot in mid-1863. This young man had had preparation for such unpleasantness over a year before at a marshaling point in Burlington, when two of his friends had been set upon by four Irishmen and one of those friends nearly killed by a blow on the head with a coupling iron. That perhaps helps explain why he all but welcomed a confrontation in New York City in August 1863. If it came, it would be one that the "mobs will remember for some time to come." Three weeks later, he was among a contingent that had gone a hundred miles up the Hudson to Rondout on the water near Kingston, expecting that the "Irishmen" might raise a "row" over a draft there. Those Irishmen did not oblige him, he informed his father, as the Vermonters' arrival on the day before the draft "dried them up badly." To dry up was now serving metaphorically for being quiet or, simply, shutting up, upon which happy project many dearly wished the Irish to embark.[63]

However great the service of Irish soldiers in Union ranks, these images tenaciously colored what many people surmised about these people who had come to loom so large and dramatically in American affairs. William M. Johnson of the Sixty-third North Carolina Regiment may have found these Yankee suspicions of the Irish puzzling. On a day in June 1863 he drew firing-squad duty for execution of a man who had twice deserted: "it seems like he did knot mind the lest in the world he was a substitute and a Irishman in the Bargon &.c." Rebel Private Johnson would have to go on in puzzlement, and for a Yankee here and there the lingering resonance of ancient religious animosities came near the surface. On July 11, 1864, Andersonville's horrors got deadly punctuation as a half-dozen of the "Raiders" were dispatched by hanging. Union servicemen gone renegade and criminal, the "Raiders" had terrorized their fellow inmates until, with official sanction of Confederate officers, "Regulators" tried two dozen of them and sentenced six to hang. A Connecticut soldier recorded the grisly conclusion in a sternly satisfied way, noting at the end of his diary entry, "A Catholic Priest Officiated on the occasion."[64]

What soldier William Jackson of Connecticut stated with terse economy, "A Catholic Priest Officiated on the occasion," MacKinlay Kantor could embroider for many pages in treating Father Peter Whelan's efforts to turn heavenward the gaze and thoughts of Willie Collins, Pat Delaney, and other convicted "Raiders." The fathers of men such as William Jackson could have been in Mexico sixteen years earlier when members of the San Patricio Brigade—Irish deserters from the United States Army fighting for Mexico—moved from time to eternity by way of a scaffold after defeat and capture at Churubusco. Here and there, the theme surfaces, vaguely intimating that the North-South vis-à-vis partook in some faint way of Protestant versus Catholic.[65]

A spirited member of a Texas cavalry unit with Kirby Smith's army had already suffered by the fall of 1862 the deprivations all but synonymous with the Confederate cause. He already knew what it was to go into battle with bare and swollen feet and to lift equipment from a fallen enemy; that Hoosier "was a dying" as his cartridge belt was removed. Still, Confederate Thomas Colman's liveliness endured. He had recently caught a glimpse of General Braxton Bragg, a consummately homely man, and he opined that "his ears would hafter be set back to make his mouth any bigger." At the end of his arresting letter, the cavalryman told that he was sending a piece from a battle flag that had been shot up in action at Richmond, Kentucky. He then described the design that had been chosen early in the war by Pierre Gustave Toussaint Beauregard, a "solid red Flag with a large Blue catholic cross." At a distance that blue cross—what others would call St. Andrew's cross and yet others the southern cross—appeared black, and "the Yankees could not comprehend the meaning of the Black X." Often misidentified as the flag of the Confederate States of America, it was the battle flag of that embattled nation which Thomas Colman described. Whatever General Beauregard's intentions were in designing that flag, one supposes that very few looked upon it as cavalryman Colman did; still, certain ethnic groups and their religion had marched much farther into common American awareness than they had theretofore.[66]

Looking sourly on the national situation in 1872, Henry Spencer, farmer and storekeeper on the Minnesota River southwest of Minneapolis–St. Paul, noted a newspaper report that a "darky" had been chosen for superintendent of public instruction in Arkansas. "It looks to me," the sixty-one-year-old former Kentuckian concluded, "verry much like the Blacks will soon rule most of the states far South and the foreigners the northern states Perhaps the Americans will be allowed to rule a few of the middle states for a few more years." In newer settlements off to the northwest some ten years later, young Minnesotan May Gorham told a friend of conducting a school of seventeen students "composed of Irish, Germans & Norwegians in about equal proportions with now & then an American sprinkled in to season the whole." May Gorham seemed to enjoy the challenge: "It is real pleasant if it is 'Dutchy.'"[67]

Henry Spencer and May Gorham took different views of the world, but both symbolized and recorded the realities that had emerged in the late nineteenth century. They recognized that the ethnic makeup of their country had changed and would change more. At least for the moments we can look over their shoulders, May Gorham appears in the posture of positive accommodation, while her predecessor Henry Spencer betrays the marks of sullen resistance. In an age when the words *Democrat* and *conservative* were intertwined if not interchangeable, resistance befit that aging Democrat. Spencer represented his party, and he represented America generally in his large and ready conversance with the political scene. Now we find run-of-the-mill citizens of this nation as fully attuned to political affairs as some of us assumed they had been all along. In fact, their political interests had grown mightily in recent times; it took a Civil War and the myriad of things deriving from that devastation to get them to heed politics to the degree that modernity would expect. For those such as Emerson who had espied and bemoaned that movement of American "genius" from, figuratively, the "temple" to the "senate," Henry Spencer offered cold comfort at best as he assessed the situation late in the election year of 1872. His summary view is partisan, but it is also analogous to Emerson's metaphor: "Gone to the D——l and Grant."[68]

7. Reprise: And On to the Twentieth Century

These common people had restricted God's role, diminished religion, and euphemized death. They had enlarged the awareness of self, had altered their notions of society accordingly, and had come to have an enhanced regard for the nation's politics and what it might do for them. A brief review will seek to show these people in some of the starker manifestations of the changed attitudes that prepared them for the new century ahead. In treating late nineteenth-century sources somewhat more elevated than those in this study, Rush Welter hit upon the centrality of "enterprise" as reflected in "venturesome individuals" making "their own way in the world untrammelled by considerations of social obligation." The writings of genuinely unelevated people of this era breathe much of that spirit, along with various ancillary qualities.[1]

That enterprising and worldly spirit fed upon the Civil War far more than one might suppose. Pure excitement provided the setting for war, as for the West. Robert Nisbet hit upon this matter in a tangential way in treating boredom: "Ghastly though the American Civil War became in its unending slaughter and epidemic disease, there was no end to the lines of young men fleeing the deadly monotony of farm and village for enlistment under one banner or the other." Another modern commentator treating a diary from that conflict offered an imaginative indication of the change in frame of mind of a New York soldier, a farmer's son, "nothing more." As the youth left the "oppressive, unrelieved flatness" of farm life, he felt "a new thrill by skirting on what, for him, was the edge of morality. The soldier's world allowed it to him. . . . He had found a release." That soldier could manage only a banality after two weeks of life in camp: " 'like Soldier life good yet.' " And, as many of the preceding pages indicate, many soldiers felt ambivalence if not downright uneasiness at their "release." Thus a Minnesota soldier with a column pursuing the Sioux in Dakota Territory in 1863 told of the death of a comrade in a setting freighted with release: "this poor soldier died in the Hospital Tent and but A few feet from it there is A gang of men pitching Horse Shoes and Swearing so loud that they can be heard all through the Camp but no one tries to stop them and they continue their game and do not stop even when the Corps is brought out in the Coffin and taken to its last resting place." Devil's Lake may have seemed an apt destination for this march.[2]

Pitching horseshoes and swearing might not fall under the rubric of enterprise, but they evince some of the same secular spirit. And, of course, unadorned enterprise enters the picture, sometimes in ways that betray the furtive and the suspect. Moving from the ludicrous on the way to Devil's Lake to the pathetic at Andersonville, we can consider the ruminations of inmate Charles Ross trying to look to God for sustenance but finding readier surcease in "the speculations of the day." This Vermonter doubted the "exact honesty" of cooking and selling pitiful little food items to fellow prisoners, but he was only doing "as others do." Charles Ross of Lower Waterford evidently saw himself as skirting the edge of morality in this venture, but there is no way to know if it thrilled him.[3]

For others, the feeling of release from the "oppressive, unrelieved flatness" of the farm came with direct assertion and clear dedication to some new fortune or enterprise, however hazardous. Another man from Vermont—Woodstock in this case—said succinctly at war's end after having been home on leave: "It seems more like home to me here than it does at Woodstock. I don't think I shall ever live in Vermont any way there is no style for me there Nothing going on, too dull altogether." He did not appear on the 1870 census for Woodstock. Exactly four months after that man from Vermont wrote that letter in 1865, a young man from New York wrote to his parents from that same area around the nation's capital, and he showed a similar spirit in comparing his lot with that of his parents. Here we have the seemingly incongruous theme of the army serving as opportunity for enterprise: "When I think how hard you have both toiled for a life time and I only 21 shall have nearly half as much as you have got by careful exertion, even if I am mustered out this fall and all mine earned in a few months, it makes me mighty suspicious of 36 acre farms." However puzzling it may be to some, the theme appears often, though probably very few said anything about it once the war had ended. In January 1862, an Indiana corporal wrote to his wife from Virginia, putting the matter unapologetically as follows: "I think I can lay up some money in this war."[4]

That young man from New York no longer felt much claim laid upon him by that small farm in Ira Township, Cayuga County; but he had not made a comprehensive rejection. In this letter and elsewhere he stated that a farm would be acceptable, but it must be a "Western farm" to be "the thing for me." A theme so hackneyed might better be left at rest were it not so central to what these lesser mortals believed. As James Bryce described, so these people illustrated, often without concern for dissimulation. From a couple at Antelope Diggings in Arizona Territory came word that "society" there left something to be desired, but they were not there for that. "We came for that which we are getting daily. Money." They had gone there, not to be miners but to mine the miners by storekeeping: "One thing I know: I see every day of my life, dust brought into the store *and falls into our hands* which is not bad to look upon."[5]

In Phoenix a few years later, an aspiring young businessman matched the enthusiasm of the couple at Antelope Diggings. He told his mother that things were looking up, and, if father were only younger, he could come out and they would do "*a smashing big business* here we would get *rich rich rich* how good it sounds." As a young man from Connecticut described these westerners, "They are all on the make." A man from Vermont used less figurative language in explaining to friends at home that, having been in California, "Vermont will never be my home again." He had not prospered in the West, far from it; but it was better than his lot would be back in Franklin County: "I should have to work for Chas. Bullard for $7.00 per month."[6]

The age-old reluctance to express themselves in terms of laying up treasures in time rather than eternity was falling into disuse.

With the major impetus coming from the war and the West, these people were adopting a business language, sometimes a mercenary language. The very word *business* was assuming a frequency and a resonance in their writings far beyond what it had had before. In turn, the word was undergoing a constriction that removed it more and more from the realm of unspecified activity. Without qualifiers or special contexts, business was coming to mean commerce, merchandising, trade. Common people assisted in the semantic change.

Something of the old, undifferentiated sense remains in the diary entry of a Connecticut soldier imprisoned at Andersonville as he told that there had been "a grand clearing out of Raiders." The hangings yet remained, but, as Henry Savage put it, Captain Wirtz "has taken hold of the business in earnest." The assertiveness of "taking hold" of some project—a term that had become a common locution—itself breathed a businesslike aura, as when an eastern soldier in March 1863 allowed that, in Grant, Vicksburg had now "got a man hold of it that can do the business right up." Long after the war, an Indiana veteran wrote to a "Comrade" to tell what the "Boys" in his locale were now doing. One was selling farm equipment; one was working "by the day wer ever he gets work"; yet another was keeping "the Wiskey from Spoiling." "So you see we are all in biusness."[7]

That fact became abbreviated and hypostasized in a particular usage. From the war experience people adopted *order of the day* as a label for the regnant concern or activity of the moment. Mary Jacacks, a housewife in Seneca County, New York, illustrates the adoption. In late 1868, she went to assist a neighbor woman who had given birth to a son: "House work & care of Sarah is the order of the day." The expression lived on, and it often served interchangeably with a civilian parallel chosen, for example, by a Civil War veteran when he described the intense cold in Delaware County, New York, late in 1890: "Ice is the business of the day." From that general usage came an abbreviated intensification. A few miles to the west of where that veteran spent his postwar years, a young man worked on a small dairy in Chenango County in the summer of 1871. He was thinking of moving on to Madison County to work as a hop picker, which would yield up to two dollars a day if done zealously. Perhaps the thought of that hard work moved him to think about a cousin who worked the "Soda Water business" at fairs and the like. This enterprising dairy worker and prospective hop picker found that an attractive alternative, and he thought he might join his cousin and "try my luck at that Biz."[8]

At one level a simple foreshortening, "Biz." serves as well as a semantic signal of shifting values. Of course, the impulse it represented had been there long, perhaps always, but common Americans had previously kept it nearly covert and, nearly always, humbly subservient to the one thing needful. A young man newly arrived in Ames, Iowa, in 1869 managed to maintain old priorities, but not very impressively. In a letter written to his partner-to-be, he did give "first place" to the condition of "Christian Society" in the village. That gave way rather abruptly to the prospects for "biz."[9]

As New Englander Henry Huntington was getting established in Ames and embarked on a "biz." that would prove fairly successful, twenty-four-year-old Eugene Wilkie spent the better part of a year fifty miles to the southeast in Leighton. Three years younger than Huntington, Wilkie betrayed even more of modernity. In the very early 1870s he was moving about, sourly refusing to return to a clerkship in South Bend, Indiana, near which he had been born and raised on a farm. Something had offended him: "they cannot come that 'gag' 'as the saying is' on me." The flippancy, the slang, even the quotation marks—for which overuse John Updike has playfully blamed Henry James—betoken times ahead. And he too liked the expression, "biz," so in August 1872 he incorporated it in this hastily written passage of a letter to his younger brother: "Tell Mother no use talking cant raise the 'spuds' for her just at present 'Biz' to dull but send them when I get them! So rest easy and keep Kool!" One surmises that those "spuds" were dollars owed, and one hopes that forty-seven-year-old Sarah Wilkie, a Civil War widow, managed to "keep Kool" that August without them.[10]

The more secular language of enterprise could assume shadings one very rarely encounters in humble writings of the earlier period, and a baker newly arrived in St. Paul offers an instance. In June 1883 he wrote a friend who remained in the Wisconsin town he had left that he had gotten a job as "second pastry baker" at the Merchants Hotel for thirty-five dollars a month and board. His letter would serve well in the old debate about whether the city or the West provided greater opportunity. In his new location, he pointed out, he could learn "something more than making ryebread and filling molasses shugs." He was enjoying himself fully, and he regretted not having left that Wisconsin town sooner. Back there, "a man has no chance to work himself up, nor in————" Given the tenor of this letter, that latter aspect of enterprise admits of only one construction. As mentioned elsewhere in this study, untoward intimations—theretofore so rare—now have an occasional place in the writings of such people as George Peterman, once of Hudson, Wisconsin.[11]

That town lay only twenty miles from St. Paul, but, attitudinally, this young baker had come a fair distance. The liveliest conveyance for working such movement was railroading far more than baking. Thus Ben Maddow depicted the railroad of that era as "one of those strange and energetic symbols that alter the subconscious of a whole people." That partakes of the undemonstrable, but it does involve an inviting thought. Simply and surely, the railroad captured the awareness of common people to an extraordinary degree in what Howard Mumford Jones aptly styled the "Age of Energy." And one can see in the ways the railroad was registered in humble writings at least some of the symbolic force Maddow ascribed to it, if not quite what Peter Gay has more venturesomely ascribed to it. "Curiously," Maddow noted, "it's not the diesel nor the electric locomotive that has such mana; they are not animal enough. The steam locomotive audibly chuffs and breathes." As the exhilarating word came in early 1866 from a small Iowa town, the "iron horse will snuff dirt & snort in Prairie City" in only a month or two.[12]

Eugene Wilkie, who could not "raise the 'spuds' just now," had become a railroad worker, probably a telegrapher, on the same branch of the Rock Island Line some thirty miles southeast of Prairie City. He had adopted the peripatetic ways of that contrivance that had come to symbolize the nation. The railroad represented not just motion but speed and force as well. Back at Ames, Henry Huntington's partner, George Tilden, described to his wife in June 1869 the performance of the Chicago and Northwestern: "They run from the switch one mile west of here to the next station—distance ten miles—in nine minutes." Nothing stood in the way. On the day he wrote, the Chicago-to-Omaha run killed a cow near Ames, and it struck a flock of sheep near Ontario just to the west—"beef at Ames and mutton at Ontario." Writing home to North Carolina from railroad shops in Birmingham, an employee of the Richmond and Danville Railroad used for stationery a form designed for "Engineman's Report of Stock Killed or Injured." "I was lucky enough," he informed his brother, "to kill a cow and that is how I came to have these on hand."[13]

The railroad loomed even larger in the southern awareness than in the northern, perhaps because, aside from those now restored lines, so much else remained in devastation. Those railroads reflected the New South, and a young man in Laurinburg, North Carolina, worked an arresting blend of the ancient and the emergent ways in a letter to his father, who, like himself, sometimes had railroad employment. Here, in February 1872, he moved from discussion of railroad work to a description of the "Tournament" that had recently taken place at or near Laurinburg. The "charge to the Knights" evoking the spirit of "chivalry" of the twelfth to fifteenth centuries, the tilting, the "Queen and maids of Honor" stood in wondrous juxtaposition to the Wilmington, Charlotte and Rutherford Rail Road. Sad to say, the event ended on a sour note as too many had been drinking too much, and some neglected to act in a "very Knightly way." Knights-errant had less and less place, even in Laurinburg, though, conceivably, the railroader provided something of a modern surrogate. A month later young William Garland, who had described the Laurinburg tournament, recalled his father's having told him that "A R.R. man and a steam Boat man would be known no matter where he would go."[14]

The world has long adopted business terms such as *first-rate* for general usage, but *first-rate* and others appear more frequently after 1860. A similar expression may have derived directly from railroading. *Right side up* and *right side up with care* made the move from freight cartons to general instructions for the proper handling of things. Thus an Indiana soldier advised a sister to "tell the girls to keepe rite side up with care untill the soldiers come home." Learning that an employee whom he had left to tend some hogs in his absence had grown dissatisfied and homesick for New York, an Illinois man sought to cajole him into staying on at the job: "poor fellow try to keep rite side up."[15]

In expressing expectations or aspirations the common language was taking on a decided upward orientation. That did not involve refinement or decorum, and we recall the enterprising George Peterman of St. Paul, who aimed to work his way "up" and "in." That qualification notwithstanding, "up" was in the air, and the impish Eugene Field stated the case of "an overworked word" in his *Chicago Daily News* column in 1886:

> And everywhere "up" 's to be heard
> > We wet up and set up,
> > But hanged if we let up
> On "up," the much overworked word.[16]

Right side up and similar terms had a positive resonance, betokening things done correctly and successfully. Even when good fortune became coy, however, an upward tilt remained. That involved not so much the prayerful recognition, as had previously been the case, that God disposed in His pleasure, but rather the calm, worldly trust that something would "turn up." In a previous chapter a Massachusetts sergeant expressed his hope of getting a commission in a "nigger regiment." He knew it was unlikely because he had no influential friends. He remained a "cheap common sergeant," but, he mused, "I can wait patiently for something to 'turn up,' as Micawber says." In August 1890, at the end of our period, J. N. Scott of Evansburgh, Pennsylvania, told a brother about harvest and about "working away like the devil" with "enough to eat and wear and that is about all." Scott persevered, "waiting for something to turn up as the saying is." The consanguinity between Dickens's Mister Micawber and Mark Twain's Colonel Sellers has often been noted.[17]

An aptness inheres in arriving at the ambience of Field, Dickens, and Mark Twain. The breezier and earthier language and attitudes breathed the spirit of enterprise. They also reflected, vastly more than prewar language and attitudes had, the world of newspapers, books, and entertainment. One of the striking things about reading the writings of common people before the war is the dearth of mentions or reflections of such things. Now the newspapers and other staples of popular culture make their appearance, often in generous amounts. Mark Twain overstated the matter in 1871 because he was angry at a "slimy, sanctimonious, self-righteous reptile," that being a clergyman who expressed distaste at officiating at an actor's funeral. The decent impulses received by "the American people to-day" come, Mark Twain insisted, "*through dramas and tragedies and comedies on the stage, and through the despised novel and the*

Christmas story, and through . . . the teeming columns of ten thousand newspapers, and NOT from the drowsy pulpit!" He exaggerated, but he told a good portion of truth too.[18]

In the case of newspapers and magazines, the coincidence of great technological advancement with the Civil War assured an immense proliferation. Great things were afoot in the land, and the desire to know registered proportionally. We can see a good instance in the previously discussed case of General Sterling Price's 1864 invasion of central Missouri and Caroline Frissell's being left to tend the farm when her father and other Union men fled. Caroline walked out toward the road on which a rebel column was passing "and hailed them to know what the News was," but "the impudent pups sayed they had no news."[19]

Rachel Dobbins of Le Claire, Iowa, illustrated the much intensified interest in news and newspapers, and she had a better medium than those "impudent pups" encountered by Carie Frissell. In a letter of early 1862 she cited Chicago and St. Louis newspapers, and at one point in her description of battle action she exclaimed, "O its awful to think about the 18th Illinois on the extreme right." Soon she resorted to paraphrasing or quoting: "the Davenport Daily Gazette says, at length the Iowa 2d has had a chance to show its valor, Fort Donelson has fallen." To a brother in Indiana she put the matter in general terms: "I read the news now more than I ever did as [I] feel interested, write soon and give the particulars." Here again, the particulars were leaving the deathbed to focus on another brother's regiment, commander, location, and the like. Rachel Dobbins was becoming the habitual American newspaper reader, and she wanted the particulars.[20]

The soldier brother about whom Rachel sought particulars wrote letters nicely illustrating a theme discussed earlier, that soldiers had seen so much but knew so little. When he made that point regarding the Battle of Fredericksburg, an engagement he had witnessed and one more susceptible to understanding than many, he wrote that his brother in Indiana would know more about it than he could at the scene of action in Virginia. An Ohio soldier wrote in the same spirit from northeast Arkansas in April 1862: "I'd give a quarter for a paper just now." A year later, another Hoosier in Virginia gave convincing testimony to the premium on newspapers as rebels and Yankees groped toward their rendezvous at Gettysburg. A train had come out from Alexandria bringing "supplies and papers," and the Hoosier said he had never observed such a scene as those newspapers created. Through connivance he and another man managed to get close enough to the "newsboy" to get a precious paper, "but generally the boys gave it up as hopeless and returned to their quarters mad and cursing some body or some thing they hardly knew what." Here we see a dramatic foreshadowing of anger felt when the newsboy fails in his rounds.[21]

Visual aspects of the graphic revolution made themselves felt also, at times more compellingly than the informative. Thus a soldier in a Massachusetts regiment assessed some North Carolina war scenes appearing in a recent publication. Writing from New Bern, Charles Kittredge felt qualified to say which illustrations appeared "natural" and which did not. *Frank Leslie's Illustrated Magazine* had the widest reputation in the war years, and a marginally literate wife of an Illinois soldier indicates that few credentials were needed to appreciate it. Her husband had recently told of an encounter with a literal hornet's nest, and Mary Labrant did what she could to reciprocate the humor of the situation: "i wish one of frank leslies artists had of ben there i should like to of se the po reformance illustrated in one of his magizeans i think it would of ben comic." Arresting things could now be referred to in terms of "a good picture for Frank Leslie," as a New York soldier put it.[22]

The "ungodly community" around San Juan Capistrano might also have made a good picture for Frank Leslie in early 1871 as a sheepherder recorded the tenor of his way: "This day has been devoted to sheep hearding that is—I have lain on my back,—on my Belly,—and loled from side to side, and read the Bulletin all day." A sheepherder's interest in the news, such as the report now reaching the San Juan Capistrano area that Paris had been taken, differed from a soldier's, but both resorted to the printed word to escape boredom. Thus a member of the Sixth Infantry Regiment stationed on the high plains kept a diary that was often little more than a record of his reading. He served on the peripheries of the scrape at the Little Big Horn, and on April 10, 1876, he "Got Custer's Life on the Plains." In the weeks ahead he found little to report, one sodomy matter aside, other than his reading of such things as the *Toledo Blade*, the "Police News," and J. W. De Forest's *Wetherell Affair*. As his column moved along the Yellowstone, he did record, two days before Custer's death on the plains, this state of affairs: "Officers drunk, noisy, and kept us awake all night."[23]

Custer had a brush with immortality in the West, but for most others that setting meant business and the boom mentality, that temper of the West that James Bryce described as "a kind of religion." Bryce marveled to find the stores of Seattle, Washington Territory, open already at 7:00 A.M., and "Booster Talk," or what Daniel Boorstin styled the "language of anticipation," had all but put to rout the old and staid modes of expression. Descriptions of things that "had not yet 'gone through the formality of taking place'" became the order of the day, and a onetime bartender and acerbic viewer of the California scene described a man who in 1867 had "found the *bottom*": "Like all smart folks he went up on mining, but principally on *show*, trying like many others to run a *thousand* dollar machine on a *hundred* dollar bottom." In such a setting, newspapers proliferated, and when Bryce wondered aloud how a small western town could sustain four newspapers he was told that four newspapers were needed to sustain the town.[24]

The language of exaggeration came more readily, and some of the pyrotechnic displays would leave a legacy of shame and distaste in those who did not recognize, as George Santayana did, that when an American was "most boastful" he was likely to have "a twinkle in his eye." Though he often had a twinkle in his eye, Richard Grant White wrote sternly in 1870 about the spread of such expressions as "loving" green peas: "We shall have deteriorated, as well as our language, when we can no longer distinguish our liking from our loving." "The line between the specific and the hyperbolic was," Daniel Boorstin noted, "anything but clear in the American experience." Common Americans were adopting the hyperbolic ways. Those newspapers they were reading so much more helped them along, as surely the western stories of Bret Harte, Mark Twain, and others did.[25]

A man well known to Bret Harte and Mark Twain offered this variant of exaggeration in a mining town paper in 1880: "The editor of the *Pioche Record* says, 'Mrs. Page's milk is delicious.' We shall soon hear that her husband has weaned him with a club. He knows too much." That contribution of "Lying Jim" Townsend illustrates another shading of what Mark Twain referred to in *Roughing It* as that "vigorous new vernacular of the occidental plains and mountains": " 'Pass the bread, you son of a skunk!' No, I forget—skunk was not the word; it seems to me it was still stronger than that; I know it was, in fact, but it is gone from my memory, apparently." Eugene Field's "Damnation Bill" grew to boyhood in "the quiet and humdrum of country life" and then slipped away at sixteen to enter the army. At war's end Bill had "no hankerin' for the old life in New England, with its quiet folks and humdrum, go-to-meetin' ways." Having gotten his training in the war, he moved on to practice and perfect in the West that which brought a name indicative of "the most salient features of his character."[26]

Coarseness was now taking its place in the written vernacular. The war furthered the work already under way in the "occidental plains and mountains." Writing from a stationer's store on East Washington Street in Indianapolis, a clerk played fast and loose with the patriotic theme embossed on the paper he used. The goddess of liberty, buxomly portrayed, appeared prominently at the top of the sheet, with sword in one hand and stars and stripes in the other, indignant, one assumes, at the perfidy of the southern states. Whatever indignation that clerk felt, he leavened it with an earthy aside begun well down the page: "(I would have commenced at the top of this paper, but I have always made it a rule to not try to feel 'Bubbies' nor impose on a *woman* in *any* way. So you see I leave her untouched My modesty compels me to do so.)" The self-restraint and decorum he parodied were indeed giving way.[27]

Self-restraint and decorum often receive rough treatment in modern depictions of our ancestors. With a blending of Marx and Melville at the outset, one such venture points accusingly at a nineteenth-century America that conditioned itself to "fear spontaneity and resist serendipity," to practice "ascetic self-control" and to "construct a culture of 'self-renunciation.' " Those people led, it would seem, a studiedly joyless existence, even to the point of attempting to be "virtuous." Worse, they had imprisoned themselves in "iron cages," and from that situation prodigious evils flowed. Thankfully, the ever-obliging Captain Ahab—although imprisoned in his own "demonic iron cage"—comes forth thaumaturgically at the end to take the whole sorry business to its grave in the " 'watery prairies' of Asia, near the 'Manilla isles.' " Aside from wishing that the much overworked Captain Ahab could be given a rest, one hardly knows what to make of it all.[28]

Perhaps one can take comfort from knowing that, whatever Captain Ahab was up to, common Americans were losing their fear of spontaneity and their resistance to serendipity. Whether the consequences were so injurious as depicted by the aforementioned scholar, the intense scrutiny and management of self was falling into disrepair. If the traditional suspicion of entertainment has been exaggerated wildly, that suspicion was real and was now markedly giving ground. We almost reach out to these hitherto benighted ancestors to greet them and welcome them to our world.

For example, the reading of novels—theretofore resisted more on theological, epistemological, and psychological than on moral grounds—now becomes far more apparent among undistinguished people. Mark Twain, Bret Harte, Harriet Beecher Stowe, Edward Eggleston, and others now surface in common writings, mostly, however, in bare mentions. At the end of the 1880s a small-town barber in Indiana and Ohio sought a copy of *Robert Elsmere*. He had richer fare than that when he read H. Rider Haggard's *She* and Emile Zola's *Nana*. What his reading meant, if anything, is hard to say. Perhaps coincidence, even serendipity, is all that can be seen in the added fact that this man's letters contain some overtly sexual material well beyond anything I had previously encountered in such sources, excepting perhaps some Far West collections. Delbert Boston's iron cage was wearing a bit thin. How salutary the consequences of his release will have to be left to the judge presiding in individual minds.[29]

In 1883 the wife of a blacksmith in Bedford, Iowa, wrote to a daughter to inform her that her older brother had become a "church goer again." Mrs. Andrew Greenlee neared sixty when she sent that news, and that lime- and brick-burning son, who, "as he sais turned over a new leaf," approached forty. It pleased Mother Greenlee to see him reading the Bible rather than "dime novels," but she had no certainty that the change would be "lasting." A year or so earlier and some eighty miles to the southeast a young Missouri woman told a cousin that she had enjoyed reading Jean Ingelow's *Sarah de Berenger*. After asking if he read novels, she went on to say that she read "every thing I get hold of except the bible, and I have not got down that far yet, as not to have anything else to read." Perhaps young Della Crosby enjoyed being "contrary, like all the other Crosbys." Perhaps also she was assuming, as so many others were, some willfulness. Contrary and willful ways were waxing, and those disturbed by visions of iron cages should take heart.[30]

When one studies sources such as these, one should attempt to follow the urging of G. M. Young, to " 'go on reading until he hears them talking.' " Then again, as the resonance and cadence of the Bible recedes to be replaced by that of, say, *Nana* and *Sarah de Berenger*, some may lose their relish for the work. Some may wonder if they do indeed wish to hear Delbert Boston and Della Crosby "talking." After all, they were starting to talk as we do, and most of us have an acquaintance with that language. Anyway, what one hears from them differs a good deal from what one hears from their counterparts thirty, forty, and more years before. Delbert Boston and Della Crosby do not exhibit much "self-renunciation," which was indeed a notable part of the mood of that earlier period. But they do exhibit a good deal more of the spirit of enterprise, Boston with his longing for a "speck" or speculation and Crosby with her admiration for a *"real go ahead* sort of a man."[31]

Most likely, Della Crosby and Delbert Boston lived decent and law-abiding lives, as surely most of the figures in this study did. Still, they exhibited the changes that had taken place in roughly a generation. They spoke a language significantly different from that of their prewar ancestors. Simply, they showed less of the godly and more of the worldly. Therefore, they could move more comfortably into the twentieth century.

Notes

INTRODUCTION

1. Nahum Trask Wood Daily Journal for the Year 1871, December 14, 1871.

2. Lewis O. Saum, *The Popular Mood of Pre–Civil War America*.

3. Milo, Carrie, and Mrs. Obadiah Ethelbert Baker to Obadiah Ethelbert Baker, September 3, 1882, Obadiah Ethelbert Baker Collection. Except where clarity was well served by a *sic*, I left misspellings unaltered and unmarked.

4. Ambrose Bierce, "Disintroductions," in *The Collected Works of Ambrose Bierce*, 9:260.

5. Letters and Papers of Charles G. Fisher; Emory Norwood Papers.

6. Elizabeth Hampsten, *Read This Only to Yourself*, pp.vii–viii. Such urgings as appear in this title were not at all confined to women's writings. The Mary Paul Letters of the Vermont Historical Society now appear in Thomas Dublin, ed., *Farm to Factory*; Jane Apostol, "Gold Rush Widow"; Jennie Akehurst Lines material in the Akehurst-Lines Collection, University of Georgia Libraries, now appears in Thomas Dyer, ed., *To Raise Myself a Little*.

7. Hampsten, *Read This Only to Yourself*, p.172; Gilman M. Ostrander, *American Civilization in the First Machine Age*, p.2.

8. Bell Irvin Wiley, *The Life of Johnny Reb*, and *The Life of Billy Yank*; Michael Barton, *Goodmen*; Randall C. Jimerson, *The Private Civil War*; Gerald F. Linderman, *Embattled Courage*; Reid Mitchell, *Civil War Soldiers*.

9. Samuel L. Clemens and Charles Dudley Warner, *The Gilded Age*, p.168; Herman Melville, *Clarel*, 2:460; Henry James, *Hawthorne*, p.144; Obadiah Ethelbert Baker Collection, folder 22.

10. "Books Received," p.362.

11. Harold Frederic, "The War Widow," in *Marsena and Other Stories of Wartime*, pp.119, 101.

12. Lemuel Hazzard to wife, August 10, 1873, Lemuel H. Hazzard Papers.

13. Richard Hofstadter, *Social Darwinism in American Thought*, p.21; Rush Welter, "Between Two Worlds," p.411.

14. Lester H. Cohen, *The Revolutionary Histories*, pp.21, 67; Gertrude Himmelfarb, "Two Nations or Five Classes," in *The New History and the Old*, p.69.

15. Ben Maddow, *A Sunday between Wars*, pp.88–89, 263.

16. Peter Gay, *The Bourgeois Experience*, pp.330–31.

Durkheim's contemporary and studious observer of America James Bryce titled a chapter of *The American Commonwealth* "The Fatalism of the Multitude," but he confined his attention to the political realm. Nevertheless, as will be pointed out in Chapter 2, he saw the West as being particularly lush in the growth of what Robert Nisbet, with Bryce's inspiration, refers to in treating "Fatalism" in *Prejudices: A Philosophical Dictionary* as that "strong faith in the power of chance, fortune, luck, and the random, and the purely fortuitous." Here there comes to mind the gravitation that William D. Howells depicted in *The Rise of Silas Lapham*. In the closing lines of chapter 9 he presented the juxtaposition of "grim antique Yankee submission" and "quaint modern American fatalism."

CHAPTER 1

1. Saum, *Popular Mood*, esp. chaps.1–4; Perry Miller, ed., *The American Puritans*, p.192; Urian Oakes, *The Soveraign Efficacy of Divine Providence*, pp.21, 37.

2. I. D. Keating to sister, February 1, 1874, James Ireland Family Correspondence; T. A. Evans to R. A. Evans, August 10, 1874, R. A. Evans Papers.

3. Zina W. Chase Diary, July 4, 1866, Zina W. Chase Papers.

4. James, *Hawthorne*, p.144; Melville, *Clarel*, 2:422.

5. James Turner, *Without God, without Creed*, p.204.

6. John C. Jackson, ed., "A Wild Mustang Campaign of 1879 in Pumpkin Creek Valley," pp.317–18; Lura C. Smith to Helen Huntting, August 18, 1862, SMI 69, Lura (Case) Smith Correspondence; Martin Mallett Diaries, June 16, 1868.

7. Fleming Fraker, Jr., ed., "To Pike's Peak by Ox-Wagon," pp.132–33; Margaret Fields to Nancy Spoon, June 29, [1868?], Frederic Stafford Papers.

8. Rebecca Skillin, ed., "William Cheney (1787–1875)," p.50; L. H. (or Mrs. L. H.) Blackwell to brother and sister, March 21, 1867, Charles Brigham Kittredge Family Papers; Unknown to Dear Children, December 27, 1872, George James Crosby and Family Papers.

9. Pauline H. Stratton Diary, January 1, March 20, 1862, and March 24, 1864; John and Triphena Henry to Dear Niece, April 14, 1869, James Diamond Family Papers.

10. M. M. Woods to Z. A. Holman, September 6, 1867, Woods-Holman Papers; Sara McAteer to Frankling McAteer, December 17, 1873, William Stevens Powell Collection; William Littlejohn to uncle, August 12, 1876, Lipscomb Family Papers; T. W. Chapman to father and mother, November 23, 1890, Chapman Family Papers.

11. Cicero Sims to James N. Sims, January 13, 1863, John Merrick Papers.

12. See George M. Fredrickson, *The Inner Civil War*, esp. chaps.7, 12–14.

13. Ray Henshaw and Glenn W. LaFantasie, eds., "Letters Home," p.107.

14. Obadiah Ethelbert Baker Collection. Baker wrote this and other poetry in an order book for a farm equipment company with dates of the 1880s. When I used the material it was in an envelope marked 1900–1923. Given the firmness of the hand of the quoted poem, I am sure that it was written no later than the early 1890s.

15. "Diary of Charles Ross 1862," p.136.

16. George H. Mellish to mother, May 2, 1862, George H. Mellish Collection; Robert Middlekauff, *The Glorious Cause*, p.498; O. D. Fogelman to aunt and uncle, March 23, 1863, Martin Moser Papers; Gorham Coffin to father and sister, July 18, 1862, in Herbert Wisbey, Jr., ed., "Civil War Letters of Gorham Coffin," p.86; Leander Huckaby to father, October 12, 1862, in Donald B. Reynolds, ed., "A Mississippian in Lee's Army," p.167.

17. Wiley, *Life of Johnny Reb*, p.183.

18. "Diary of Charles Ross 1862," p.136.

19. John Sharp to Helen Maria Sharp, April 12, 1862, and May 28, 1865, in George Mills, ed., "The Sharp Family Civil War Letters," pp.493, 521.

20. Perry Miller, *The New England Mind*, p.208; Joseph T. Glatthaar, *The March to the Sea and Beyond*, p.xii; Helen Maria Sharp to John Sharp, January 14, 1862, in Mills, ed., "The Sharp Family Civil War Letters," p.489.

21. T. M. Wilson to wife, December 13, 1864, Mary Ann (Covington) Wilson Papers.

22. Charles B. Kittredge to father and mother, December 22, 1862, Kittredge Family Papers; Sara Sims, J. B. Sims, and Cicero Sims to James Sims, January 9, 1863, Merrick Papers; W. R. Coffee Diary, March 13 and April 7, 1863.

23. Mary A. Easterwood and Martha Burgess to Nancy E. Burgess, October 8, 1868, Lipscomb Family Papers; William Garland, Jr., to father, December 12, 1871, William Harris Garland Papers.

24. William W. Shepherd to Cousin Lissie, May 10, 1865, George Washington Lambert Papers; H. C. Kendrick to brother, August 16, 1861, H. C. Kendrick Letters; Marinda Silsby to Russell Dutton Silsby, May 14, 1863,

Russell Dutton Silsby Letters; Thomas J. Dooley to father and mother, March 1, 1862, Thomas J. Dooley Letters.

25. David D. Danbom, " 'Dear Companion,' " p.542.

26. Joseph G. Hyde to Cousin Henrietta, December 31, 1866, Darwin G. Seeley Papers; Charles E. Perkins to brother-in-law, July 17, 1862, in Henshaw and LaFantasie, "Letters Home," p.117; H. C. Kendrick to father, February 16, 1862, Kendrick Letters.

27. Arthur M. Schlesinger, ed., "A Blue Bluejacket's Letters Home," p.554; Stephen Crane, *The Red Badge of Courage*, p.41; George M. Wilkie to Dear Sarah, October 20, 1862, Wilkie Family Correspondence and Diaries.

28. Richard D. Rowen, ed., "The Second Nebraska's Campaign against the Sioux," p.30; Nathan Buck to sister, July 9, 1864, HM 27885, Saxton Family Collection; T. H. Colman to parents, November 18, 1861, Coleman-Hayter Letters; H. C. Kendrick to brother and sister, February 2(?), 1862, Kendrick Letters.

29. H. C. Kendrick to parents, January 24, 1863, Kendrick Letters; Warren Slesinger, "Other Voices Than Their Own," p.247; Andrew James Morrison to brother and sister, September 22, 1862, Main File, HM 20873.

30. Ransom Perkins to friends, May 14, 1864, Main File, HM 36791; George W. Lambert to brother and sister, May 17, 1863, Lambert Papers; George H. Mellish to mother, December 20, 1862, and April 22, 1863, Mellish Collection.

31. Sarah P. Harlan to mother and father, June 9, 1865, Bond and Fentriss Family Papers.

32. Linderman, *Embattled Courage*, p.110.

33. Tommy R. Thompson, "Letters Home," p.246; Ohio sergeant quoted in Mitchell, *Civil War Soldiers*, p.187.

34. Thompson, "Letters Home," p.245; Benjamin Mabrey to Louisa Mabrey, May 29, 1864, Benjamin Benn Mabrey Papers; Granville Alspaugh to mother, April 29 and June 14, 1862, in Mary Elizabeth Sanders, ed., "Letters of a Confederate Soldier," pp.1230, 1233.

35. Harvey A. Marckres to brother and to father and mother, July 4 and 5, 1864, Main File, HM 30504 (6–7).

36. "Diary of Charles Ross 1863," pp.6, 29, 46, 48, 57, 61; Charles E. Perkins to sister, December 19, 1862, in Henshaw and LaFantasie, "Letters Home," p.129.

37. Amory K. Allen to wife, October 15 and November 2, 1862, in "Civil War Letters of Amory K. Allen," pp.357, 360.

38. Amory K. Allen to wife, June 2, 12, and May 15, 1864, ibid., pp.375–77.

39. Maurice Kendall, "Chance," in Philip P. Wiener, ed., *Dictionary of the History of Ideas*, p.336.

40. George Hudson to John Fry, March 8, 1863, Fry-Rhue Papers.

41. Turner, *Without God, without Creed*, pp.204–5.

42. Ibid., p.97.

43. George H. Mellish to mother and sister, March 13, 1864, Mellish Collection.

44. Turner, *Without God, without Creed*, p.207.

45. Frank Wilkeson, *Recollections of a Private Soldier in the Army of the Potomoc*, pp.202–3.

46. Thomas Colman to father and mother, August 21, 1864, Coleman-Hayter Letters.

47. Mother to Dear Charles, June 13, 1864, in C. M. Destler, ed., "An Andersonville Prison Diary," p.58.

48. Ibid., pp.58, 64–65.

49. Ibid., pp.65, 72, 73, 75, 76.

50. Joseph Flower, Jr., Diary, August 5 and May 16, 1864; Henry H. Adams Diary, September 19–20, 1864.

51. Donald F. Danker, ed., "Imprisoned at Andersonville," pp. 104, 122; William B. Hesseltine, *Civil War Prisons*, p.153.

52. Clemens L. Clendenen to Louisa Clendenen, April 4, 1864, Clendenen Family Collection.

53. Hellkiah McHenry to "Friends and Fellow Soldiers," August 24, 1863, Main File, HM 28814.

54. Lizzie Fentriss to Mrs. Uriah Bond, August 15, 1865, Bond and Fentriss Family Papers.

55. George H. Mellish to mother, June 12, 1863, Mellish Collection; Harry Morgan to Ellen Morgan, March 1863 and undated letter probably mid-1863, in John A. Cawthon, ed., "Letters of a North Louisiana Private to His Wife," pp.541, 543; Benjamin Mabrey to Louisa Mabrey, November 24, 1862, Mabrey Papers; David Boilard and Joseph Carvalho III, "Private John E. Bisbee, the 52nd Mass. Volunteers, and the Banks Expedition," p.41.

56. Russell Kirk, ed., "A Michigan Soldier's Diary," p.238; John C. Ransdell to Robert Banta, November 23, 1863, Robert M. Banta Papers.

57. A. Reed Taylor, "The War History of Two Soldiers," p.103; "A Solger in the Ind. Sixteenth," pp.111–12.

58. Jonathan Labrant to wife, September 3, 1862, January 18, 1864, June 14, 1862, and April 6, 1864, Jonathan Labrant Papers.

59. Jonathan Labrant to wife, March 20, May 1 and 24, 1864, Labrant Papers.

60. Barton, *Goodmen*, p.81.

61. Whitman quoted in F. O. Matthiessen, *American Renaissance*, p.603.

CHAPTER 2

1. Angeline (Mitchell) Brown, Diary of a School Teacher on the Arizona Frontier, December 26, 1880.

2. J. S. Holliday, *The World Rushed In*, p.495, chaps.11, 12.

3. Ira Butterfield to foster mother, April 18 and 23, 1863, in "The Correspondence of Ira Butterfield," pp.139, 141.

4. Albert E. Bugbie to George B. Greene, February 6, 1870, in B.L.H., "Pioneering in Stearns County," p.323.

5. Everitt Judson to Phileta Judson, November 16, 1863, and Sophia Smith to Mrs. Everitt Judson, May 25, 1865(?), Judson-Fairbanks Correspondence.

6. William Carroll to wife and children, June 3, 1860, HM 19802, and June 13, 1860(?), HM 19803, Saxton Family Collection; George Tilden to wife, April 11, 1869, George G. Tilden Letters.

7. Leonard Dibble to mother, January 1865(?), Leonard W. Dibble Papers; William Carroll to wife and children, June 3, 1860, HM 19802, Saxton Family Collection; Ephraim Morse to father, March 7, 1867, HM 26545, Ephraim W. Morse Letters and Diary.

8. Frederick Jackson Turner, "The Significance of the Frontier in American History," in *The Frontier in American History*, p.38; John M. Findlay, *People of Chance*, p.3, chap.3.

9. John R. Carmine to Robert M. Banta, June 30, 1864, Banta Papers.

10. Diary of John W. Grannis, as quoted in Maddow, *A Sunday between Wars*, p.96; Zina W. Chase Diary, June 16, 1866, Chase Papers; George Loring Diary, May 30, 1876, George Loring to mother, May 28, 1876, and to wife, June 25, 1876, Loring Family Collection.

11. John Fiske to wife, June 3, 1887, in John Spencer Clark, *The Life and Letters of John Fiske*, 2:358–59; Joseph A(llan) Nevins Diary, January 12, 1874; Fraker, ed., "To Pike's Peak by Ox-Wagon," p.135; A. H. (Howard) Cutting, Journal of a trip by overland route, May 25, 1863.

12. James T. Jones to sister, April 16, 1869, JTJ 17 and to sister, September 13, 1869, JTJ 6, James T. Jones Papers; Minnie Harney to Ella Mitchell, May 6, 1883, Mitchell Family Papers.

13. William S. Pritchard to niece, July 17, 1866, September 12, 1868, and February 7, 1869, in "Pioneer Letters," pp.9–11; Diary of John W. Grannis, as quoted in Maddow, *A Sunday between Wars*, pp.91, 96.

14. Leonard W. Dibble to father, February 19, 1868, and to family, June 28, 1868, Dibble Papers.

15. David Ludlum, *Social Ferment in Vermont*, p.274; T. D. Seymour Bassett, "500 Miles of Trouble and Excitement," pp.133, 135.

16. Donald W. Davis to father, April 14, June 9 and 13, 1867, Lyman Stuart Papers.

17. Donald W. Davis to mother, February 23, 1870, ibid.

18. Donald W. Davis to father, January 17, 1869, ibid. For a fuller treatment of Davis as a representative figure, see Lewis O. Saum, "From Vermont to Whoop-Up Country."

19. Herman Melville, *Israel Potter*, p.244; Rodman W. Paul, *The Far West and the Great Plains in Transition*, p.299; Ludlum, *Social Ferment in Vermont*, p.274.

20. Maddow, *A Sunday between Wars*, 115, 108, 116.

21. Joseph A(llan) Nevins Diary, January 14–15, 1874.

22. W. H. Taylor to wife, July 10, 1866, Mitchell Family Papers.

23. Edgar Allan Poe, "Never Bet the Devil Your Head," in *Edgar Allan Poe*, pp.460–61.

24. Andrew Jackson Stone to Wesley Stone, September 2, 1860, Andrew J. Stone Correspondence; George Loring to mother, September 26, 1876, Loring Family Collection.

25. As cited in John Samuel Ezell, *Fortune's Merry Wheel*, p.12.

26. Minnie Harney to Ella Mitchell, May 6, 1883, Mitchell Family Papers.

27. Nahum Trask Wood, Daily Journal, January 1, 8, 1871.

28. Ibid., January 10, 22, 24, and May 11, 1871.

29. Ibid., May 7, June 11, 22, July 10, and September 8, 1871.

30. Ibid., September 2, 1871; Charles H. Tyler to Andrew Jackson Stone, December 22, 1861, Stone Correspondence.

31. Josie [Mitchell] and Kate [Schieffer] to Ella [Mitchell], and Kate Schieffer to Josie Mitchell, June 26, Mitchell Family Papers. These letters are in a file marked "c. 1876–1879."

32. J. H. Hooper to friends, February 2, 1880, ibid.

33. George S. Mooers to Charles Smith, October 16, 1876, John L. Smith Papers.

34. Turner, *Without God, without Creed*, p.92; Harriet Beecher Stowe, *Poganuc People*, p.265; Harriet Beecher Stowe, *Sam Lawson's Oldtown Fireside Stories*, pp.205–6.

35. Samuel Clemens, *The Man That Corrupted Hadleyburg*, pp.18, 29; Samuel Clemens, *Roughing It*, pp.388–89.

36. Francis Bret Harte, *The Luck of Roaring Camp*, pp.11, 18.

37. John Wallace Crawford, *Whar' the Hand o' God Is Seen*, pp.118–21.

38. Ibid., p.118; Paul A. Carter, *The Spiritual Crisis of the Gilded Age*, chap.7. In slightly different form "Rattlin' Joe's Prayer" appeared in 1879 in Crawford's first book, *The Poet Scout*. It has no mention of Henry Ward Beecher.

39. *Brooklyn Daily Eagle*, June 20, 1880; Carter, *Spiritual Crisis of the Gilded Age*, p.132.

40. *Brooklyn Daily Eagle*, January 25, 1880. Huntley's humorous poetry and prose appeared in several book forms in the 1880s and 1890s. For a recent sampling and assessment, see Lewis O. Saum, comp., "Spoopendyke's Dakota."

41. Henry Ward Beecher, *Lectures to Young Men on Important Subjects*, pp.135, 169. *Seven* was dropped from the title as Beecher added lectures to later editions.

42. Ben Innis, ed., "The Fort Buford Diary of Wilmot P. Sanford," pp.369, 373; Lemuel Hazzard to wife, August 31, 1873, Hazzard Papers.

43. Eric F. Goldman, *Rendezvous with Destiny*, p.3; Henry Queripel to Caleb Carr [late 1864] and Queripel to Carr [early 1865], Caleb M. Carr Letters.

44. Henry Queripel to Caleb Carr [early 1865], Carr Letters.

45. Bryce, *American Commonwealth*, chap.121; Henry Queripel to Caleb Carr, September 20, 1864, Carr Letters.

46. Leonard W. Dibble to father, April 2, 1865, and Rose G. Dayton to Lucile Kane, August 9, 1954, Dibble Papers; Henry Nash Smith, *Virgin Land*. Dayton's letter provided some information about Dibble's later life.

47. Martin E. Marty, *Righteous Empire*, pp.188–98.

48. Zina W. Chase Diary, July 4, 1866, Chase Papers; T. A. Evans to R. A. Evans, August 10, 1874, Evans Papers. An Iowa diarist occasionally heard challenging sermons at Unitarian meetings in Iowa City, including mention of "nebular hypothesis." She probably reacted as she did on another occasion: "I probably could not comprehend it" (Adaline Kimball Jones Diaries, November 13, 30, 1879, and January 18, 1880).

49. William Preston Longley Letter. Sheriff Jim Brown of Lee County, Texas, probably received this in 1877, and he presided at Longley's hanging shortly thereafter.

50. Carter, *Spiritual Crisis of the Gilded Age*, p.85; Leonard Hawley to Hannah Hawley, April 20, 1862, HM 47929, Main File; Melville, *Clarel*, 2:483.

51. Turner, *Without God, without Creed*, p.xiii; Benjamin Harris to wife and children, December 13, 1862, Benjamin Harris Letters.

52. "Aug. 1866 Home Musings," George B. C. Ingraham Journal. George Ingraham died in 1860, and his widow occasionally wrote in unused parts of his journal.

53. James E. Glazier Diaries, December 31, 1891, James Edward Glazier Collection.

54. Mary E. L. Carpenter to aunt, July 10, 1873, in Peg Meier, coll., *Bring Warm Clothes*, pp.126, 128.

55. Ibid., p.128.

56. Harry Cooley Diary, January 5, 1876, Milo H. Cooley Diaries; Philena and James Milton Pearson to uncle, September 12, 1879, John Scott Papers; Uriah W. Oblinger to wife and child, February 9, 1873, Uriah W. Oblinger Papers.

57. James J. Heslin, ed., "The Diary of a Union Soldier in Confederate Prisons," p.267.

58. Rose Williams to Mrs. Lettie Mosher, February 12, 1888, in Elizabeth Hampsten, comp., *To All Inquiring Friends*, pp.124–25; Eliza Nutting to Lois Nutting Dane, February 5, 1872, Dane Papers.

59. Julia Raine to "My Darling Little Daughter," October 8, 1878, Todd-Austin Family Papers.

60. Louisa Jane Phifer to husband and parent, March 15, 1865, in Carol Benson Pye, intro. and annot., "Letters from an Illinois Farm," pp.398–99.

61. L.S. [Lizzie Scaper], "In Memory of the Epidemic of 1878," Scaper-Handwerker Family Scrapbook; Almeda Arrowsmith to mother, October 6, 1886, Arrowsmith Collection; W. B. Bradley School Account Book, January 9, 1882, W. B. Bradley Papers.

62. Allenson Study to Sarah Bailey, February 27, 1865, Sarah Bailey Papers; Augustine, *The City of God*, bk. 4, chap.1 ; Miller, ed., *The American Puritans*, p.192.

CHAPTER 3

1. Ralph Waldo Emerson, "Divinity School Address," in *The Complete Works of Ralph Waldo Emerson*, p.143.

2. A. P. Tannehill to J. C. Tannehill, July 30, 1860, Jesse C. Tannehill Papers.

3. Charles H. Flanders to Brother Judson, September 20, 1862, Judson-Fairbanks Correspondence; Arngi (?) L. Demaree to Robert Banta, May 19, 1862, Banta Papers; Elias M. Wood to wife, June 13 (or 15), 1864, Elias M. Wood Letters and Papers; Uriah Oblinger to Martha Thomas, Oblinger Papers.

4. Annis Pierce to Emily Pierce Carr, November 1862, Carr Letters; Unknown to John W. Van Scyoc, February 19, 1865, Ralph Shackelford Collection.

5. Nellie Nutting to Lois Nutting Dane, June 6–11, 1864, Dane Papers, Box 9; Thomas and Margaret Stafford to sister, April 14, 1872, Stafford Papers; R. B. Smith to father, December 8, 1867, Ralph S. Smith Letter; William Carroll to Ann Buck, June 27, 1860, HM 19804, Saxton Family Collection.

6. Sarah F. Morse to sisters, September 20, 1862, Morse Family Letters; T. C. Oatts Diary, June 30, 1871.

7. Henry E. Savage Diary, June 26–27, 1864; H. J. Hightower to sister, March 14, 1864, in Dewey W. Grantham, Jr., ed., "Letters from H. J. Hightower, A Confederate Soldier," p.187. I excluded the writings of officers, but this "son of a yeoman farmer" (p.174) had very recently, through exigencies of war, been elevated to lieutenant.

8. Mathew Andrew Dunn to wife, November 7, 1863, in Weymouth T. Jordan, ed., "Mathew Andrew Dunn Letters," p.115; Granville W. Hough, ed., "Diary of a Soldier in Grant's Rear Guard," p.202; James M. Forbes to sister, March 1, 1863, FO 11, James Monro Forbes Collection.

9. Mary Jacacks Diary, memorandum pages at end of 1868 diary, Jacacks Diaries; C.I.S. (?) to M.A.I. (Mary Ann Ireland), July 13, 1873, Ireland Family Correspondence; Callie Coble to sister, August 27, 1882, Bond and Fentriss Family Papers.

10. John H. Yzenbaard and John Hoffmann, eds., "'Between Hope and Fear': The Life of Lettie Teeple 2: 1850–1868," p.325; Robert S. McCully, "Letter from a Reconstruction Renegade," p.36; Uriah Oblinger to wife, December 22, 1872, Oblinger Papers.

11. Joseph Haroutunian, *Piety versus Moralism*, p.xxii; C. H. Essy to D. W. Ireland, October 21, 1869, Ireland Family Correspondence; Joel Triplett to Susan Shockly and children, June 9, 1874, David Shockly Papers.

12. Francis W. Squires Diaries, November 3, 1861; M.K. to George James Crosby, December 28, 1883, Crosby and Family Papers.

13. Margaret Fields to cousin, March 8, 1868, Stafford Papers; George H. Mellish to mother, July 6, 1862, Mellish Collection.

14. Jane Whiteman Dallas to Mahala Whiteman Williams, September 11, 1864, HM 16818, Whiteman Family Letters; Elijah M. Odom to wife, July 15, 1862, Elijah Odom Letters; Martin Bone, Sanford Sheilds [sic], John L. Smith, and James B. Parten to William Bone, August 27, 1861, Adams Collection.

15. Raymond Williams, *Keywords*, pp.11–12.

16. Elizabeth Stevens to husband, October 12, 1862, in Richard N. Ellis, ed., "The Civil War Letters of an Iowa Family," p.576.

17. Angeline Van Scyoc to John Van Scyoc, July 2, 1862, Shackelford Collection; Sarah Jane and James Clendenen to Louisa Clendenen, July 1, 1861, HM 21765, Clendenen Family Collection; George Loring to wife, July 23, 1876, Loring Family Collection.

18. Unknown to Sallie Neu, November 6, 1868, Sallie Neu Correspondence; Anne Bailey and Carrie Study to Sarah Bailey, February 4, 1863, Bailey Papers; Austin Carrell Diary, December 28, 1862, Samuel D. Carrell and Family Papers.

19. W. C. Pierce Diary, April 13, June 4 and 8, 1879, Pierce Family Collection; Ruben Abbott to brother and sister, December 3, 1870, John Scott Papers.

20. John K. Baldwin Diary, December 6, 1868, January 3, 28, and May 2, 1869.

21. Ibid., February 18, 1871; B. F. Cloyes Diary, May 31, 1878.

22. B. F. Cloyes Diary, January 10, 1864; Mary Jacacks Diary, September 20, 1868, Jacacks Diaries.

23. Moses Coit Tyler, *A History of American Literature during the Colonial Period*, 1:192.

24. Mary Labrant to husband, September 2, 1862, Labrant Papers; Amos W. Ames, "A Diary of Prison Life in Southern Prisons," p.2; William H. Jackson Diary, July 17 and 28, 1864.

25. David S. Reynolds, "From Doctrine to Narrative," p.480; Anna Furnas to unknown, November 27, 1870, John M. Furnas Letters; Adaline Kimball Jones Diaries, March 7 and 14, 1880.

26. Milo H. Cooley Diaries, June 15, 1878.

27. Ibid., December 31, 1882, January 7, 21, and 28, and February 11, 1883; Richard S. Storrs, "Contributions Made to Our National Development by Plain Men," p.63.

28. Hattie E. Mason Diaries, January 6, 1884; Nettie Comins Diaries, September 6 and October 4, 1885; Nancy Nash Holeman Diary, June 4, 1871, Nancy Nash Holeman Papers.

29. Nathan Buck to sister, July 9, 1864, HM 27885, Saxton Family Collection; Ann Douglas, The Feminization of American Culture, p.6; Willard L. Clendenen to Mary Cowan, October 4, 1887, HM 46706(c), Clendenen Family Collection.

30. B. F. Cloyes Diaries, December 31, 1878; Alonzo Teed Diaries, December 31, 1890, Teed Family Papers; Thomas Faucett Diaries, December 31, 1880.

31. Marvin C. Snell Diary, January 1, 6, 7, and 22, 1873, Snell Family Papers; I. D. Keating to sister, May 4, 1873, Ireland Family Correspondence.

32. Lois Nutting Dane to Ezra Dane, June 3, 1876, Dane Papers, Box 12; Marlene Springer and Haskell Springer, eds., Plains Woman, pp.62–63, 70.

33. Mrs. T. W. Chapman to mother, February 25, 1890, Chapman Family Papers, Mississippi.

34. Charles W. Hicks to Robert E. Chapman, September 24, 1868, ibid.

35. Ada Nutting Baker to Lois Nutting Dane, June 27 and July 16, 1868, Dane Papers, Box 4.

36. I. D. Keating to sister, May 4, 1873, Ireland Family Correspondence; James Colby to John Anderson, January 1, 1863, HM 4253, California File (I surmise that John Anderson was Colby's son and had been adopted by the Andersons); Ada Nutting Baker to Lois Nutting Dane, January 7, 1869, Dane Papers, Box 4.

37. Lorenzo Dow Chillson Diaries, November 6, 1865.

38. Bryce, American Commonwealth, 2:894–95; John Hyde to Moses Hyde, September 27, 1868, HM 16599, California File.

39. W. D. Robertson to Emma Perry, May 4, 1878, Dow Perry Family Papers; Rebecca Colby to Rebecca Anderson, May 20, 1860, HM 4244, California File.

40. Margaret Fields to Nancy Spoon, June 29 (probably 1868), Stafford Papers.

41. Anne M. Boylan, Sunday School, p.87; Moses Puterbaugh to Uriah Oblinger, June 26, 1868, Oblinger Papers.

42. Lois Nutting Dane to Eliza Nutting, December 7, 1869, Dane Papers, Box 12; Dwight Bartlett to sister, January 18, 1871, HM 26640, California File;

James Edward Glazier Diaries, November 27 and December 25, 1873, GZ 126, Glazier Collection.

43. Harriet Beecher Stowe, *Oldtown Folks*, pp.280, 337; Stowe, *Poganuc People*, p.364.

44. Springer and Springer, eds., *Plains Woman*, pp.65–66.

45. George H. Mellish to mother, December 26, 1862, Mellish Collection; Henry E. Savage Diary, October 9, 1864.

46. Kattie Rowzee to sister, n.d., John Scott and Justina Rowzee Pickle Family Papers (content leaves no doubt that this is wartime Christmas letter, probably early in the war); Stowe, *Oldtown Folks*, p.280.

47. Hattie to Nettie, Edie, and sister, December 26, 1876, Nettie A. Snow Letters; Johnny Parrott Diary, December 24, 1887.

48. Nettie Comins Diaries, December 24, 1885; I. D. Keating to sister, February 1, 1874, Ireland Family Correspondence; Mamie A. James to Edie, December 1876, Snow Letters.

49. "Christmas 1876," Mary Bennett Papers.

50. Ibid.

51. Francis Bret Harte, "How Santa Claus Came to Simpson's Bar," in *The Works of Bret Harte*, 3:11–12.

52. Josie Beckman to Ella Mitchell, December 29, 1878, Mitchell Family Papers; Innis, ed., "Fort Buford Diary of Private Wilmot P. Sanford," p.352; Donald W. Davis to mother, December 24, 1871, Stuart Papers; G. S. Mooers to unknown, December 27, 1874, John L. Smith Papers.

53. H. H. Raymond Diary, December 26, 1873; Venola Lewis Bivans, ed., "The Diary of Luna E. Warner, a Kansas Teenager of the Early 1870's," p.300; Springer and Springer, eds., *Plains Woman*, p.66.

54. Thomas R. Johnson to wife, December 18, 1870, Thomas R. Johnson Letter; William Garland to father, December 25, 1871, Garland Papers; Zina W. Chase Diary, June 25, 1866, Chase Papers.

55. Sarah Colby to John William Colby, January 4, 1860, HM 4236, California File; Alonzo Teed Diaries, March 17, 1864, Teed Family Papers.

56. Mattie Oblinger to father and mother, January 11, 1880, Oblinger Papers; Alice D. Watson to sister, December 22 and 23, 1889, Ida Greenlee Houck Letters.

57. Stowe, *Oldtown Folks*, pp.336–37.

58. Bertha R. Wright, intro., "Diary of Charles Ross, 1861," p.78; Donald F. Carmony, ed., "Jacob W. Bartness Civil War Letters," p.50.

59. Wiley, *Life of Johnny Reb*, pp.183–84; Milton W. Woodford to wife, April 5, 1865, in Vaughn D. Bornet, "A Yankee after Olustee," p.396.

60. Benjamin Mabrey to wife, March 11, May 18, 1864, April 1, 1865, and to brother and sister, wife and baby, May 6, 1864, Mabrey Papers.

61. Robert T. Wood to wife and children, July 15, 1864, Wood Papers.

62. John W. Truss to wife, February 21, 1864, in Johnette Highsmith Ray, ed., "Civil War Letters from Parsons' Texas Cavalry," p.222; Harry Morgan to wife, August 21, September 18, 1862, and January 31, February 19, 1865, in Cawthon, ed., "Letters of a North Louisiana Private," pp.534–35, 545, 547.

63. Thomas H. Colman to father and mother, August 21, 1864, Coleman-Hayter Letters.

64. William Garland to father, January 18 and December 11, 1871, Garland Papers; William and Anna Evans to Mary Ann Wilson, August 31, 1866, Wilson Papers.

65. W. J. Cash, *The Mind of the South*, p.131.

66. Mrs. E. P. Henslee to husband, January 28, 1865, Mrs. E. P. Henslee Letter.

67. Chard Powers Smith, *Yankees and God*, p.451; Fannie Ross to Mrs. Bond, September 20, 1882, and Lizzie Coble to sister, October 2, 1882, Bond and Fentriss Family Papers.

68. Cash, *Mind of the South*, p.130.

69. As quoted in Maggie Aldridge Smith, *Big Wah of Seminole County*, p.2.

70. Barton, *Goodmen*, p.133; Hampsten, *Read This Only to Yourself*, p.99.

71. William A. Clebsch, *From Sacred to Profane America*, p.ix; Ruben Abbott to brother and sister, December 3, 1870, John Scott Papers.

CHAPTER 4

1. Knut Hamsun, *The Cultural Life of Modern America*, p.76; Emerson, "Divinity School Address," p.143; James J. Farrell, *Inventing the American Way of Death*, p.4.

2. Henry Wadsworth Longfellow, "A Psalm of Life," in *The Complete Poetical Works of Henry Wadsworth Longfellow*, pp.2–3; Eunice Brown to brother, March 28, 1864, Eunice A. Brown Papers; Mrs. John Colyer to Henry Colyer, February 21, 1864, HM 29053, Henry Isaac Colyer Collection. In discussing my depiction of the prewar mood, Philippe Ariès employs the term *thanatophilia* (*The Hour of Our Death*, p.447), but that term does not seem altogether apt.

3. Farrell, *Inventing the American Way of Death*, pp.73, 44.

4. Mathew Andrew Dunn to wife, October 13, 1864, in Jordan, ed., "Mathew Andrew Dunn Letters," p.112; J. W. Forbes to J. B. Landreth and W. Fulliton, November 27, 1870, and Forbes to aunt, March 24, 1871, J. Berryman Papers.

5. Yzenbaard and Hoffmann, eds., "Between Hope and Fear," p.331.

6. EEM to Lizzy, December 18, 1863, and Lizzy to brother, December 24, 1863, Vermillion and Kittredge Civil War Letters. EEM wrote from Maine to Iowa, and Lizzy wrote more on the same letter and sent it to her brother.

7. L. A. Gushee to brother, December 20, 1881, Llewellyn Amos Gushee Papers; Canan and Mary Duitt to Susan Shockly, May 23, 1873, Shockly Papers; Aggie to Lem, May 13, 1866, Hazzard Papers.

8. Richard O'Connor, *Ambrose Bierce*, p.3; N. B. Booth to sister, April 19 and May 3, 1874, George E. Beers Collection.

9. John Hunt to niece, March 14, 1873, Emily R. Ewing Day Papers.

10. Geoffrey Gorer, "The Pornography of Death"; James Edward Glazier Diaries, GZ 126, March 4–10, 1881, Glazier Collection. Of course, he may have written letters containing such material, but his diary was the natural, self-evident place for such reflection.

11. M. Van Tassel to Mahala Whiteman Williams, May 6, 1864, HM 16824, Whiteman Family Letters; Abbie T. Griffin Diary, February 10, 1885.

12. Susannah Scott to children, September 20, 1890, Ransom D. Scott Papers.

13. Mrs. A. B. Wambaugh to "My Dear Madam," January 27, 1867, Seeley Papers.

14. Linderman, *Embattled Courage*, p.248, chap.12.

15. Wilkeson, *Recollections*, pp.203–4.

16. Ibid., p.197; L. Humphrey to John Black, September 14, 1862, Black Family Letters; Leroy H. Streetman to William Bone, September 10, 1861, Adams Collection.

17. Wilkeson, *Recollections*, p.205; Levi Sowers to Emily Huckaby, October 5, 1863, in Reynolds, ed., "A Mississippian in Lee's Army," p.287.

18. Harriet H. A. Eaton Diaries, October 18, 1862.

19. Fredrickson, *Inner Civil War*, p.96; Smith and Sally Lipscomb to William Lipscomb, September 24, 1861, Lipscomb Family Papers.

20. Walt Whitman, *Specimen Days in America*, pp.125–26. On Whitman's failure to do more with his war experience, see Fredrickson, *Inner Civil War*, pp.93–97; Daniel Aaron, *The Unwritten War*, pp.62–73; and Edmund Wilson, *Patriotic Gore*, pp.479–81.

21. Mrs. A. B. Wambaugh to "My Dear Madam," January 27, 1867, Seeley Papers; Lucy Dawson to Lois Nutting Dane, n.d., Dane Papers, Box 9. Cataloging identifies this as an 1883 letter.

22. Francis W. Squires Diaries, January 11, 1861.

23. Henry Ruechel to Jonathan Labrant, March 25, 1887, Labrant Papers; A. J. Powell to sister, April 1, 1872, in "Levi Powell and A. J. Powell Letters," p.33.

24. Jane Freeland to Eliza Keyes, February 23, 1869, in Hampsten, comp., *To All Inquiring Friends*, p.143. Content of the succeeding letter suggests that this was written in 1869 rather than 1868, as dated.

25. Fredrickson, *Inner Civil War*, pp.107–8.

26. Henry B. Williams to Sue Fisher, October 5, 9, 1878, Letters and

Papers of Charles G. Fisher. The Memphis city directory of 1878 has a Henry T. Williams listed as white. Six Henry Williamses were black, and I assume that Henry B. Williams was one of them.

27. Rena Steadman to uncle and aunt, September 8, 1890, Ransom D. Scott Papers.

28. J. T. Gregg to mother, January 1, 1889, Mrs. J. B. Rhea Family Papers; Emma to sister, May 28, 1888, Smith-Hamilton Families Papers; S. L. and Louisa Gitchel to brother and sister, May 19, 1884, Gitchel-Larsen Family Papers.

29. S. L. and Louisa Gitchel to brother and sister, May 19, 1884, Gitchel-Larsen Family Papers; Stowe, *Oldtown Folks*, p.35.

30. Stowe, *Oldtown Folks*, pp.28, 35–37.

31. Harold Frederic, *Seth's Brother's Wife*, p.35.

32. Farrell, *Inventing the American Way of Death*, chap.6.

33. Truman Pierce Diary, October 1, 1865, August 30, 1873, and August 9, 1874, and W. C. Pierce Diary, August 30, 1873, January 6–7, 1879, Pierce Family Collection.

34. James Russell Lowell to Mrs.———, April 19, 1876, in Charles Eliot Norton, ed., *Letters of James Russell Lowell*, 2:163–64; Mary Jacacks Diary, September 9–18, 1868, Jacacks Diaries.

35. Abbie Griffin Diary, July 4, 1882.

36. George B. C. Ingraham Journal, HM 16955; Obadiah Ethelbert Baker Collection, folder 19. George Ingraham's widow made various entries in his unfilled journal.

37. Lemuel Raye Poem.

38. Undated poem, Mabrey Papers; T. M. Wilson to wife, December 13, 1864, Wilson Papers.

39. Abraham Lincoln to Andrew Johnston, April 18, 1846, in David D. Anderson, ed., *The Literary Works of Abraham Lincoln*, p.66; William Van Scyoc to John W. Van Scyoc, May 5, 1879, Ralph Shackelford Collection.

40. Narcisa L. Black Diaries, June 2, 1882. In 1878 widow Black married a man named Johnson.

41. Henry Colyer to sister, May 17, 1865, Colyer Collection. This is a typed transcript. Apparently, the original was never acquired by the Huntington Library. Perhaps it remained in the hands of Colyer descendants. A direct descendant of Henry Colyer, Mary Louise Brown of 5956 West 74th Street, Los Angeles, California, has given me permission to quote from the transcript of the apparently misplaced letter.

42. S. L. and Louisa Gitchel to brother and sister, May 19, 1884, Gitchel-Larsen Family Papers; Autograph Book #3, Elizabeth E. Breckenridge and Family Papers; Narcisa L. Black Diaries, June 2, 1882.

43. Samuel Clemens, *The Adventures of Huckleberry Finn*, title page, pp.139–40.

44. Ibid., 217–18, 232–33.

45. Clemens, *Roughing It*, pp.329–33.

46. Max Eastman, *The Sense of Humor*, p.24.

47. *Brooklyn Daily Eagle*, March 7, 1880.

48. Ibid., May 29, 1881; Sally M. Rike to brother, April 18, 1869, Andrew Jackson Rike Papers; Printed obituary for Mrs. Sarah Wells, September 4, 1873, Michael Shoffner Papers, folder 7.

49. Undated folder, Boody and Mowers Family Papers.

50. Alexander Borthwick to brother, July 29, 1865, HM 39263(7), Main File.

51. H. C. Kendrick to parents (February 2, 1863), Kendrick Letters. Kendrick did not date this letter. A different hand penciled the above date, but it seems too early by several days.

52. C. S. Turner to John P. Turner, April 2, 1877, Calvin S. Turner Family Papers; Mason and Mary Arrowsmith to Mrs. Lucy Arrowsmith and family, October 3, 1869, Arrowsmith Collection; Oglethorpe County Diary, January 1, 1867, and October 23, 1868. The Arrowsmith letter was evidently written by Mason, though it was also signed by Mary.

53. James Morse to brother, September 8, 1868, Morse Family Letters.

54. Dyer, ed., *To Raise Myself a Little*, pp.207–8.

55. Springer and Springer, eds., *Plains Woman*, p.37.

56. Ibid., pp.37–38.

57. Douglas, *Feminization of American Culture*, p.205.

58. Springer and Springer, eds., *Plains Woman*, p.39; Clara Madan to friend, May 4, 1874, Stuart Papers.

59. Aileen L. Fentriss to aunt, June 29, 1883, Bond and Fentriss Family Papers.

60. Nathaniel Hawthorne, *The Blithedale Romance*, pp.271–72. Thirty years later in the Riverside Edition of *The Complete Works of Nathaniel Hawthorne* (Boston and New York, 1883) the "evil one" seemed to need some accentuation of identity. There he became the "Evil One" (5:584), and there he remains in uppercase on into an age ever less able to recognize the devil without some hint or emphasis.

61. Barsina (Rogers) French Journal.

62. H. C., Y. H., and S. J. Cruson to brother and sister, April 29, 1868, John Scott Papers.

63. Turner, *Without God, without Creed*, pp.71, 143.

64. *Santa Cruz Sentinel*, February 16, 1878; Zina W. Chase Diary, September 19, 1866, Chase Papers.

65. Farrell, *Inventing the American Way of Death*, p.218.

66. Mary to sister, June 5, 1882, William Harper Papers; Callie Coble to sister, November 13, 1882, and October 14, 1884, Bond and Fentriss Family Papers; William H. Garland to father, May 31 and June 1, 1871, Garland Papers.

67. Michael Barton, "Painful Duties," p.127.

68. Obituary of W. B. Powell, Kendrick Letters.

69. Lewis Atherton, *Main Street on the Middle Border*, chap.6, pp.190–92; Michael Lesy, *Wisconsin Death Trip*. This work is unpaginated. By my count, this passage is on the thirteenth page of the "Conclusion."

70. Douglas, *Feminization of American Culture*, chap.6; Julia M. Keyes to Lois Nutting Dane, June 8, 1877, Dane Papers; John K. Baldwin Diary, June 20–25, 1873.

CHAPTER 5

1. Ralph Waldo Emerson, "Society and Solitude," in Emerson, *Society and Solitude*, p.8; Williams, *Keywords*, p.291. The minor variations between the 1857 and the 1870 versions of the Emerson essay are nearly all stylistic.

2. Andrew Jackson Stone to Wesley Stone, March 1, 1860, SN 41, Stone Correspondence; F. Attwood to Nettie Snow, March 28, 1870, Snow Letters.

3. C. Carver to parents, July 23, 1870, Stuart Papers; Jacob and Eliza Beth Hufford to John Scott, May 30, 1869, John Scott Papers; *Brooklyn Daily Eagle*, March 7, 1880.

4. Nettie Comins Diaries, November 12, 1873.

5. John K. Baldwin Diary, December 31, 1868.

6. Henry David Thoreau, *Walden*, in *The Writings of Henry David Thoreau*, 2:150. This assertion comes in the "Solitude" chapter of *Walden*.

7. M. Van Tassel to Mahala Whiteman Williams, July 15, 1864, HM 16825, Whiteman Family Letters.

8. Edward Lipscomb to brother, October 3, 1875, Lipscomb Family Papers.

9. Douglas, *Feminization of American Culture*, pp.213–14, 220–26; "Married May 18th 1879," Scaper-Handwerker Family Scrapbook.

10. Douglas, *Feminization of American Culture*, p.12.

11. James P. Sampson Diary. This is a photocopy of the original. The poem appears to have been written inside the front cover and dated August 2, 1867.

12. Jesse M. Sears to Ella Springer, August 16 and September 6, 1869, and Ella and Jesse Sears to Mr. and Mrs. Springer, September 20, 1870, Brayton Papers.

13. *New York Times* quoted in Carter, *Spiritual Crisis of the Gilded Age*, p.132; Delbert Boston to Ella Furney, September 26, 1889, Delbert D. Boston Papers.

14. Delbert Boston to Ella Furney, October 2, 1889, Boston Papers; Mary Mellish to George H. Mellish, January 1, 1865, Mellish Collection; Sylvester Smith to wife, September 4, 1862, Smith-Hamilton Families Papers.

15. Henry Wight to "My Darling 'Parents,'" December 14, 1889, Levi Lamoni Wight Papers.

16. Douglas, *Feminization of American Culture*, p.6; Dwight Bartlett to mother, March 5, 1870, HM 26635 and October 2, 1871, HM 26643, California File.

17. [Mary Ann Wilson] to mother and sisters, September 11, 1868, Wilson Papers.

18. Lemuel Raye Poem.

19. "Rock Me to Sleep Mother," John J. Robacher Papers.

20. Mamie Reynolds to George Crosby, March 23, 1883, and Sarah Reynolds to George Crosby, April 8, 1883, Crosby and Family Papers.

21. Sarah Reynolds to George Crosby, May 13, 1883, and February 19, 1884, ibid.

22. Sarah Reynolds to George Crosby, February 19, 1884, Crosby and Family Papers.

23. Lucy Nutting to Lois Nutting Dane, January 2, 1869, Dane Papers, Box 1.

24. Ada Nutting Baker to Lois Nutting Dane, July 8, 1865, Dane Papers, Box 3.

25. Ada Nutting Baker to Lois Nutting Dane, September 29, ca. 1865, Dane Papers, Box 3.

26. Judy Nolte Lensink, Christine M. Kirkham, and Karen Pauba Witzke, " 'My Only Confidant'—The Life and Diary of Emily Hawley Gillespie," pp.309, 311.

27. Unknown to Stella Atkins, April 25, 1872, Kittredge Family Papers; John Mack Faragher, *Women and Men on the Overland Trail*, p.151.

28. Adaline Kimball Jones Diaries, October 26, 1879; Carroll Smith-Rosenberg, *Disorderly Conduct*; Carl N. Degler, *At Odds*.

29. Elaine Tyler May, *Great Expectations*.

30. Albina Wilson to brother, August 21, 1864, Labrant Papers.

31. Americus Buck to Marco Buck and mother, August 25, 1865, HM 27909, Saxton Family Collection.

32. Leonard Dibble to family, July 17, 1867, Dibble Papers.

33. Melissa Baker to Obadiah Ethelbert Baker, November 12, 1882, Obadiah Ethelbert Baker Collection.

34. Melissa Baker to Obadiah Ethelbert Baker, February [1883], and Milo Baker to mother, February 3, 1889, ibid.

35. George Loring to wife, July 31, 1876, and George Loring to mother, September 26, 1876, Loring Family Collection; Ada Nutting Baker to Lois Nutting Dane, September 29, ca. 1865, Dane Papers, Box 3.

36. Columbus Furnas to sister, February 7, 1872, Furnas Letters; Emma to sister, July 1, 1888, Smith-Hamilton Families Papers; J. M. Aldridge to brother and family, April 11, 1881, Aldridge (J. M.) and Family Letters.

37. Unknown to brother, May 23, 1875, and Carter Page to Mrs. Isabella

Page, July 10, 1876, Thomas D. Page Family Letters. The May 23, 1875, letter may have been written by another brother to Carter.

38. Stephen Barron to wife, June 25, 1870(?), and July 27, 1872(?), in Robert W. Lovett, ed., "A Maine Man in the West," pp.69, 70.

39. "lizzie morr" to Nellie Kittredge, November 6, 1883, and R.S. to Nellie Kittredge, February 17, 1884, Kittredge Family Papers.

40. Mabel B. Johnson to Nellie Kittredge, October 7, 1883, ibid.

41. Diary and school account book of W. B. Bradley, 1872, 1873, Bradley Papers.

42. David Perrin to James Canfield Howlett, May 20, ca. 1877, HM 20880, Main File; Nellie Nutting to Lois Nutting Dane, January 14, 1862, Dane Papers, Box 9.

43. Wright, intro., "Diary of Charles Ross, 1861," pp.75–77; Article of agreement, Ireland Family Correspondence.

44. Emerson, "Society and Solitude," pp.7–8.

45. Schlesinger, ed., "A Blue Bluejacket's Letters Home," pp.557, 565.

46. Glatthaar, *The March to the Sea and Beyond*, pp.164–65, 173; Henry H. Bailey to Sarah Bailey, February 4, 1863, Bailey Papers.

47. Henry I. Colyer to sister, October 18, 1862, HM 29023(2), Colyer Collection.

48. Tom H. Coleman to parents, December 6, 1862, Coleman-Hayter Letters; H. C. Kendrick to mother, August 25, 1861, Kendrick Letters.

49. Schlesinger, ed., "A Blue Bluejacket's Letters Home," p.565; John W. Truss to wife, February 21, 1864, in Johnette Highsmith Ray, ed., "Civil War Letters from Parsons' Texas Cavalry," p.222.

50. Philip N. Racine, "Emily Lyles Harris," p.390.

51. Hezekiah Mowers to wife, February 5, 1863, Boody and Mowers Family Papers.

52. T. M. Wilson to wife, November 25–26, 1864, Wilson Papers; George Phifer to Louisa Jane Phifer, January 2, 1865, in Carol Benson Pye, intro. and annot., "Letters From an Illinois Farm," p.400; H. C. Kendrick to sister, August 25, 1861, Kendrick Letters.

53. Mary Labrant to Jonathan Labrant, August 3, 1862, and Jonathan Labrant to Mary Labrant, July 26, 1863, Labrant Papers.

54. Caroline Frissell to sister, October 30, 1864, Reppy, Frissell, and Drake Papers.

55. Edward Spencer to Jennie Spencer, February 14, May 28, and July 9, 1862, HM 27867, 27869, and 27872, Saxton Family Collection. That truly astronomical figure came in the last of these three letters.

56. Edward Spencer to Jennie Spencer, February 14, May 28, July 9, and August 4, 1862, HM 27867, 27869, 27872, and 27873, and Edward Spencer to Barney Barker, January 31, 1862, HM 27865, Saxton Family Collection.

57. W. H. Bothrick(?) to Charles Smith, November 11, 1873, John L. Smith Papers. This difficult signature may be that of Will Bottriel, who is mentioned in other letters in this collection from about this time.

58. Linda Peavey and Ursula Smith, "Women in Waiting in the Westward Movement," pp.2, 17.

59. Jefferson Martenet to mother, January 30, 1861, Jefferson Martenet Collection; George Loring to sister, June 1 (or July 1), 1876, Loring Family Collection.

60. Josie Mitchell to Ella Mitchell, November 6, Mitchell Family Papers. This item is in a folder marked 1878–79, and that seems appropriate.

61. Hattie Kingman to aunt and uncle, March 30, 1863, Hattie H. Kingman Letter.

62. Melissa and Carrie Baker to Obadiah Ethelbert Baker, April 29, 1883, Obadiah Ethelbert Baker Collection; C.A.P. to cousin, November 5, 1884, Crosby and Family Papers. C.A.P. was almost certainly Cornelia Perrigo.

63. Maggie Sepper to Willie, April 25, 1867, Chapman Family Papers. The addressee was probably William G. Chapman.

64. Springer and Springer, eds., *Plains Woman*, pp.3–5.

65. Ibid., pp.43–45, 31.

66. Hampsten, *Read This Only to Yourself*, pp.89, 92, 81.

67. Clara Conron Diary, March 22, 1885.

68. Ella Boston to Delbert Boston, October 13, 1890, Boston Papers.

69. Willard Frissell to Eliza Frissell, April 11 and 12, 1862, Reppy, Frissell, and Drake Papers.

70. Edward and Fannie Rust to Ada Nutting Baker, January 11, 1880, Dane Papers, Box 14.

71. Lensink, Kirkham, and Witzke, " 'My Only Confidant,' " pp.290, 312; Willard L. Clendenen to Mary Cowan, November 13, 1887, HM 46707(c), and Amos Clendenen to Willard L. Clendenen, September 20, 1908, HM 46712, Clendenen Family Collection.

72. Uriah Oblinger to wife, January 12, 1873, Oblinger Papers; Leonard W. Dibble to family, December 4, 1865, Dibble Papers.

73. Alonzo Choate to Hubbel Pierce, January 16, 1866, in Hampsten, comp., *To All Inquiring Friends*, p.72; Sophia Chapin Tunnell Diary, November 29, 1878, Chapin and Tunnell Family Papers; "Hebdomidal Thunderbolt"; Irvin G. Wyllie, *The Self-Made Man in America*, p.7.

74. Matt B. Lane to cousin, November 5, 1867, Wilson Papers; Harold Frederic, *The Damnation of Theron Ware*, pp.288, 294, 300.

75. Chauncey E. Stearns to William Stearns, April 17, 1866, HM 21306, California File.

76. Kent Packard, ed., "Jottings by the Way," p.248.

77. "A Voyage to the Mediterranean," Snow Letters.

78. Edward Eggleston, *The Hoosier School-Master*, pp.17–18; Minutes of the Mount Hope Debating Society, December 22, 1856, Leander Crawford and Louisa (Canfield) Purdy, *Collectors*, Family Papers.

79. Dwight Bartlett to sister, October 2, 1871, HM 26643, California File.

80. Nancy Williams to cousins and uncle, February 26, 1861, Boody and Mowers Family Papers; Harold Frederic, *Marsena and Other Stories of Wartime*, p.10.

81. Nancy Williams and Jacob Williams to cousins and aunt, June 22, [1865], Boody and Mowers Family Papers; L. C. Fogelman to cousin, July 17, 1872, Moser Papers; William H. Crist to Margaret and Keziah Loop, February 22, 1863, Uriah J. Loop Papers.

82. Maddow, *A Sunday between Wars*, p.269; Marjorie Hope Nicolson, *Mountain Gloom and Mountain Glory*, p.95.

83. Benjamin Mabrey to Louisa Mabrey, September 24, 1863, and January 20, 1864, Mabrey Papers.

84. E. Roach to cousin, March 27, 1884, Rhea Family Papers; Anna Furnas to unknown, November 27, 1870, Furnas Letters.

85. Aunt Hattie to Nellie Kittredge, December 27, 1869, Kittredge Family Papers; W. S. and Malinda Burton to Sarah and Malinda Stafford, May 31, 1868, Stafford Papers; E. C. Wells to brother, December 23, 1878, Chapman Family Papers, Mississippi.

86. G. L. Seligmann, ed., "North to New Mexico," p.282.

87. Stowe, *Oldtown Folks*, p.36; Nettie Comins Diaries, August 14, 1884; Rachel and Fannie Ross to sister and aunt, August 2, 1884, and E. Callie Coble to sister, August 15, 1884, Bond and Fentriss Family Papers.

88. Herman Melville, *Pierre*, p.347; Richard Rudisill, *Mirror Image*, p.238.

89. Robert Elliot Fitch, *Odyssey of the Self-Centered Self*; Tom Wolfe, "The Me Decade and the Third Great Awakening," in *Mauve Gloves & Madmen, Clutter & Vine, and Other Stories, Sketches, and Essays*, p.167.

CHAPTER 6

1. Emerson, "Divinity School Address," p.143.

Michael E. McGerr's *Decline of Popular Politics* pays little attention to the Civil War as an energizing agent. Using data regarding voter turnout as his point of departure, McGerr devotes most of his pages "to the political strategies of the rich" (p.11). McGerr contends that the high interest had long been there. My sources have led me to the conclusion that the war and its ramifications had great significance in moving common people to a greater political awareness.

That greater awareness came against a backdrop of wretchedness and hatred, and one is moved to wonder why it is that lessened political interest is so insistently seen as dysgenic. At the end of McGerr's account of the decline in interest from the post–Civil War heights we are left on the verge of salutary revitalization of political interest, with only a panic, a depression, and widespread suffering necessary to work the unfolding. Perhaps some aspect of the romantic impulse moves us to see the vibrant spirit brought by suffering as nigh unto justification for the suffering, as a gallows speech might justify a hanging.

2. Ralph Waldo Emerson, "Politics," in *The Works of Ralph Waldo Emerson*, 1:200–201. For an elaborate and persuasive depiction of this tension, see Rush Welter, *The Mind of America*.

3. T. H. Colman to parents, April 3, 1862, Coleman-Hayter Letters.

4. Hugh Scott to John Scott, February 2, 1866, John Scott Papers.

5. James Caseley to Sarah Bailey, May 4, 1861, Bailey Papers.

6. For an instance of the use of *Tory*, see T. M. Wilson to Mary, November 25–26, 1864, Wilson Papers.

7. Harold Frederic, *The Copperhead*, p.193.

8. Ibid., pp.5, 8.

9. Andrew Jackson Stone to Wesley Stone, September 2, 1860, SN 42, Stone Correspondence.

10. Sarah Kenyon to brother and sister, February 23, 1861, John Kenyon Letters.

11. Ibid.

12. Sarah Kenyon to [brother and sister?], October 11, 1861, ibid.; Thomas J. Gurr to Sophronia Thompson, February 8, 1864, Gurr Family Papers.

13. Nellie Nutting to Lois Nutting Dane, September 17, 1861, and January 14, 1862, Dane Papers, Box 9.

14. Becky Baye to Lizzie, December 1, 1861, Mitchell Family Papers; Gustave Genthner to father, February 20, 1864, HM 16658, California File.

15. Wiley, *Life of Billy Yank*, pp.358, 286–88. Earl J. Hess's *Liberty, Virtue, and Progress* does far more with politics, in large part by going to intellectuals.

16. George W. Lambert Diary, June 26, 1863, Lambert Papers.

17. George H. Mellish to mother, April 22, 1863, Mellish Collection; Ezra A. Glazier to James Edward Glazier, November 24, 1864, GZ 4, Glazier Collection.

18. [Isaac Banta] to Robert M. Banta, August 23, 1863, Banta Papers; George W. Lambert to brother and sister, November 14, 1862, Lambert Papers. The Banta letter is incomplete, but it is almost surely the handiwork of Isaac writing to his brother.

19. P. G. Wheeler to brother, July 23, 1861, George R. Wheeler Papers; Americus Buck to mother, September 5, 17, 1865, and Americus Buck to parents, July 5, 1865, HM 27898, HM 27899, and HM 27891, Saxton Family

Collection; Mollie Wetherald to Sallie Bradford, November 10, 1864, Bailey Papers.

20. A. J. McRoberts to wife, July 5, November 18, 1863, A. J. McRoberts Family Letters; Sarah P. Harlan to mother and father, November 1, 1864, and to sister, November 17, 1865, Bond and Fentriss Family Papers; Henry Colman to Jackson Colman, January 13, 1867, Coleman-Hayter Letters.

21. Leonard W. Dibble to Willard Dibble, August 11, 1865, Dibble Papers.

22. Leonard W. Dibble to father, May 13, 1867, Dibble Papers; Joanna D. Cowden, "The Politics of Dissent," p.552.

23. Zina W. Chase to Lydia Chase, September 14, 15, 16, and 17, 1866, Chase Papers. The quoted segment of this journal-like letter was penned on September 15.

24. Uriah Oblinger to Martha Thomas, October 29, 1865, and January 6, 1866, Oblinger Papers.

25. Martha Thomas to Uriah Oblinger, October 6, 1866, ibid.; John D. Hicks, "Oliver Perry Morton," in *Dictionary of American Biography*, 13:263.

26. Uriah Oblinger to Martha Thomas, October 25, 1866, Oblinger Papers.

27. Uriah Oblinger to Martha Thomas, July 18, 1868, and Martha Thomas to Uriah Oblinger, July 18, 1868, ibid.

28. Uriah Oblinger to Martha Thomas, August 3, 1868, ibid.

29. H. P. Shumway to friend, May 8, 1876, Henry V. Arnold Papers; Poem, "Oh hearing the news that Blaine was elected President," Obadiah Ethelbert Baker Collection.

30. T. M. Goodman to brother, November 8, 1884, and T. M. Goodman to Ellen Goodman, February 8, 1883, Powell Collection; Ella Furney to Delbert Boston, December 14, 1888, and Delbert Boston to Ella Furney, October 1, 1889, Boston Papers.

31. Nettie Rowzee to sister, March 13, 1882, John Scott and Justina Rowzee Pickle Family Papers.

32. George H. Mellish to mother, March 28, 1862, Mellish Collection; Packard, ed., "Jottings by the Way," p.261.

33. George H. Mellish to mother, January 24, October 31, 1863, Mellish Collection; Marion Shappell to cousin, December 1, 1862, Ireland Family Correspondence; Alonzo Teed Diary, September 23, 1864, Teed Family Papers.

34. Myron G. Love to sister, December 8, 1861, Myron G. Love Collection.

35. Abram Hayne Young to sister, April 21, 1864, in Mary Wyche Burgess, ed., "Civil War Letters of Abram Hayne Young," p.69; Fredrickson, *Inner Civil War*, chap.7; Henry E. Savage Diary, October 20, 1864; Henry I. Colyer to aunt, February 11, 1863, HM 29043, Colyer Collection.

36. Charles Carver to mother, August 7, 1864, Stuart Papers; Wright, intro., "Diary of Charles Ross, 1861," p.138; Russell Dutton Silsby to wife, May 19, 1863, Silsby Letters; John Sharp to wife, May 28, 1865, in Mills, ed., "Sharp Family War Letters," p.521.

37. Americus Buck to mother, August 8, 1865, HM 27895, Saxton Family Collection.

38. Eggleston, *Hoosier School-Master*, p.45; George Loring to Frank Loring, September 11, 1876, Loring Family Collection; *Brooklyn Daily Eagle*, August 22, 1880.

39. William Harper to wife, August 17, 1864, Harper Papers; Mary Crapo to Sarah Mowers, n.d., Boody and Mowers Family Papers. Content of the Crapo letter clearly indicates 1864.

40. A. J. Adams to William Harper, September 15, 1885, Harper Papers; M. M. Brinegar to Perry Rhue, July 28, 1888, Fry-Rhue Papers; John Henry Van Scyoc to John Van Scyoc, October 20, 1884, Shackelford Collection.

41. John T. Brewster to Samuel Conklin, December 15, 1889, Samuel Conklin Papers. For a succinct treatment of the setting in which Tanner operated, see Leonard D. White, *The Republican Era*, pp.208–21. White used a variant version of the fabled Tanner remark.

42. Eddie to sister, July 2, 1886, Robacher Papers; S. D. Roberts to Addie, January 5, 1885, Rhea Family Papers.

43. T. C. Bradway to Charles Kittredge, April 1, 1878, Kittredge Family Papers.

44. E. K. Lee to John (Jonathan Labrant?), March 24, 1878, Labrant Papers; John Winsell to friend, September 13, 1874, Eunice A. Brown Papers.

45. William Littlejohn to uncle, August 12, 1876, Lipscomb Family Papers.

46. Robert H. Wiebe, *The Search for Order*, pp.9, 12; Jacques Ellul, *The Political Illusion*, p.187.

47. S. H. Parsons to ——— Tuthill, October 21, 1867, Freegift Tuthill Papers; N. B. Booth to sister, December 1, 1872, and June 21, 1871, Beers Collection.

48. James Edward Glazier Diaries, January 21 and 25, 1883, November 4, 1884, and November 6, 1888, GZ 126, Glazier Collection.

49. Rachel Atteberry to Mrs. Ireland, November 30, 1873, and Aaron Stryker to David Ireland, March 29, 1874, Ireland Family Correspondence.

50. Delbert Boston to Ella Furney, October 13, 24, 1890, Boston Papers; Adaline Kimball Jones Diaries, March 26, 1879.

51. Ossian Scott to John Scott, August 28, 1873, John Scott Papers.

52. Mary Mellish to George Mellish, March 22, April 16, 1865, Mellish Collection.

53. Mary Mellish to George Mellish, April 26, 1865, Mellish Collection; Adaline Kimball Jones Diaries, October 15, 1879; George B. King to aunt,

December 23, 1879, Powell Collection; William Van Scyoc to John W. Van Scyoc, February 11, 1880, Shackelford Collection.

54. Anna Cook Cooper Diary, September 22, 1888; B. S. Gitchell to father and mother, February 10, 1888, Gitchel-Larsen Family Papers.

55. Milton H. Townsend to sister, March 31, 1867, Milton H. Townsend Letters; Theodore Wilkie Diary, June 10, 1869, Wilkie Family Correspondence and Diaries.

56. Obadiah Ethelbert Baker Collection, Poetry Folder.

57. Wiley, *Life of Billy Yank*, p.109. In *The March to the Sea and Beyond*, Joseph T. Glatthaar arrives at somewhat different conclusions (pp.64–65). I agree fully with Wiley.

58. Thomas S. Hawley to Caleb Hawley, July 30, 1863, HM 47931, Main File; George O. Jewett to Dexter Jewett, July 20, 1862, HM 20887, ibid.; Henry I. Colyer to brother, February 3, 1865, HM 28982, Colyer Collection; George R. Wheeler to mother, April 23, 1864, Wheeler Papers.

59. C. Vann Woodward, *The Strange Career of Jim Crow*, chap.2; Benjamin Harris to wife and children, December 13, 1862, Harris Letters; Alonzo E. Smith Diaries, February 22, 1870.

60. Henry Colyer to mother, October 12, 1864, HM 28968, Colyer Collection; Alonzo D. Teed Diaries, March 17, 1864, Teed Family Papers.

61. W. R. Coffee Diary, March 17, 1863; George H. Shirk, "Campaigning with Sheridan," p.102.

62. Elizabeth Mitchell Kinney to Eliza Taylor, March 17, 1869, Mitchell Family Papers; R. A. Burchell, *The San Francisco Irish*, p.4.

63. Americus Buck to mother, November 8, 1865, HM 27905, Saxton Family Collection; Charles M. Snyder, "A Teen-Age G.I. in the Civil War," p.21; George Mellish to father, April 3, 1862, to parents, August 22, 1863, and to father, September 11, 1863, Mellish Collection.

64. William M. Johnson to uncle, June 29, 1863, Moser Papers; William H. Jackson Diary, July 11, 1864.

65. MacKinlay Kantor, *Andersonville*, pp.337–80.

66. Thomas H. Colman to parents, November 6, 1862, Coleman-Hayter Letters.

67. Henry Spencer Commonplace Book, p.166, H. H. Spencer Papers (Spencer had converted what had apparently been an account book into a scrapbook, pasting clippings and then editorializing as he did here); May Gorham to Nellie [Kittredge], November 30, 1884, Kittredge Family Papers.

68. Henry Spencer Commonplace Book, p.168, H. H. Spencer Papers.

CHAPTER 7

1. Welter, "Between Two Worlds," p.412.

2. Nisbet, *Prejudices*, p.27; Dino Fabris, "A Civil War Diary," pp.76, 82;

John Perry Pritchett, "Sidelights on the Sibley Expedition from the Diary of a Private," p.332.

3. Destler, ed., "An Andersonville Prison Diary," pp.64–65.

4. George H. Mellish to mother, June 15, 1865, Mellish Collection; Americus Buck to family, October 15, 1865, HM 27903, Saxton Family Collection; Amory K. Allen to wife, January 5, 1862, in "Civil War Letters of Amory K. Allen," p.346.

5. Americus Buck to family, October 15, 1865, HM 27903, Saxton Family Collection; M. Van Tassel to Mahala Whiteman Williams, November 15, 1863, HM 16823, Whiteman Family Letters.

6. George Loring to mother, August 20, 1876, Loring Family Collection; Dwight Bartlett to mother, March 5, 1870, HM 26635, California File; Chauncey E. Stearns to friends, December 1, 1861, HM 21303, ibid.

7. Henry E. Savage Diary, June 29, 1864; George H. Mellish to mother, March 5, 1863, Mellish Collection; George Weil to Perry Rhue, June 1889, Fry-Rhue Papers.

8. Mary Jacacks Diary, December 1, 1868, Jacacks Diaries; Alonzo D. Teed Diary, December 19, 1890, Teed Family Papers; J. D. Stanton to C. L. Smith, July 7, 1871, John L. Smith Papers.

9. Henry Huntington to George Tilden, February 15, 1869, George G. Tilden Letters.

10. Eugene Wilkie to Theodore Wilkie, August 13, 1871, and August 9, 1872, Wilkie Family Correspondence and Diaries; John Updike, "A Mild Complaint," p.39.

11. George Peterman to George Crosby, June 6, 1883, Crosby and Family Papers.

12. Maddow, *A Sunday between Wars*, p.45; Howard Mumford Jones, *The Age of Energy*; Peter Gay, *The Bourgeois Experience*, pp.320–28; Hugh Scott to John Scott, March 31, 1866, John Scott Papers.

13. George Tilden to wife, June 7, 1869, Tilden Letters; T. M. Goodman to G. E. Goodman, September 28, 1889, Powell Collection.

14. William Garland to father, February 24 and March 22, 1872, Garland Papers.

15. EMS to sister, October 1862, Lambert Papers; John Mooers to friend, November 18, 1873, John L. Smith Papers.

16. Eugene Field, *Sharps and Flats*, 2:43. This item originally appeared on March 6, 1886.

17. George O. Jewett to Dexter Jewett, April 19, 1863, HM 20887, Main File; J. N. Scott to R. D. Scott, August 12, 1890, Ransom D. Scott Papers.

18. Samuel Clemens, "The Indignity Put upon the Remains of George Holland by the Rev. Mr. Sabine," pp.320–21.

19. Carie Frissell to sister, October 30, 1864, Reppy, Frissell, and Drake Papers.

20. Rachel Dobbins to brother, March 6, 1862, and Rachel Dobbins to Robert M. Banta, February 1862, Banta Papers.

21. Isaac Banta to Robert M. Banta, December 25, 1862, ibid.; Myron G. Love to sister, April 23, 1862, Love Collection; George W. Lambert to unknown, June 23, 1863, Lambert Papers.

22. Charles B. Kittredge to father and mother, January 17, 1863, Charles Brigham Kittredge and Family Papers; Mary Labrant to Jonathan Labrant, July 23, 1862, Labrant Papers; Henry Isaac Colyer to friends, November 4, 1862, HM 29042, Henry Isaac Colyer Collection.

23. Nahum Trask Wood Daily Journal, March 12, 1871, HM 16766; Michael D. Hill and Ben Innis, eds., "The Fort Buford Diary of Private Sanford," pp.6–7, 13–15. The editors took Sanford's April 17 entry (p.7) to read: "Witherd Affair by P. W. DeForest." I take that to be a reference to J. W. De Forest's *Wetherell Affair*.

24. Bryce, *American Commonwealth*, 2:892–93, 895, 898; Daniel J. Boorstin, *The Americans*, pp.296–97; James T. Jones to sister, February 22, 1867, JTJ 5, James T. Jones Papers.

25. George Santayana, *Character and Opinion in the United States*, p.213; Richard Grant White, *Words and Their Uses, Past and Present*, pp.138–39; Boorstin, *The Americans*, p.292.

26. Richard A. Dwyer and Richard E. Lingenfelter, *Lying on the Eastern Slope*, p.42; Clemens, *Roughing It*, p.45; Field, *Sharps and Flats*, 2:246, 249. The Field item originally appeared on May 16, 1893.

27. J. H. P. Smith to friend, May 25, 1861, Banta Papers.

28. Ronald T. Takaki, *Iron Cages*, pp.xvii, 3–11, 288.

29. Delbert Boston to Ella Furney, December 5, 1888, and February 18, 1889, Boston Papers. The destruction of offending items by descendants or by manuscript repositories seems well beyond reckoning. Here and there one finds that part of a document has been excised, but what was on it cannot be known. In some cases, it was probably blank and was cut away for other use. Contrarily, those many letters bearing instructions to the receivers to destroy them after reading bear testimony to neglected intentions and to a researcher's good fortune. One assumes that destruction and emending have fallen more and more out of use. That only echoes the gravitation in mood here discussed.

30. Mrs. Andrew Greenlee to Ida Greenlee Houck, ⸺ 13, 1883, Houck Letters; Della Crosby to George Crosby, November 20, 1881, Crosby and Family Papers.

31. G. M. Young, quoted in C. V. Wedgwood, *The Common Man in the Great Civil War*, p.3; Delbert Boston to wife, September 1, 1890, Boston Papers; Della Crosby to George Crosby, November 20, 1881, Crosby and Family Papers.

Bibliography

MANUSCRIPTS

Adams Collection. University of Georgia Libraries. Athens, Georgia.

Adams, Henry H., Diary. Connecticut Historical Society. Hartford, Connecticut.

Aelmore, A. S., Letter. Miscellaneous Collection, Manuscript Department. Kansas State Historical Society. Topeka, Kansas.

Albin, S. E., Diary. Iowa State Historical Department, Office of the State Historical Society. Iowa City, Iowa.

Albright Family Papers. E. C. Barker Texas History Center. University of Texas. Austin, Texas.

Aldridge Family Letters. State of Mississippi. Department of Archives and History. Jackson, Mississippi.

Aldridge (J. M.) and Family Letters. State of Mississippi. Department of Archives and History. Jackson, Mississippi.

Allen, George H., Diary. E. C. Barker Texas History Center. University of Texas. Austin, Texas.

Allen-Derbius Papers, 1877–88. Joint Collection, University of Missouri Western Historical Manuscript Collection–Columbia and State Historical Society of Missouri Manuscripts. Columbia, Missouri.

Ansley Family Letters. University of Georgia Libraries. Athens, Georgia.

Arnold, Henry V., Papers. Minnesota Historical Society. St. Paul, Minnesota.

Arrowsmith Collection. Iowa State Historical Department, Office of the State Historical Society. Iowa City, Iowa.

Baechtel, Luther S., Diary. State of Mississippi. Department of Archives and History. Jackson, Mississippi.

Bailey, Sarah, Papers, 1820–95, sc 40. Indiana Historical Society. Indianapolis, Indiana.

Baker, Neil A., Papers, 1861–63. Joint Collection, University of Missouri Western Historical Manuscript Collection–Columbia and State Historical Society of Missouri Manuscripts. Columbia, Missouri.

Baker, Obadiah Ethelbert, Collection. Henry E. Huntington Library and Art Gallery. San Marino, California.

Baldwin, John K., Diary. Southern Historical Collection, University of North Carolina. Chapel Hill, North Carolina.

Banta, Robert M., Papers, 1860–65, M 317. Indiana Historical Society. Indianapolis, Indiana.

Barnacastle Papers. State of Mississippi. Department of Archives and History. Jackson, Mississippi.

Bassett, Erasmus E., Diary, 1863. Accession #490. Department of Manuscripts and University Archives, Cornell University Libraries. Ithaca, New York.

Beal Family Letters, 1851–72. Accession #2468. Department of Manuscripts and University Archives, Cornell University Libraries. Ithaca, New York.

Bean, William E., Papers, 1864–81. Joint Collection, University of Missouri Western Historical Manuscript Collection–Columbia and State Historical Society of Missouri Manuscripts. Columbia, Missouri.

Beers, George E., Collection, 1813–76. Connecticut State Library. Hartford, Connecticut.

Bell, James Alvin, Collection. Henry E. Huntington Library and Art Gallery. San Marino, California.

Bennett, Mary, Papers, 1866–74. Accession #121. Department of Manuscripts and University Archives, Cornell University Libraries. Ithaca, New York.

Berryman, J., Papers. Miscellaneous Manuscripts, Manuscript Department. Kansas State Historical Society. Topeka, Kansas.

Binnon, John R., Letters. University of Georgia Libraries. Athens, Georgia.

Black Family Letters, 1861–70. Joint Collection, University of Missouri Western Historical Manuscript Collection–Columbia and State Historical Society of Missouri Manuscripts. Columbia, Missouri.

Black, Narcisa L., Diaries. State of Mississippi. Department of Archives and History. Jackson, Mississippi.

Blackwell, Agnes, Diary. Miscellaneous Manuscripts AM 10:4. Mississippi Valley Collection. Memphis State University. Memphis, Tennessee.

Bond and Fentriss Family Papers. Southern Historical Collection, University of North Carolina. Chapel Hill, North Carolina.

Boody and Mowers Family Papers, 1856–1915. Accession #788. Department of Manuscripts and University Archives, Cornell University Libraries. Ithaca, New York.

Boston, Delbert D., Papers, 1881–1960, M 314. Indiana Historical Society. Indianapolis, Indiana.

Bradley, W. B., Papers. E. C. Barker Texas History Center. University of Texas. Austin, Texas.

Brayton Papers. Indiana Division of the Indiana State Library. Indianapolis, Indiana.

Breckenridge, Elizabeth E., and Family Papers. Minnesota Historical Society. St. Paul, Minnesota.

Broat, Willard, Diary. Iowa State Historical Department, Office of the State Historical Society. Iowa City, Iowa.

Brophy-Beeson Papers, BB 1–218. Henry E. Huntington Library and Art Gallery, San Marino, California.

Brown, Angeline (Mitchell), Diary of a School Teacher on the Arizona Frontier, FAC 309. Henry E. Huntington Library and Art Gallery. San Marino, California.

Brown, Eunice A., Papers, 1852–74, SC 137. Indiana Historical Society. Indianapolis, Indiana.

Buchanan, Mrs. William, Papers. Southern Historical Collection, University of North Carolina. Chapel Hill, North Carolina.

Burgess, Emsley, Diary and Papers. Southern Historical Collection, University of North Carolina. Chapel Hill, North Carolina.

Burney, John G., Papers. Nebraska State Historical Society. Lincoln, Nebraska.

California File. Henry E. Huntington Library and Art Gallery. San Marino, California.

Campbell, James McGinley, Diary. E. C. Barker Texas History Center. University of Texas. Austin, Texas.

Caplinger, Leonard J., Collection, HM 28385–96. Henry E. Huntington Library and Art Gallery. San Marino, California.

Capron, Edward, Correspondence. Nebraska State Historical Society. Lincoln, Nebraska.

Carothers, Sam D., Family Papers. E. C. Barker Texas History Center. University of Texas. Austin, Texas.

Carpenter, Jake, Book. Southern Historical Collection, University of North Carolina. Chapel Hill, North Carolina.

Carpenter, John C., Letters, 1868–70. Joint Collection, University of Missouri Western Historical Manuscript Collection–Columbia and State Historical Society of Missouri Manuscripts. Columbia, Missouri.

Carr, Caleb M., Letters. Accession #2386. Department of Manuscripts and University Archives, Cornell University Libraries. Ithaca, New York.

Carrell, Samuel D., and Family Papers. Minnesota Historical Society. St. Paul, Minnesota.

Chandler, Alice Victoria, Papers. E. C. Barker Texas History Center. University of Texas. Austin, Texas.

Chapin and Tunnell Family Papers. Southern Historical Collection, University of North Carolina. Chapel Hill, North Carolina.

Chapin, Arthur T., Papers. Nebraska State Historical Society. Lincoln, Nebraska.

Chapman Family Papers. Nebraska State Historical Society. Lincoln, Nebraska.

Chapman Family Papers. State of Mississippi. Department of Archives and History. Jackson, Mississippi.

Chase, Zina W., Papers. Minnesota Historical Society. St. Paul, Minnesota.

Chillson, Lorenzo Dow, Diaries, HM 4295. Henry E. Huntington Library and Art Gallery. San Marino, California.

Civil War Letters, 1860–62. Joint Collection, University of Missouri Western Historical Manuscript Collection–Columbia and State Historical Society of Missouri Manuscripts. Columbia, Missouri.

Clendenen Family Collection, HM 21722–82. Henry E. Huntington Library and Art Gallery. San Marino, California.

Cloyes, B. F., Diaries, 1864, 1868. Accession #2155. Department of Manuscripts and University Archives, Cornell University Libraries. Ithaca, New York.

Coffee, W. R., Diary. E. C. Barker Texas History Center. University of Texas. Austin, Texas.

Coleman-Hayter Letters, 1840–1900. Joint Collection, University of Missouri Western Historical Manuscript Collection–Columbia and State Historical Society of Missouri Manuscripts. Columbia, Missouri.

Columbus, Texas, Letters. E. C. Barker Texas History Center. University of Texas. Austin, Texas.

Colyer, Henry Isaac, Collection, HM 28943–29056. Henry E. Huntington Library and Art Gallery. San Marino, California.

Comins, Nettie, Diaries. Connecticut Historical Society. Hartford, Connecticut.

Coney, Delphine, Diaries, 1866–76. Accession #2313. Department of Manuscripts and University Archives, Cornell University Libraries. Ithaca, New York.

Conklin, Samuel, Papers. Miscellaneous Manuscripts, Manuscript Department. Kansas State Historical Society. Topeka, Kansas.

Connor, Aaron, Letters. Miscellaneous Manuscripts, Manuscript Department. Kansas State Historical Society. Topeka, Kansas.

Connor, Elias H., Papers. Minnesota Historical Society. St. Paul, Minnesota.

Conner, Wesley, Letter. Miscellaneous Manuscripts, Manuscript Department. Kansas State Historical Society. Topeka, Kansas.

Conron, Clara, Diary. Miscellaneous Manuscripts, Manuscript Department. Kansas State Historical Society. Topeka, Kansas.

Cooley, Henry, Diaries, 1867–77. Accession #1703. Department of Manuscripts and University Archives, Cornell University Libraries. Ithaca, New York.

Cooley, Milo H., Diaries. Connecticut Historical Society. Hartford, Connecticut.

Cooper, Anna Cook, Diary. Miscellaneous Manuscripts, Manuscript Department. Kansas State Historical Society. Topeka, Kansas.

Cooper, Elijah, and Family Letters. State of Mississippi. Department of Archives and History. Jackson, Mississippi.

Coppernoll, Ferdinando H., Diaries. University of Georgia Libraries. Athens, Georgia.

Cornatzer, C. A., Letter. Miscellaneous Manuscripts, Manuscript Department. Kansas State Historical Society. Topeka, Kansas.

Corum, Robert W., Papers, 1878–92. Joint Collection, University of Missouri Western Historical Manuscript Collection–Columbia and State Historical Society of Missouri Manuscripts. Columbia, Missouri.

Country Store Journal from M. Jones Mercantile. Miscellaneous Manuscripts 54:45. Mississippi Valley Collection. Memphis State University. Memphis, Tennessee.

Coverstone, David, Letters, HM 16840–57. Henry E. Huntington Library and Art Gallery. San Marino, California.

Covert, J., Papers. Miscellaneous Manuscripts, Manuscript Department. Kansas State Historical Society. Topeka, Kansas.

Crane, Joel, Papers, 1819–1904, SC 457. Indiana Historical Society. Indianapolis, Indiana.

Crosby, George James, and Family Papers. Minnesota Historical Society. St. Paul, Minnesota.

Cutting, A. H. (Howard), Journal of a trip by overland route, HM 652. Henry E. Huntington Library and Art Gallery. San Marino, California.

Dane Papers. Henry E. Huntington Library and Art Gallery. San Marino, California.

Day, Emily R. Ewing, Papers. Minnesota Historical Society. St. Paul, Minnesota.

Diamond, James, Family Papers. University of Georgia Libraries. Athens, Georgia.

Dibble, Leonard W., Papers. Minnesota Historical Society. St. Paul, Minnesota.

Dooley, Thomas J., Letters. E. C. Barker Texas History Center. University of Texas. Austin, Texas.

Earnest, Frank B., Diary. E. C. Barker Texas History Center. University of Texas. Austin, Texas.

Eaton, Harriet H. A., Diaries. Southern Historical Collection, University of North Carolina. Chapel Hill, North Carolina.

Evans, R. A., Papers. State of Mississippi. Department of Archives and History. Jackson, Mississippi.

Faile, Edward G., Diary, HM 40042. Henry E. Huntington Library and Art Gallery. San Marino, California.

Faucett, Thomas, Diaries, 1873–81, M 103. Indiana Historical Society. Indianapolis, Indiana.

Fisher, Charles G., Letters and Papers. Miscellaneous Manuscripts 54:32. Mississippi Valley Collection. Memphis State University. Memphis, Tennessee.

Flower, Joseph, Jr., Diary. Connecticut State Library. Hartford, Connecticut.

Forbes, James Monroe, Collection, FO 1–56. Henry E. Huntington Library and Art Gallery. San Marino, California.

Frank Family Letters. Southern Historical Collection, University of North Carolina. Chapel Hill, North Carolina.

Freeman Family Papers. University of Georgia Libraries. Athens, Georgia.

French, Barsina (Rogers), Journal of a wagon trip from Evansville, Indiana, to Prescott, Arizona, HM 26058. Henry E. Huntington Library and Art Gallery. San Marino, California.

French, George Q., Letters. E. C. Barker Texas History Center. University of Texas. Austin, Texas.

Friend, Andrew, Diary. Minnesota Historical Society. St. Paul, Minnesota.

Forehand, Lloyd D., Papers. Nebraska State Historical Society. Lincoln, Nebraska.

Fry-Rhue Papers, 1843–1969, M 111. Indiana Historical Society. Indianapolis, Indiana.

Fuller, John L., Diaries, 1875–1900. Accession #1065. Department of Manuscripts and University Archives, Cornell University Libraries. Ithaca, New York.

Furnas, John M., Letters. Iowa State Historical Department, Office of the State Historical Society. Iowa City, Iowa.

Gardiner, John Williams, Diary. Miscellaneous Manuscripts, Manuscript Department. Kansas State Historical Society. Topeka, Kansas.

Garland, William Harris, Papers. Southern Historical Collection, University of North Carolina. Chapel Hill, North Carolina.

Gigous Family Papers, 1875–77, Joint Collection, University of Missouri Western Historical Manuscript Collection–Columbia and State Historical Society of Missouri Manuscripts. Columbia, Missouri.

Gillespie, George A., Papers, GI 1–115. Henry E. Huntington Library and Art Gallery. San Marino, California.

Gilliam, Charles Wesley, Diary, 1856–76. Joint Collection, University of Missouri Western Historical Manuscript Collection–Columbia and State Historical Society of Missouri Manuscripts. Columbia, Missouri.

Gilligan, Arthur E., Diary. E. C. Barker Texas History Center. University of Texas. Austin, Texas.

Gitchel-Larsen Family Papers. Nebraska State Historical Society. Lincoln, Nebraska.

Glazier, James Edward, Collection, GZ 1–126. Henry E. Huntington Library and Art Gallery. San Marino, California.

Glenn Family Papers. Joint Collection, University of Missouri Western Historical Manuscript Collection–Columbia and State Historical Society of Missouri Manuscripts. Columbia, Missouri.

Greene, Edmund B., Diary. Connecticut State Library. Hartford, Connecticut.

Griffin, Abbie T., Diary. Minnesota Historical Society. St. Paul, Minnesota.

Gurr Family Papers. University of Georgia Libraries. Athens, Georgia.

Gushee, Lewellyn Amos, Papers. Nebraska State Historical Society. Lincoln, Nebraska.

Hamilton, Gideon Anthony, Collection, HM 26463–26512. Henry E. Huntington Library and Art Gallery. San Marino, California.

Harper, William, Papers, 1861–90, SC 697. Indiana Historical Society. Indianapolis, Indiana.

Harris, Benjamin, Letters. Nebraska State Historical Society. Lincoln, Nebraska.

Hazzard, Lemuel H., Papers. Henry E. Huntington Library and Art Gallery. San Marino, California.

Head Gift. University of Georgia Libraries. Athens, Georgia.

"Hebdomidal Thunderbolt." Miscellaneous Manuscripts, Manuscript Department. Kansas State Historical Society. Topeka, Kansas.

Henslee, Mrs. E. P., Letter. University of Georgia Libraries. Athens, Georgia.

Herndon Family Letters, 1859–79. Joint Collection, University of Missouri Western Historical Manuscript Collection–Columbia and State Historical Society of Missouri Manuscripts. Columbia, Missouri.

Herrington Diaries, 1864–65. Accession #1664. Department of Manuscripts and University Archives, Cornell University Libraries. Ithaca, New York.

Holeman, Nancy Nash Papers, 1865–77. Joint Collection, University of Missouri Western Historical Manuscript Collection–Columbia and State Historical Society of Missouri Manuscripts. Columbia, Missouri.

Houck, Ida Greenlee, Letters, 1869–1927. Joint Collection, University of Missouri Western Historical Manuscript Collection–Columbia and State Historical Society of Missouri Manuscripts. Columbia, Missouri.

Howard, George W., Diary. University of Georgia Libraries. Athens, Georgia.

Hunter, John T., Diary. State of Mississippi. Department of Archives and History. Jackson, Mississippi.

Huntsinger, Samuel Kessler, Papers. Nebraska State Historical Society. Lincoln, Nebraska.

Ingraham, George B. C., Journal, HM 16955. Henry E. Huntington Library and Art Gallery. San Marino, California.

Ireland, James, Family Correspondence, 1849–80, M 169. Indiana Historical Society. Indianapolis, Indiana.

Irvin, George Washington, Letter. University of Georgia Libraries. Athens, Georgia.

Jacacks Diaries, 1859–68. Accession #1566. Department of Manuscripts and University Archives, Cornell University Libraries. Ithaca, New York.

Jackson, William H., Diary. Connecticut State Library. Hartford, Connecticut.

Jennings, W. T., Notebook. State of Mississippi. Department of Archives and History. Jackson, Mississippi.

Johnson, Thomas R., Letter. University of Georgia Libraries. Athens, Georgia.

Jones, Adaline Kimball, Diaries. Iowa State Historical Department, Office of the State Historical Society. Iowa City, Iowa.

Jones Family Papers, 1861–62. Joint Collection, University of Missouri Western Historical Manuscript Collection–Columbia and State Historical Society of Missouri Manuscripts. Columbia, Missouri.

Jones, Hugh N., Papers. E. C. Barker Texas History Center. University of Texas. Austin, Texas.

Jones, James T., Papers, JTJ 1–67. Henry E. Huntington Library and Art Gallery. San Marino, California.

Judd, Frederick, Diary, 1848–73. Connecticut State Library. Hartford, Connecticut.

Judson-Fairbanks Correspondence. Henry E. Huntington Library and Art Gallery. San Marino, California.

Kendrick, H. C., Letters. Southern Historical Collection, University of North Carolina. Chapel Hill, North Carolina.

Kenyon, John, Letters. Iowa State Historical Department, Office of the State Historical Society. Iowa City, Iowa.

Ketchum, Ami Whitney, Papers. Nebraska State Historical Society. Lincoln, Nebraska.

Kingman, Hattie H., Letter. Nebraska State Historical Society. Lincoln, Nebraska.

Kinkade, John Thompson, Collection, KI 1–91. Henry E. Huntington Library and Art Gallery. San Marino, California.

Kinsland, Mary, Letter. University of Georgia Libraries. Athens, Georgia.

Kittredge, Charles Brigham, Family Papers in the personal possession of Kathleen Lopp Smith, 6534 17th Avenue Northeast, Seattle, Washington.

Labrant, Jonathan, Papers. Henry E. Huntington Library and Art Gallery. San Marino, California.

Lambert, George Washington, Papers, 1828–1951, M 178. Indiana Historical Society. Indianapolis, Indiana.

Leaver, Celestia A., Letter. Iowa State Historical Department, Office of the State Historical Society. Iowa City, Iowa.

Ledbetter Family Papers. Southern Historical Collection, University of North Carolina. Chapel Hill, North Carolina.

Lippincott, Joshua C., Papers. Nebraska State Historical Society. Lincoln, Nebraska.

Lipscomb Family Papers. Southern Historical Collection, University of North Carolina. Chapel Hill, North Carolina.

Lloyd, John A., Diaries, 1867–76, M 187. Indiana Historical Society. Indianapolis, Indiana.

Long, Ira, Papers. E. C. Barker Texas History Center. University of Texas. Austin, Texas.

Longley, William Preston, Letter. E. C. Barker Texas History Center. University of Texas. Austin, Texas.

Loop, Uriah J., Papers, 1862–64, M 189. Indiana Historical Society. Indianapolis, Indiana.

Loring Family Collection. Henry E. Huntington Library and Art Gallery. San Marino, California.

Love, Myron G., Collection. University of Georgia Libraries. Athens, Georgia.

Lowrey, James H., Account Books. Miscellaneous Manuscripts 54:46. Mississippi Valley Collection. Memphis State University. Memphis, Tennessee.

Luark, Michael Fleenan, Diary, 1846–99. University of Washington Manuscript Collection. Seattle, Washington.

McCormick, Daniel Washington, Diary. State of Mississippi. Department of Archives and History. Jackson, Mississippi.

McRoberts, A. J., Family Letters, 1862–76. Joint Collection, University of Missouri Western Historical Manuscript Collection–Columbia and State Historical Society of Missouri Manuscripts. Columbia, Missouri.

Mabrey, Benjamin Benn, Papers, 1862–65, M 190. Indiana Historical Society. Indianapolis, Indiana.

Main File. Henry E. Huntington Library and Art Gallery. San Marino, California.

Mallett, Martin, Diaries. Connecticut Historical Society. Hartford, Connecticut.

Martenet, Jefferson, Collection. Henry E. Huntington Library and Art Gallery. San Marino, California.

Mason, Hattie E., Diaries, 1883–84. Connecticut Historical Society. Hartford, Connecticut.

Mellish, George H., Collection. Henry E. Huntington Library and Art Gallery. San Marino, California.

Meroney, Philip F., Papers. Southern Historical Collection, University of North Carolina. Chapel Hill, North Carolina.

Merrick, John, Papers, 1831–98, M 313, BV 1629–30. Indiana Historical Society. Indianapolis, Indiana.

Merrill, Luke Tuttle, Diary, 1864. Accession #478. Department of Manuscripts and University Archives, Cornell University Libraries. Ithaca, New York.

Mitchell Family Papers. Henry E. Huntington Library and Art Gallery. San Marino, California.

Moore, Henry F., Papers. State of Mississippi. Department of Archives and History. Jackson, Mississippi.

Morse, Ephraim W., Letters and Diary, HM 26543–58. Henry E. Huntington Library and Art Gallery. San Marino, California.

Morse Family Letters. Iowa State Historical Department, Office of the State Historical Society. Iowa City, Iowa.

Moser, Martin, Papers. Southern Historical Collection, University of North Carolina. Chapel Hill, North Carolina.

Mulholland, Olive Helms, Papers. Henry E. Huntington Library and Art Gallery. San Marino, California.

Nabors Family Collection. University of Georgia Libraries. Athens, Georgia.

Neu, Sallie, Correspondence. E. C. Barker Texas History Center. University of Texas. Austin, Texas.

Nevins, Joseph A(llan), Diary, HM 26339. Henry E. Huntington Library and Art Gallery. San Marino, California.

Newton, E. L., Letter. University of Georgia Libraries. Athens, Georgia.

Norwood, Emory, Papers. E. C. Barker Texas History Center. University of Texas. Austin, Texas.

Oatts, T. C., Diary. E. C. Barker Texas History Center. University of Texas. Austin, Texas.

Oblinger, Uriah W., Papers. Nebraska State Historical Society. Lincoln, Nebraska.

Odom, Elijah, Letters. State of Mississippi. Department of Archives and History. Jackson, Mississippi.

Oglethorpe County Diary. University of Georgia Libraries. Athens, Georgia.

Page, Thomas D., Family Letters, 1854–87. Joint Collection, University of Missouri Western Historical Manuscript Collection–Columbia and State Historical Society of Missouri Manuscripts. Columbia, Missouri.

Parrott, Johnny, Diary. State of Mississippi. Department of Archives and History. Jackson, Mississippi.

Perry, Dow, Family Papers. E. C. Barker Texas History Center. University of Texas. Austin, Texas.

Phillips, D. W., Letters. University of Georgia Libraries. Athens, Georgia.

Pierce Family Collection. Accession #858. Department of Manuscripts and University Archives, Cornell University Libraries. Ithaca, New York.

Pomeroy, Calvin, Letters. Nebraska State Historical Society. Lincoln, Nebraska.

Powell, William Stevens, Collection. Southern Historical Collection, University of North Carolina. Chapel Hill, North Carolina.

Preece, Richard Lincoln, Papers. E. C. Barker Texas History Center. University of Texas. Austin, Texas.

Purdy, Leander Crawford and Louisa (Canfield), *Collectors*, Family Papers, 1738–1925. Accession #2523. Department of Manuscripts and University Archives, Cornell University Libraries. Ithaca, New York.

Rall, J. C., Correspondence. Nebraska State Historical Society. Lincoln, Nebraska.

Rankin, D. W., Letters, HM 48322–26. Henry E. Huntington Library and Art Gallery. San Marino, California.

Ransdell, Edward Chinn, Letters, 1824–90. Joint Collection, University of Missouri Western Historical Manuscript Collection–Columbia and State Historical Society of Missouri Manuscripts. Columbia, Missouri.

Raye, Lemuel, Poem. State of Mississippi. Department of Archives and History. Jackson, Mississippi.

Raymond, H. H., Diary. E. C. Barker Texas History Center. University of Texas. Austin, Texas.

Redman, Wesley, Papers. E. C. Barker Texas History Center. University of Texas. Austin, Texas.

Reppy, Frissell, and Drake Papers, 1860–1930. Joint Collection, University of Missouri Western Historical Manuscript Collection–Columbia and State Historical Society of Missouri Manuscripts. Columbia, Missouri.

Rhea, Mrs. J. B., Family Papers. E. C. Barker Texas History Center. University of Texas. Austin, Texas.

Rike, Andrew Jackson, Papers. Southern Historical Collection, University of North Carolina. Chapel Hill, North Carolina.

Robacher, John J., Papers. State of Mississippi. Department of Archives and History. Jackson, Mississippi.

Rogers Family Letters, 1865–97. Joint Collection, University of Missouri Western Historical Manuscript Collection–Columbia and State Historical Society of Missouri Manuscripts. Columbia, Missouri.

Sampson, James P., Diary. State of Mississippi. Department of Archives and History. Jackson, Mississippi.

Savage, Henry E., Diary. Connecticut State Library. Hartford, Connecticut.

Saxton Family Collection, HM 19802–13 and HM 27863–27911. Henry E. Huntington Library and Art Gallery. San Marino, California.

Scaper-Handwerker Family Scrapbook, 1864–1925. Miscellaneous Manuscripts 54:82. Mississippi Valley Collection. Memphis State University. Memphis, Tennessee.

Scott, John, Papers, 1841–94, SC 1319. Indiana Historical Society. Indianapolis, Indiana.

Scott, John, and Justina Rowzee Pickle Family Papers. E. C. Barker Texas History Center. University of Texas. Austin, Texas.

Scott, Ransom D., Papers, 1886–1908, M 247. Indiana Historical Society. Indianapolis, Indiana.

Scoville, Ralph I., Diary. Connecticut Historical Society. Hartford, Connecticut.

Seeley, Darwin G., Papers. E. C. Barker Texas History Center. University of Texas. Austin, Texas.

Seymour, Alfred P., Diaries. Nebraska State Historical Society. Lincoln, Nebraska.

Shackelford Family Letters. E. C. Barker Texas History Center. University of Texas. Austin, Texas.

Shackelford, Ralph, Collection. Indiana Division of the Indiana State Library. Indianapolis, Indiana.

Shockly, David, Papers, 1859–95. Indiana Historical Society. Indianapolis, Indiana.

Shoffner, Michael, Papers. Southern Historical Collection, University of North Carolina. Chapel Hill, North Carolina.

Silsby, Russell Dutton, Letters. Nebraska State Historical Society. Lincoln, Nebraska.

Smith, Alonzo E., Diaries, Archives RG 69:67. Connecticut State Library. Hartford, Connecticut.

Smith, John L., Papers, 1848–1917. Accession #813. Department of Manuscripts and University Archives, Cornell University Libraries. Ithaca, New York.

Smith, Lura (Case), Correspondence, SMI 1–80. Henry E. Huntington Library and Art Gallery. San Marino, California.

Smith, Ralph S., Letter. Nebraska State Historical Society. Lincoln, Nebraska.

Smith-Hamilton Families Papers. University of Georgia Libraries. Athens, Georgia.

Smithson, Fred, Letter. Nebraska State Historical Society. Lincoln, Nebraska.

Snell Family Papers, 1766–1942. Accession #1170. Department of Manuscripts and University Archives, Cornell University Libraries. Ithaca, New York.

Snow, Nettie A., Letters. Connecticut Historical Society. Hartford, Connecticut.

Spencer, C. L., Poem. E. C. Barker Texas History Center. University of Texas. Austin, Texas.

Spencer, H. H., Papers. Minnesota Historical Society. St. Paul, Minnesota.

Squires, Francis W., Diaries, 1840–97. Accession #1638. Department of Manuscripts and University Archives, Cornell University Libraries. Ithaca, New York.

Stafford, Frederic, Papers. Southern Historical Collection, University of North Carolina. Chapel Hill, North Carolina.

Stearns, O. E., Diaries. Nebraska State Historical Society. Lincoln, Nebraska.

Steele, Horace B., Diaries. Connecticut State Library. Hartford, Connecticut.

Stewart, Walter Preston, Diaries. E. C. Barker Texas History Center. University of Texas. Austin, Texas.

Stillson, Sadie, Diary. Iowa State Historical Department, Office of the State Historical Society. Iowa City, Iowa.

Stone, Andrew J., Correspondence, sn 1–45. Henry E. Huntington Library and Art Gallery. San Marino, California.

Stratton, Pauline H., Diary, 1846–70. Joint Collection, University of Missouri Western Historical Manuscript Collection–Columbia and State Historical Society of Missouri Manuscripts. Columbia, Missouri.

Stuart, Lyman, Papers, 1806–81. Accession #1283. Department of Manuscripts and University Archives, Cornell University Libraries. Ithaca, New York.

Swathel, George C., Diary. Connecticut State Library. Hartford, Connecticut.

Tannehill, Jesse C., Papers. E. C. Barker Texas History Center. University of Texas. Austin, Texas.

Teed Family Papers, 1864–1908. Accession #2110. Department of Manuscripts and University Archives, Cornell University Libraries. Ithaca, New York.

Tilden, George G., Letters. Iowa State Historical Department, Office of the State Historical Society. Iowa City, Iowa.

Tilley, Belle and Henry, Correspondence. Miscellaneous Manuscripts, Manuscript Department. Kansas State Historical Society. Topeka, Kansas.

Todd-Austin Family Papers. Miscellaneous Manuscripts 54:73. Mississippi Valley Collection. Memphis State University. Memphis, Tennessee.

Townsend, Milton H., Letters. Miscellaneous Manuscripts, Manuscript Department. Kansas State Historical Society. Topeka, Kansas.

Turner, Calvin S., Family Papers. E. C. Barker Texas History Center. University of Texas. Austin, Texas.

Tuthill, Freegift, Papers, 1810–89. Accession #1823. Department of Manuscripts and University Archives, Cornell University Libraries. Ithaca, New York.

Upshaw Collection. University of Georgia Libraries. Athens, Georgia.

Vermillion and Kittredge Civil War Letters. Mississippi Valley Collection. Memphis State University. Memphis, Tennessee.

Wall, Charles, Letters, 1857–69. Accession #2012. Department of Manuscripts and University Archives, Cornell University Libraries. Ithaca, New York.

Warren Collection. Henry E. Huntington Library and Art Gallery. San Marino, California.

Wheeler, George R., Papers. Nebraska State Historical Society. Lincoln, Nebraska.

White, George H., Letter. University of Georgia Libraries. Athens, Georgia.

Whiteman Family Letters, HM 16809–39. Henry E. Huntington Library and Art Gallery. San Marino, California.

Wight, Levi Lamoni, Papers. E. C. Barker Texas History Center. University of Texas. Austin, Texas.

Wilkie Family Correspondence and Diaries. Manuscript Department. Kansas State Historical Society. Topeka, Kansas.

Williams, John, and Family Papers. Minnesota Historical Society. St. Paul, Minnesota.

Williams, Robert, Collection. University of Georgia Libraries. Athens, Georgia.

Wilson, Mary Ann (Covington), Papers. Southern Historical Collection, University of North Carolina. Chapel Hill, North Carolina.

Wood Papers. University of Georgia Libraries. Athens, Georgia.

Wood, Elias M., Letters and Papers. Nebraska State Historical Society. Lincoln, Nebraska.

Wood, Nahum Trask, Daily Journal for the Year 1871, HM 16766. Henry E. Huntington Library and Art Gallery. San Marino, California.

Woods-Holman Papers, 1805–1906. Joint Collection, University of Missouri Western Historical Manuscript Collection–Columbia and State Historical Society of Missouri Manuscripts. Columbia, Missouri.

Wright Gift. University of Georgia Libraries. Athens, Georgia.

Wright, William Alexander, Papers. Nebraska State Historical Society. Lincoln, Nebraska.

Wylie, Lee Ray, Letter. E. C. Barker Texas History Center. University of Texas. Austin, Texas.

BOOKS

Aaron, Daniel. *The Unwritten War: American Writers and the Civil War*. 1973. Reprint. New York: Oxford University Press, 1975.

Anderson, David D., ed.. *The Literary Works of Abraham Lincoln*. Columbus, Ohio: Charles E. Merrill, 1970.

Ariès, Philippe. *The Hour of Our Death*. Translated by Helen Weaver. New York: Knopf, 1981.

Atherton, Lewis. *Main Street on the Middle Border*. Bloomington: Indiana University Press, 1954.

Augustine. *The City of God*. in Robert Maynard Hutchins, Editor in Chief, *Great Books of the Western World*, 18 *Augustine*. William Benton, Publisher, Encyclopaedia Britannica, Inc. Chicago, 1952.

Barton, Michael. *Goodmen: The Character of Civil War Soldiers*. University Park: Pennsylvania State University Press, 1981.

Beecher, Henry Ward. *Lectures to Young Men, on Important Subjects*. Boston: Ticknor and Fields, 1868.

Bierce, Ambrose. "Disintroductions." In *The Collected Works of Ambrose Bierce*, vol.9, *Tangential Views*. New York: Neale, 1911.

––––––. *The Enlarged Devil's Dictionary*. Research and Editing by Ernest Jerome Hopkins. Garden City, N.Y.: Doubleday, 1967.

Boorstin, Daniel. *The Americans: The National Experience*. New York: Random House, 1965.

Boylan, Anne M. *Sunday School: The Formation of an American Institution*. New Haven: Yale University Press, 1988.

Bryce, James. *The American Commonwealth*. 2 vols. Rev. ed. New York: Macmillan, 1923.

Burchell, R. A. *The San Francisco Irish, 1848–1880*. Manchester, Eng.: Manchester University Press, 1979.

Carter, Paul A. *The Spiritual Crisis of the Gilded Age*. DeKalb: Northern Illinois University Press, 1971.

Cash, W. J. *The Mind of the South*. New York: Knopf, 1941.

Clark, John Spencer. *The Life and Letters of John Fiske*. 2 vols. Boston: Houghton, 1917.

Clebsch, William A. *From Sacred to Profane America: The Role of Religion in American History*. New York: Harper & Row, 1968.

Clemens, Samuel L. [Mark Twain]. *Adventures of Huckleberry Finn: Tom Sawyer's Comrade*. Edited by Walter Blair and Victor Fischer. Berkeley and Los Angeles: University of California Press, 1985.

––––––. *The Man That Corrupted Hadleyburg and Other Stories and Essays*. New York: Harper and Brothers, 1928.

––––––. *Roughing It*. Hartford, Conn.: American Publishing Company, 1872.

Clemens, Samuel L., and Charles Dudley Warner. *The Gilded Age: A Tale of To-Day*. Hartford, Conn.: American Publishing Company, 1873.

Cohen, Lester H. *The Revolutionary Histories: Contemporary Narratives of the American Revolution*. Ithaca: Cornell University Press, 1980.

Crane, Stephen. *The Red Badge of Courage: An Episode of the American Civil War.* New York: D. Appleton & Company, 1895.

Crawford, John Wallace. *The Poet Scout: Being a Selection of Incidental and Illustrative Verses and Songs.* San Francisco: H. Keller & Company, 1879.

———. *Whar' the Hand o' God Is Seen, and Other Poems.* New York: Lyceum Publishing Company, 1910.

Degler, Carl N. *At Odds: Women and Family in America from the Revolution to the Present.* New York: Oxford University Press, 1980.

Douglas, Ann. *The Feminization of American Culture.* New York: Knopf, 1977.

Dublin, Thomas, ed. *Farm to Factory: Women's Letters, 1830–1860.* New York: Columbia University Press, 1981.

Dwyer, Richard A., and Richard Lingenfelter. *Lying on the Eastern Slope: James Townsend's Comic Journalism on the Mining Frontier.* Miami: University Presses of Florida and Florida International University Press, 1984.

Dyer, Thomas, ed. *To Raise Myself a Little: The Diaries and Letters of Jennie, a Georgia Teacher, 1851–1886: Amelia Akehurst Lines.* Athens: University of Georgia Press, 1982.

Eastman, Max. *The Sense of Humor.* New York: Charles Scribner's Sons, 1936.

Eggleston, Edward. *The Hoosier School-Master: A Novel.* New York: Orange Judd, 1871.

Ellul, Jacques. *The Political Illusion.* Translated by Konrad Kellen. New York: Knopf, 1967.

Emerson, Ralph Waldo. "Divinity School Address." In *The Complete Works of Ralph Waldo Emerson,* vol. 1. Autograph Centenary Edition. Cambridge, Mass.: Riverside Press, 1903.

———. "Politics." In *The Works of Ralph Waldo Emerson,* vol. 1. Standard Library Edition. Boston: Houghton Mifflin, 1883.

———. *Society and Solitude: Twelve Chapters.* Boston: Fields, Osgood and Company, 1870.

Ezell, John Samuel. *Fortune's Merry Wheel: The Lottery in America.* Cambridge, Mass.: Harvard University Press, 1960.

Faragher, John Mack. *Women and Men on the Overland Trail.* New Haven: Yale University Press, 1979.

Farrell, James J. *Inventing the American Way of Death.* Philadelphia: Temple University Press, 1980.

Field, Eugene. *Sharps and Flats,* Vols. 11 and 12 of *The Writings in Prose and Verse of Eugene Field.* New York: Charles Scribner's Sons, 1901.

Findlay, John M. *People of Chance: Gambling in American Society from Jamestown to Las Vegas.* New York: Oxford University Press, 1986.

Fitch, Robert Elliot. *Odyssey of the Self-Centered Self, or Rake's Progress in Religion.* New York: Harcourt, Brace & World, 1960.

Frederic, Harold. *The Copperhead.* New York: Charles Scribner's Sons, 1893.

————. *The Damnation of Theron Ware*. Chicago: Stone and Kimball, 1896.

————. *Marsena and Other Stories of Wartime*. New York: Charles Scribner's Sons, 1894.

————. *Seth's Brother's Wife: A Study of Life in Greater New York*. New York: Charles Scribner's Sons, 1887.

Fredrickson, George M. *The Inner Civil War: Northern Intellectuals and the Crisis of the Union*. New York: Harper & Row, 1965.

Gay, Peter. *The Bourgeois Experience: Victoria to Freud*, vol. 2, *The Tender Passion*. New York: Oxford University Press, 1986.

Glatthaar, Joseph T. *The March to the Sea and Beyond: Sherman's Troops in the Savannah and Carolinas Campaigns*. New York: New York University Press, 1985.

Goldman, Eric F. *Rendezvous with Destiny: A History of Modern American Reform*. New York: Knopf, 1952.

Griffith, Lucille, ed. *Yours Till Death: Civil War Letters of John W. Cotton*. University, Ala.: University of Alabama Press, 1951.

Hampsten, Elizabeth. *Read This Only to Yourself: The Private Writings of Midwestern Women, 1880–1910*. Bloomington: Indiana University Press, 1982.

————, comp. *To All Inquiring Friends: Letters, Diaries and Essays in North Dakota, 1880–1910*. Grand Forks: University of North Dakota, 1979.

Hamsun, Knut. *The Cultural Life of Modern America*. Edited and translated by Barbara Gordon Morgridge. Cambridge, Mass.: Harvard University Press, 1969.

Haroutunian, Joseph. *Piety versus Moralism: The Passing of the New England Theology*. 1932. Reprint. New York: Harper Torchbooks, 1970.

Harte, Francis Bret. "How Santa Claus Came to Simpson's Bar." In *The Works of Bret Harte*, vol. 3, *Tales of Argonauts and Eastern Sketches*. Boston: Houghton Mifflin, 1883.

————. *The Luck of Roaring Camp and Other Stories*. Boston: Fields, Osgood & Company, 1870.

Hawthorne, Nathaniel. *The Blithedale Romance*. Boston: Ticknor, Reed and Fields, 1852.

Hess, Earl J. *Liberty, Virtue, and Progress: Northerners and Their War for the Union*. New York: New York University Press, 1988.

Hesseltine, William B. *Civil War Prisons: A Study in War Psychology*. Columbus: Ohio State University Press, 1930.

Hicks, John D. "Oliver Perry Morton." In *Dictionary of American Biography*, 13:262–64. New York: Charles Scribner's Sons, 1934.

Himmelfarb, Gertrude. "Two Nations or Five Classes: The Historian as Sociologist." In *The New History and the Old: Critical Essays and Reappraisals*. Cambridge, Mass.: Harvard University Press, 1987.

Hofstadter, Richard. *Social Darwinism in American Thought, 1860–1915*. Philadelphia: University of Pennsylvania Press, 1944.

Holliday, J. S. *The World Rushed In: The California Gold Rush Experience.* New York: Simon and Schuster, 1981.

Howells, William D. *The Rise of Silas Lapham.* Boston: Houghton Mifflin, 1884.

James, Henry. *Hawthorne.* London: Macmillan, 1870.

Jimerson, Randall C. *The Private Civil War: Popular Thought during the Sectional Conflict.* Baton Rouge: Louisiana State University Press, 1988.

Jones, Howard Mumford. *The Age of Energy: Varieties of American Experience, 1865–1915.* New York: Viking Press, 1971.

Kantor, MacKinlay. *Andersonville.* Cleveland: World Publishing Company, 1955.

Kendall, Maurice. "Chance." In Philip P. Wiener, ed., *Dictionary of the History of Ideas: Studies of Selected Pivotal Ideas,* 1:335–40. New York: Charles Scribner's Sons, 1968.

Lesy, Michael. *Wisconsin Death Trip.* New York: Pantheon, 1973.

Levy, Leonard V. *Treason against God: A History of the Offense of Blasphemy.* New York: Schocken Books, 1981.

Linderman, Gerald F. *Embattled Courage: The Experience of Combat in the American Civil War.* New York: Free Press, 1987.

Longfellow, Henry Wadsworth. "A Psalm of Life." In *The Complete Poetical Works of Henry Wadsworth Longfellow.* Cambridge edition. Boston: Houghton Mifflin, 1893.

Luchetti, Cathy, in collaboration with Carol Olwell. *Women of the West.* St. George, Utah: Antelope Island Press, 1982.

Ludlum, David. *Social Ferment in Vermont, 1791–1850.* New York: Columbia University Press, 1939.

McGerr, Michael E. *The Decline of Popular Politics: The American North, 1865–1928.* New York: Oxford University Press, 1986.

Maddow, Ben. *A Sunday between Wars: The Course of American Life from 1865 to 1917.* New York: Norton, 1979.

Marty, Martin E. *Righteous Empire: The Protestant Experience in America.* New York: Dial Press, 1970.

Matthiessen, F. O. *American Renaissance: Art and Expression in the Age of Emerson and Whitman.* London: Oxford University Press, 1941.

May, Elaine Tyler. *Great Expectations: Marriage and Divorce in Post-Victorian America.* Chicago: University of Chicago Press, 1980.

Meier, Peg, coll. *Bring Warm Clothes: Letters and Photos from Minnesota's Past.* Minneapolis: Minneapolis Tribune, 1981.

Melville, Herman. *Clarel: A Poem and a Pilgrimage in the Holy Land.* 2 vols. New York: G. P. Putnam's Sons, 1876.

———. *Israel Potter: His Fifty Years of Exile.* New York: G. P. Putnam and Company, 1855.

———. *Pierre; or, The Ambiguities.* New York: Harper and Brothers, 1852.

Middlekauff, Robert. *The Glorious Cause: The American Revolution, 1763–1789*. New York: Oxford University Press, 1981.

Miller, Perry. *The New England Mind: The Seventeenth Century*. 1939. Reprint. Cambridge, Mass.: Harvard University Press, 1954, 1963.

———, ed. *The American Puritans: Their Poetry and Prose*. Garden City, N.Y.: Anchor Books, 1956.

Mitchell, Reid. *Civil War Soldiers*. New York: Viking, 1988.

Myres, Sandra L. *Westering Women and the Frontier Experience, 1800–1915*. Albuquerque: University of New Mexico Press, 1982.

———, ed. and annot. *Ho for California: Women's Diaries from the Huntington Library*. San Marino, Calif.: Huntington Library, 1980.

Nicolson, Marjorie Hope. *Mountain Gloom and Mountain Glory: The Development of the Aesthetics of the Infinite*. Ithaca: Cornell University Press, 1959.

Nisbet, Robert. *Prejudices: A Philosophical Dictionary*. Cambridge, Mass.: Harvard University Press, 1982.

Norton, Charles Eliot, ed. *Letters of James Russell Lowell*. 2 vols. New York: Harper & Brothers, 1893.

Oakes, Urian. *The Soveraign Efficacy of Divine Providence [1682]*. Introduction by Joseph L. Blau. Los Angeles: University of California Press, 1955.

O'Connor, Richard. *Ambrose Bierce: A Biography*. Boston: Little, Brown, 1967.

Ostrander, Gilman M. *American Civilization in the First Machine Age, 1890–1940*. New York: Harper & Row, 1970.

Paul, Rodman W. *The Far West and the Great Plains in Transition, 1859–1900*. New York: Harper & Row, 1988.

Poe, Edgar Allan. "Never Bet the Devil Your Head: A Tale with a Moral." In *Edgar Allan Poe: Poetry and Tales*. New York: Library of America Edition, 1984.

Rudisill, Richard. *Mirror Image: The Influence of the Daguerreotype on American Society*. Albuquerque: University of New Mexico Press, 1971.

Santayana, George. *Character and Opinion in the United States*. 1920. Reprint. New York: Norton Library Paperback, 1967.

Saum, Lewis O. *The Popular Mood of Pre–Civil War America, 1830–1860*. Westport, Conn.: Greenwood Press, 1980.

Smith, Chard Powers. *Yankees and God*. New York: Hermitage Press, 1954.

Smith, Henry Nash. *Virgin Land: The American West as Symbol and Myth*. New York: Vintage Books, 1950.

Smith, Maggie Aldridge. *Big Wah of Seminole County*. N.p.: N.p., n.d.

Smith-Rosenberg, Carroll. *Disorderly Conduct: Visions of Gender in Victorian America*. New York: Knopf, 1985.

Springer, Marlene, and Haskell Springer, eds. *Plains Woman: The Diary of Martha Farnsworth, 1882–1922*. Bloomington: Indiana University Press, 1986.

Stowe, Harriet Beecher. *Oldtown Folks*. Boston: Fields, Osgood and Company, 1869.

———. *Poganuc People: Their Loves and Lives*. New York: Fords, Howard and Hulbert, 1878.

———. *Sam Lawson's Oldtown Fireside Stories*. Boston: Houghton Mifflin, 1881.

Takaki, Ronald T. *Iron Cages: Race and Culture in Nineteenth-Century America*. New York: Knopf, 1979.

Thoreau, Henry David. *Walden*. In *The Writings of Henry David Thoreau*, vol.2. Boston: Houghton Mifflin, 1906.

Turner, Frederick Jackson. "The Significance of the Frontier in American History." In *The Frontier in American History*. New York: Henry Holt, 1920.

Turner, James. *Without God, without Creed: The Origins of Unbelief in America*. Baltimore: Johns Hopkins University Press, 1985.

Tyler, Moses Coit. *A History of American Literature during the Colonial Period, 1607–1765*. 2 vols. Rev. ed. New York: G. P. Putnams, 1898.

Wedgwood, C. V. *The Common Man in the Great Civil War*. Leicester, Eng.: Leicester University Press, 1957.

Welter, Rush. *The Mind of America, 1820–1860*. New York: Columbia University Press, 1975.

White, Leonard D. *The Republican Era: A Study in Administrative History, 1869–1901*. New York: Macmillan, 1958.

White, Richard Grant. *Words and Their Uses, Past and Present: A Study of the English Language*. New York: Sheldon and Company, 1870.

Whitman, Walt. *Specimen Days in America*. Rev. ed. London: Walter Scott, 1887.

Wiebe, Robert H. *The Search for Order, 1877–1920*. New York: Hill and Wang, 1967.

Wiley, Bell Irvin. *The Life of Billy Yank: The Common Soldier of the Union*. Indianapolis: Bobbs, Merrill, 1951.

———. *The Life of Johnny Reb: The Common Soldier of the Confederacy*. Indianapolis: Bobbs, Merrill, 1943.

Wilkeson, Frank. *Recollections of a Private Soldier in the Army of the Potomac*. New York: G. P. Putnam's Sons, 1887.

Williams, Raymond. *Keywords: A Vocabulary of Culture and Society*. Rev. ed. New York: Oxford University Press, 1983.

Wilson, Edmund. *Patriotic Gore: Studies in the Literature of the American Civil War*. 1962. Reprint. New York: Galaxy Paperback Edition, 1966.

Wolfe, Tom. "The Me Decade and the Third Great Awakening." In *Mauve Gloves & Madmen, Clutter & Vine and Other Stories, Sketches, and Essays*. New York: Farrar, Straus & Giroux, 1976.

Woodward, C. Vann. *The Strange Career of Jim Crow*. New York: Oxford University Press, 1955.

Wyllie, Irvin G. *The Self-Made Man in America: The Myth of Rags to Riches*. New Brunswick: Rutgers University Press, 1955.

PERIODICALS

Adams, Ida Bright, ed. "The Civil War Letters of James Rush Holmes." *Western Pennsylvania Historical Magazine* 44 (June 1961): 105–27.

Ames, Amos W. "A Diary of Prison Life in Southern Prisons." *Annals of Iowa* 40 (Summer 1969): 1–19.

Apostol, Jane. "Gold Rush Widow." *Pacific Historian* 28 (Summer 1984): 49–55.

Athearn, Robert G., ed. "From Illinois to Montana in 1866: The Diary of Perry A. Burgess." *Pacific Northwest Quarterly* 41 (January 1950): 43–65.

Bailey, Hugh C., ed. "An Alabamian at Shiloh: The Diary of Liberty Independence Nixon," *Alabama Review: A Quarterly Journal of Alabama History* 11 (April 1958): 144–55.

Baker, Donald E., ed. "The Conine Family Letters, 1852–1863: 'Just Think How We Are Scattered.'" *Indiana Magazine of History* 70 (June 1974): 122–78.

"A Baltimore Volunteer of 1864." *Maryland Historical Magazine* 36 (March 1941): 22–33.

Barr, Alwyn, ed. "The Civil War Diary of James Allen Hamilton, 1861–1864." *Texana* 2 (Summer 1964): 132–45.

Barton, Michael. "Painful Duties: Art, Character, and Culture in Confederate Letters of Condolence," *Southern Quarterly: A Journal of the Arts in the South* 17 (Winter 1979): 123–34.

Bassett, T. D. Seymour. "500 Miles of Trouble and Excitement: Vermont Railroads, 1848–1861," *Vermont History* 49 (Summer 1981): 133–54.

Bearss, Edwin C., ed. "The Civil War Diary of Sgt. Levi I. Hoag." *Annals of Iowa* 39 (Winter 1968): 168–93.

———. "Pvt. Charles E. Affeld Reports Action West of the Mississippi." *Illinois State Historical Society Journal* 60 (Autumn 1967): 267–96.

Beck, Harry R., ed. "Some Leaves from a Civil War Diary." *Western Pennsylvania Historical Magazine* 42 (December 1959): 363–82.

Berry, Charles R. "Prospecting in the Reese River Mines of Nevada in 1864: The Diary of John Green Berry, Jr." *Nevada Historical Society Quarterly* 24 (Spring 1981): 51–78.

Biel, John G., ed. "The Battle of Shiloh: From the Letters and Diary of Joseph Dimmit Thompson." *Tennessee Historical Quarterly* 17 (September 1958): 250–74.

Bigelow, Edwin L. "Eliakim Bigelow: A Stowe Farmer." *Vermont History* 31 (October 1963): 253–71.

Bivans, Venola Lewis, ed. "The Diary of Luna E. Warner, a Kansas Teenager of the Early 1870's." *Kansas Historical Quarterly* 35 (Autumn 1969): 276–311; (Winter 1969): 411–41.

Black, Wilfred W., ed. "Civil War Letters of George Washington McMillen and Jefferson O. McMillen 122nd Regiment, O.V.I." *West Virginia History* 32 (April 1971): 171–93.

———. "Marching with Sherman through Georgia and the Carolinas: Civil War Diary of Jesse L. Dozer." *Georgia Historical Quarterly* 52 (September 1968): 308–36 and (December 1968): 451–79.

B.L.H. "Pioneering in Stearns County." *Minnesota History: A Quarterly Magazine* 19 (September 1938): 321–27.

Boilard, David, and Joseph Carvalho III. "Private John E. Bisbee, the 52nd Mass. Volunteers, and the Banks Expedition." *Historical Journal of Western Massachusetts* 3 (Fall 1974): 39–49.

"Books Received." *Journal of the History of Ideas* 42 (April–June 1981): 362.

Bornet, Vaughn D. "A Connecticut Yankee Fights at Olustee." *Florida Historical Quarterly* 27 (January 1949): 237–59, and "A Yankee after Olustee" (April 1949): 385–403.

Bratcher, James T., ed. "An 1866 Letter on War and Reconstruction." *Tennessee Historical Quarterly* 22 (March 1963): 83–86.

Brooklyn Daily Eagle, March 7, April 18, June 20, and August 22, 1880.

Brown, Louis A., ed. "The Correspondence of David Olando McRaven and Amanda Nantz McRaven, 1864–1865." *North Carolina Historical Review* 26 (January 1949): 41–98.

Brownell, Adelia, ed. "Civil War Service in Selma, Alabama," *Cincinatti Historical Society Bulletin* 24 (October 1966): 321–26.

Burgess, Mary Wyche, ed. "Civil War Letters of Abram Hayne Young." *South Carolina Historical Magazine* 78 (January 1977): 56–70.

Carmony, Donald, F., ed. "Jacob W. Bartness Civil War Letters." *Indiana Magazine of History* 52 (March 1956): 49–73.

Cavanaugh, Lawrence R., ed. "A Civil War Diary: The Diary of Isaac R. Rathbun 'Co. D.' 86th N.Y. Volunteers Aug 23, 1862–Jan. 20, 1863." *New York History: The Quarterly Journal of the New York State Historical Association* 36 (July 1955): 336–45.

Cawthon, John A., ed. "Letters of a North Louisiana Private to His Wife, 1862–1865." *Mississippi Valley Historical Review* 30 (March 1944): 533–50.

"The Civil War Diary of William M. Macy." *Indiana Magazine of History* 30 (June 1934): 181–97.

"Civil War Letters." *Register of the Kentucky Historical Society* 72 (July 1974): 262–71.

"Civil War Letters of Amory K Allen." *Indiana Magazine of History* 31 (December 1935): 338–86.

Clark, Robert D. "Ada Harris, Teenager: Oswego County, New York, 1873," *New York History: The Quarterly Journal of the New York State Historical Association* 66 (January 1985): 29–47.

Clemens, Samuel L. "The Indignity Put upon the Remains of George Holland by the Rev. Mr. Sabine." *Galaxy: An Illustrated Magazine of Entertaining Reading* 11 (February 1871): 320–21.

Coan, Donald J., ed. "Civil War Diary of an Ohio Volunteer." *Western Pennsylvania Historical Magazine* 50 (July 1967): 171–86.

Coffman, Edward M., ed. "Henry M. West's 'Political Letter.' September 10, 1864." *Filson Club History Quarterly* 30 (October 1956): 340–42.

"The Correspondence of Ira Butterfield." *North Dakota Historical Quarterly* 3 (January 1929): 129–44.

Cowden, Joanna D. "The Politics of Dissent: Civil War Democrats in Connecticut." *New England Quarterly* 56 (December 1983): 538–54.

Cox, William E. "The Civil War Letters of Laban Gwinn: A Union Refugee." *West Virginia History* 43 (Spring 1982): 227–45.

Danbom, David B. " 'Dear Companion': Civil War Letters of a Story County Farmer." *Annals of Iowa: A Quarterly Journal of History* 47 (Fall 1984): 537–43.

Danker, Donald F., ed. "Imprisoned at Andersonville: The Diary of Albert Harry Shatzel, May 4, 1864–September 12, 1864." *Nebraska History: A Quarterly Magazine* 38 (June 1957): 81–125.

De Aumente, Vesta Kelly, and Orton A. Jones, eds. "A Letter from B. F. Kelly." *West Virginia History* 37 (July 1976): 325–27.

Delaney, Norman C., ed. "Letters of a Maine Soldier Boy." *Civil War History* 5 (March 1959): 45–61.

Destler, Chester McArthur, ed. "An Andersonville Prison Diary," *Georgia Historical Quarterly* 24 (March, 1940), 56–76.

———. "The Second Michigan Volunteer Infantry Joins the Army of the Potomac." *Michigan History Magazine* 41 (December 1957): 385–412.

"The Diary of an Eighty-Niner." *Chronicles of Oklahoma* 15 (March 1937): 66–69.

"Diary of Charles Ross 1862." *Vermont History* 30 (April 1962): 65–78.

"Diary of Charles Ross 1863." *Vermont History* 31 (January 1963): 5–64.

"Diary of Jake Pennock." *Annals of Wyoming* 23 (July 1951): 4–29.

"Diary Kept by Silas L. Hopper, Blandinsville, Illinois, April 20th, 1863." *Annals of Wyoming* 3 (October 1925): 117–26.

Disbrow, Donald W., ed. "Vett Noble of Ypsilanti: A Clerk for General Sherman." *Civil War History* 14 (March 1968): 15–39.

Dublin, Thomas, ed. "The Letters of Mary Paul, 1845–1849." *Vermont History* 48 (Spring 1980): 77–88.

Eisenberg, Albert C. " 'The 3rd Vermont *has won a name*': Corporal George Q.

French's Account of the Battle of Lee's Mills, Virginia." *Vermont History* 49 (Fall 1981): 223–31.

Ellis, John N., and Robert E. Stowers, eds. "The Nevada Indian Uprising of 1860 as Seen by Private Charles A. Scott." *Arizona and the West* 3 (Winter 1961): 355–76.

Ellis, Richard N., ed. "The Civil War Letters of an Iowa Family." *Annals of Iowa* 39 (Spring 1969): 561–86.

Engel, Paul J., ed. "A Letter from the Front." *New York History: The Quarterly Journal of the New York State Historical Association* 34 (April 1953): 204–10.

Fabris, Dino. "A Civil War Diary." *New York History: The Quarterly Journal of the New York State Historical Association* 49 (January 1968): 76–89.

Fatout, Paul, ed. "Letters of John Traub, Twenty-ninth Indiana Infantry." *Indiana Magazine of History* 53 (June 1957): 171–74.

Fite, Gilbert C., ed. "Some Farmers' Accounts of Hardship on the Frontier." *Minnesota History* 37 (March 1961): 204–11.

Fleming, Elvis E., ed. "A Young Confederate Stationed in Texas: The Letters of Joseph David Wilson, 1864–1865." *Texana* 7 (1970): 352–61.

"Footnotes to Vermont History: A Department." *Vermont History* 24 (January 1956): 64–69.

Fraker, Fleming, Jr., ed. "To Pike's Peak by Ox-Wagon: The Harriet A. Smith Day-Book," *Annals of Iowa* 35, 3rd series, (Fall 1959): 113–48.

Frederick, J. V., ed. "An Illinois Soldier in North Mississippi: Diary of John Wilson, February 15–December 30, 1862." *Journal of Mississippi History*, 1 (July 1939): 182–94.

———. "War Diary of W. C. Porter," *Arkansas Historical Quarterly* 11 (Winter 1952): 286–314.

Goodwin, Carol G. "The Letters of Private Milton Spencer, 1862–1865: A Soldier's View of Military Life on the Northern Plains." *North Dakota History: Journal of the Northern Plains* 37 (Fall 1970): 233–69.

Gorer, Geoffrey. "The Pornography of Death." *Encounter* 5 (October 1955): 49–52.

Grantham, Dewey, W., Jr., ed. "Letters from H. J. Hightower, A Confederate Soldier, 1862–1864." *Georgia Historical Quarterly* 40 (June 1956): 174–89.

Guyer, Max Hendricks. "The Journal and Letters of Corporal William O. Gulick," *Iowa Journal of History and Politics* 28 (April 1930): 194–267.

Hackett, Roger C., ed. "Civil War Diary of Sergeant James Louis Matthews." *Indiana Magazine of History* 24 (December 1928): 306–16.

Hall, Joseph F., ed. "Horace M. Hall's Letters from Gillespie County, Texas, 1871–1873." *Southwestern Historical Quarterly* 62 (January 1959): 336–55.

Hammett, Evelyn Allen. "With Pen in Hand: Letters of Malachi and Alvine Groves (1860–1867)." *Journal of Mississippi History* 33 (August 1971): 219–29.

Harmon, George D. "The Military Experiences of James A. Peifer." *North Carolina Historical Review* 32 (July 1955): 385–409, and (October 1955): 544–72.

Harrison, Lowell H. "The Diary of an 'Average' Confederate Soldier." *Tennessee Historical Quarterly* 29 (Fall 1970): 256–71.

Hauberg, John H., ed. "A Confederate Prisoner at Rock Island: The Diary of Lafayette Rogan." *Illinois State Historical Society Journal* 34 (March 1941): 26–49.

Hedren, Paul L., ed. "Campaigning with the 5th Cavalry: Private James B. Frew's Diary and Letters from the Great Sioux War of 1876." *Nebraska History* 65 (Winter 1984): 443–66.

Heinritz, Stuart, ed. and Walter H. Thompson, Intro. "The Life of a Vermont Farmer and Lumberman: The Diaries of Henry A. Thompson of Grafton and Saxons River." *Vermont History* 42 (Spring 1974): 89–139.

Henshaw, Ray, and Glenn W. LaFantasie, eds. "Letters Home: Sergeant Charles E. Perkins in Virginia, 1862." *Rhode Island History* 39 (November 1980): 106–31.

Heslin, James J., ed. "The Diary of a Union Soldier in Confederate Prisons." *New-York Historical Society Quarterly* 41 (July 1957): 233–78.

Hill, Michael D., and Ben Innis, eds. "The Fort Buford Diary of Private Sanford, 1876–1877," *North Dakota History: Journal of the Northern Plains* 52 (Summer 1985): 2–40.

Hood, Brenda, ed. " 'This Worry I Have': Mary Herren Journal." *Oregon Historical Quarterly* 80 (Fall 1979): 229–57.

Horton, John T., ed. "Folk of the Finger Lake Country during the Presidential Campaign of 1868: From the Diary of Theodore M. Horton of Barrington, Yates County." *New York History: The Quarterly Journal of the New York State Historical Association* 32 (October 1951): 425–34.

Hough, Granville W., ed. "Diary of a Soldier in Grant's Rear Guard (1862–1863)." *Journal of Mississippi History* 45 (August 1983): 194–214.

Huch, Ronald K., ed. "The Civil War Letters of Herbert Saunders." *Register of the Kentucky Historical Society* 69 (January 1971): 17–29.

Hull, Myra E., ed. "Soldiering on the High Plains: The Diary of Lewis Byram Hill, 1864–1866." *Kansas Historical Quarterly* 7 (February 1938): 3–53.

Innis, Ben, ed. "The Fort Buford Diary of Private Wilmot P. Sanford." *North Dakota History: Journal of the Northern Plains* 33 (Fall 1966): 335–78.

Jackson, John C., ed. "A Wild Mustang Campaign of 1879 in Pumpkin Creek Valley: The Memorandum Book of James Robert Jacobsen." *Nebraska History* 57 (Fall 1976): 315–30.

Jenkins, John H., ed. "Texas Letters and Documents." *Texana* 1 (Spring 1963): 175.

Jennings, Warren A., ed. "Prisoner of the Confederacy; Diary of a Union Artilleryman." *West Virginia History* 36 (July 1975): 309–23.

Johnson, Kenneth R., ed. "The Early Civil War in Southern Kentucky as Experienced by Confederate Sympathizers." *Register of the Kentucky Historical Society* 68 (April 1970): 176–79.

Johnston, Hugh Buckner. "The Vinson Confederate Letters." *North Carolina Historical Review* 25 (January 1948): 100–110.

Jones, James P., ed. "A New Yorker in Florida in 1862: War Letters of John M. Olivett to His Sister in Duchess County." *New York History: The Quarterly Journal of the New York State Historical Association* 42 (April 1961): 169–76.

Jones, Robert Leslie, ed. "Flatboating down the Ohio and Mississippi, 1867–1873: Correspondence and Diaries of the William Dudley Devol Family of Marietta, Ohio." *Ohio State Archaeological and Historical Quarterly* 59 (July 1950): 287–309, and (October 1950): 385–418.

Jordan, Weymouth T., ed. "Mathew Andrew Dunn Letters." *Journal of Mississippi History* 1 (April 1939): 110–27.

"Journals of Travel of Will H. Young, 1865." *Annals of Wyoming* 7 (October 1930): 378–82.

"A Journey across the Plains in 1863." *Nevada Historical Society Quarterly* 1 (July 1958): 145–73.

Joyner, F. B. contributor. "With Sherman in Georgia—A Letter from the Coast," *Georgia Historical Quarterly* 42 (December 1958): 440–41.

Kaiser, Leo M., ed. "Civil War Letters of Charles W. Carr of the 21st Wisconsin Volunteers." *Wisconsin Magazine of History* 43 (Summer 1960): 264–72.

———. "A Letter from Georgia." *Civil War History* 6 (June 1960): 201–2.

Keiffer, Elizabeth, ed. "A Lancaster Schoolboy Views the Civil War," *Papers of the Lancaster County Historical Society* 54 (1950): 17–37.

King, James T. "The Civil War of Private Morton." *North Dakota History: Journal of the Northern Plains* 35 (Winter 1968): 9–19.

King, Spencer B., Jr., ed. "Yankee Letters from Andersonville Prison," *Georgia Historical Quarterly* 38 (December 1954): 394–98.

Kirk, Russell, ed. "A Michigan Soldier's Diary, 1863." *Michigan History Magazine* 28 (April–June 1944): 231–45.

Layne, J. Gregg, ed. "Overland by Ox-Train in 1870: The Diary of Maria Hargave Shrode." *Historical Society of Southern California Quarterly* 26 (March 1944): 9–37.

Lensink, Judy Nolte, Christine M. Kirkham, and Karen Pauba Witzke. " 'My Only Confidant'—The Life and Diary of Emily Hawley Gillespie." *Annals of Iowa* 3d ser., 45 (Spring 1980): 288–312.

"Letter of a Confederate Soldier to His Wife in 1864." *West Virginia History* 19 (October 1957): 69–70.

"Letters from the Front: An Aunt's Civil War Soldier Boys." *Indiana History Bulletin* 51 (June 1974): 81–84.

"Letters of John Adams to Catherine Varner, 1864–65." *North Dakota Quarterly* 4 (July 1930): 266–70.

"Levi Powell and A. J. Powell Letters." *Annals of Wyoming* 23 (July 1951): 30–40.

Longacre, Edward G., ed. " 'Dear and Mutch Loved One'—An Iowan's Vicksburg Letters." *Annals of Iowa* 43 (Summer 1975): 49–61.

Lovett, Robert W., ed. "A Maine Man in the West: Letters of Stephen C. Barron, 1867–1874." *Montana: The Magazine of Western History* 32 (Spring 1982): 67–70.

McCully, Robert S. "Letter from a Reconstruction Renegade." *South Carolina Historical Magazine* 77 (January 1976): 34–40.

McLaughlin, Florence C., ed. "Diary of Sailsbury Prison by James W. Eberhart, Sergt. Co 'G' 8th Pa. Res. Vol. Cor(ps) Also Co 'G' 191st Pa. *Vet. Volounter.*" *Western Pennsylvania Historical Magazine* 56 (July 1973): 211–51.

Madden, Robert R., ed. "Letter from an Illinois Drummer Boy." *Journal of Mississippi History* 26 (May 1964): 152–57.

Marchman, Watt P., ed. "The Journal of Sergt. Wm. J. McKell." *Civil War History* 3 (September 1957): 315–39.

Martin, Charles W., ed. "Joseph Warren Arnold's Journal of His Trip to and from Montana, 1864–1866." *Nebraska History* 55 (Winter 1974): 463–552.

Mayer, Mabel Watkins, ed. "Into the Breach: Civil War Letters of Wallace W. Chadwick." *Ohio State Archaeological and Historical Quarterly* 52 (April–June 1943): 158–80.

Mellon, Knox, Jr., ed. "Letters of James Greenalch." *Michigan History* 44 (June 1960): 188–240.

Mills, George, ed. "The Sharp Family Civil War Letters." *Annals of Iowa*, 3d ser., 34 (January 1959): 481–532.

Mitchell, Enoch L., ed. "The Civil War Letters of Thomas Jefferson Newberry." *Journal of Mississippi History* 10 (January 1948): 44–80.

Monnett, Howard Norman, ed. " 'The Awfulest Time I Ever Seen': A Letter from Sherman's Army." *Civil War History* 8 (September 1962): 283–89.

Monroe, Haskell, ed. "The Road to Gettysburg: The Diary and Letters of Leonidas Torrence of the Gaston Guards," *North Carolina Historical Review* 36 (October 1959): 476–517.

Olson, James C., ed. "From Nebraska City to Montana, 1866: The Diary of Thomas Alfred Creigh," *Nebraska History: A Quarterly Magazine* 29 (September 1948): 208–37.

Osborn, George C. "A Confederate Prisoner at Camp Chase: Letters and a Diary of Private James W. Anderson." *Ohio State Archaeological and Historical Quarterly* 59 (January 1950): 38–57.

Packard, Kent, ed. "Jottings by the Way: A Sailor's Log—1862–1864." *Pennsylvania Magazine of History and Biography* 71 (April 1947): 121–51, and (July 1947): 242–82.

Padgett, James A., ed. "Reconstruction Letters from North Carolina, Part IX,

Letters to Benjamin Franklin Butler." *North Carolina Historical Review* 20 (October 1943): 341–70.

Palmer, Ralph S. "Rufus Philbrook, Trapper." *New England Quarterly* 22 (December 1949): 452–74.

Peavy, Linda, and Ursula Smith, "Women in Waiting in the Westward Movement: Pamelia Dillin Fergus and Emma Stratton Christie." *Montana: The Magazine of Western History* 35 (Spring 1985): 2–17.

Piehl, Charles K., ed. " 'It Is a Singular Country in Many Respects': A New Texan Writes about His Experiences, 1876." *Texana*, vol.11, pp.73–76.

"Pioneer Letters: The Letter as Literature." *Northwest Review* 19, Nos. 1 and 2 (1981): 2–50.

Pritchett, John Perry. "Sidelights on the Sibley Expedition from the Diary of a Private." *Minnesota History: A Quarterly Magazine* 7 (December 1926): 326–35.

————, ed. "On the March with Sibley in 1863, The Diary of Private Henry J. Hagadorn." *North Dakota Historical Quarterly* 5 (January 1931): 103–29.

Pye, Carol Benson, intro. and annot. "Letters from an Illinois Farm, 1864–1865: By Louisa Jane Phifer." *Journal of the Illinois State Historical Society* 66 (Winter 1973): 387–403.

Racine, Philip N. "Emily Lyles Harris: A Piedmont Farmer during the Civil War." *South Atlantic Quarterly* 79 (Autumn 1980): 386–97.

Ray, Johnette Highsmith, ed. "Civil War Letters from Parsons' Texas Cavalry." *Southwestern Historical Quarterly* 69 (October 1965): 21–23.

Rea, Ralph R., ed. "Diary of Private John P. Wright, U.S.A., 1864–1865." *Arkansas Historical Quarterly* 16 (Autumn 1957): 304–18.

Reynolds, David S. "From Doctrine to Narrative: The Rise of Pulpit Storytelling in America." *American Quarterly* 32 (Winter 1980): 479–98.

Reynolds, Donald B., ed. "A Mississippian in Lee's Army: The Letters of Leander Huckaby." *Journal of Mississippi History* 36 (February 1974): 53–67; (May 1974): 165–78; (August 1974): 273–88.

Riley, Glenda. "Women's History from Women's Sources: Three Examples from Northern Dakota." *North Dakota History: Journal of the Northern Plains* 52 (Spring 1985): 2–9.

————, ed. "Pioneer Migration: The Diary of Mary Alice Shutes." *Annals of Iowa*, 3d ser., 43 (Winter 1977): 487–514, and (Spring 1977): 567–92.

Robertson, James I., Jr., ed. "The Roanoke Island Expedition: Observations of a Massachusetts Soldier." *Civil War History* 12 (December 1966): 321–46.

————. " 'Such is War': The Letters of an Orderly in the 7th Iowa Infantry," *Iowa Journal of History* 58 (October 1960): 321–56.

Rosenberger, H. E., ed. "Ohiowa Soldier." *Annals of Iowa*, 3d ser., 36 (Fall 1961): 111–48.

Rowen, Richard D., ed. "The Second Nebraska's Campaign against the Sioux." *Nebraska History: A Quarterly Magazine* 44 (March 1963): 3–82.

Russell, Don, ed. "Letters of a Drummer Boy." *Indiana Magazine of History* 34 (September 1938): 324–39.

Sanders, James, ed. "Times Hard but Grit Good: Lydia Moxley's 1877 Diary." *Annals of Iowa: A Quarterly Journal of History* 47 (Winter 1984): 270–90.

Sanders, Mary Elizabeth, ed. "Letters of a Confederate Soldier, 1862–1863." *Louisiana Historical Quarterly* 29 (October 1946): 1229–40.

Santa Cruz Sentinel, February 16, 1878.

Saum, Lewis O. "From Vermont to Whoop-Up Country: Some Letters of D. W. Davis." *Montana: The Magazine of Western History* 35 (Summer 1985): 56–71.

———, comp. "Spoopendyke's Dakota: Some Humorous Prose and Verse of Stanley Huntley." *North Dakota History: Journal of the Northern Plains* 51 (Spring 1984): 14–31.

Schlesinger, Arthur M., ed. "A Blue Bluejacket's Letters Home, 1863–1864." *New England Quarterly* 1 (October 1928): 554–67.

Scrimsher, Lila Gravatt, ed. "The Diary of Anna Webber: Early Day Teacher of Mitchell County." *Kansas Historical Quarterly* 38 (Autumn 1972): 320–37.

Seligmann, G. L., Jr., ed. "North to New Mexico." *Red River Valley Historical Review* 1 (Summer 1974): 165–77, (Autumn 1974): 281–93.

Shirk, George H. "Campaigning with Sheridan: A Farrier's Diary." *Chronicles of Oklahoma* 37 (Spring 1959): 68–105.

Skillin, Rebecca, ed. "William Cheney (1787–1875): The Life of a Vermont Woodsman and Farmer." *Vermont History* 39 (Winter 1971): 43–50.

Slesinger, Warren. "Other Voices Than Their Own." *Northwest Review* 19, nos. 1 and 2 (1981): 246–53.

Smith, H. A., ed. "Letters of Privates Cook and Ball." *Indiana Magazine of History* 27 (September 1931): 243–68.

Smith, Thomas H., ed. "A Letter from Cedar Falls." *Iowa Journal of History* 55 (July 1957): 275–78.

Smith, Twil M. W., ed. " 'Mother I Don't Frollick Now . . . ' " *Southwestern Historical Quarterly* 75 (July 1971): 77–79.

Snell, Joseph W., ed. "Diary of a Dodge City Buffalo Hunter, 1872–1873." *Kansas Historical Quarterly* 31 (Winter 1965): 345–95.

Snyder, Charles M. "A Teen-Age G.I. in the Civil War." *New York History: The Quarterly Journal of the New York State Historical Association* 35 (January 1954): 14–31.

———. "They Lay Where They Fell: The Everests, Father and Son." *Vermont History* 32 (July 1964): 154–62.

"A Solger in the Ind. Sixteenth." *Indiana History Bulletin* 38 (June 1961): 111–12.

Stewart, Norman, ed. "Eight Months in Missouri: The Civil War Letters of Philander H. Nesbit." *Missouri Historical Review* 75 (April 1981): 261–84.

Storey, George C. " 'My Trip West in 1881.' " *Colorado Magazine* 49 (Fall 1972): 314–25.

Storrs, Richard S. "Contributions Made to Our National Development by Plain Men." *American Historical Association Annual Report* 1 (1896): 35–63.

Taylor, A. Reed. "The War History of Two Soldiers: A Two-Sided View of the Civil War." *Alabama Review: A Quarterly Journal of Alabama History* 23 (April 1970): 83–109.

Thompson, Tommy, R. "Letters Home: From Private Thomas Henry Lochridge, 1861–1862." *Arkansas Historical Quarterly* 33 (Autumn 1974): 239–51.

Throne, Mildred, ed. "The Civil War Diary of John Mackley." *Iowa Journal of History* 48 (April 1950): 141–68.

———. "Civil War Letters of Abner Dunham, 12th Iowa Infantry." *Iowa Journal of History* 53 (October 1955): 303–40.

———. "Iowa Farm Letters, 1856–1865." *Iowa Journal of History* 58 (January 1960): 37–88.

"A Trip from Atchison, Kansas, to Laurette, Colorado: Diary of G. S. McCain." *Colorado Magazine* 27 (April 1950): 95–102.

"Trip over the Plains of Dakota in 1865, from the Diary of L. K. Raymond, Company I, Third Illinois Cavalry." *North Dakota Historical Quarterly* 2 (April 1928): 220–26.

Tripp, Wendell., ed. "A Memory: Lincoln's Body Comes to Albany." *New York History: The Quarterly Journal of the New York State Historical Association* 46 (April 1965): 187–88.

Updike, John. "A Mild Complaint." *New Yorker* 58 (April 19, 1982): 39.

Vandiver, Frank E., ed. "A Collection of Louisiana Confederate Letters." *Louisiana Historical Quarterly* 26 (October 1943): 937–74.

Welter, Rush. "Between Two Worlds: American Social Thought after the Civil War." *Prospects: The Annual of American Cultural Studies* 6 (1981): 411–31.

Westermeier, Clifford P., ed. "Our Western Journey: Journal of Martha Wilson McGregor Aber." *Annals of Wyoming* 22 (July 1950): 91–100.

Weston, Daphne. "Colorado Letters of Marion Cook." *Colorado Magazine* 40 (July 1963): 193–207.

Wiley, Bell Irvin, ed. "The Confederate Letters of John W. Hagan." *Georgia Historical Quarterly* 38 (June 1954): 170–200, and (September 1954): 268–90.

Wilkerson, Charles J., ed. "The Letters of Ed Donnell, Nebraska Pioneer." *Nebraska History: A Quarterly Magazine* 41 (June 1960): 123–51.

Williams, Charles G., ed. "Down the Rivers: Civil War Diary of Thomas Benton White." *Register of the Kentucky Historical Society* 67 (April 1969): 134–74.

Williams, Frank B., Jr., ed. "From Sumter to the Wilderness: Letters of Sergeant James Butler Suddath, Co. E, 7th Regiment, S.C.V." *South Carolina Historical Magazine* 63 (January 1962): 1–11, and (April 1962): 92–104.

Williamson, Hugh P. "Corporal Martin V. Smith U.S.A. 1861." *Bulletin of the Missouri Historical Society* 17 (July 1961): 346–51.

Wisbey, Herbert, Jr., ed. "Civil War Letters of Gorham Coffin." *Essex Institute Historical Collections* 43 (January 1957): 58–92.

"With the U.S. Army along the Oregon Trail, 1863–66: Diary by Jno. J. Pattison." *Nebraska History Magazine* 15 (April–June 1934): 79–93.

Wooster, Ralph A., and Robert Wooster. " 'Rarin' for a Fight': Texans in the Confederate Army." *Southwestern Historical Quarterly* 84 (April 1981): 387–426.

Wright, Bertha R. Intro. "Diary of Charles Ross, 1861." *Vermont History* 29 (April 1961): 65–78.

Yzenbaard, John H., and John Hoffmann, eds. " 'Between Hope and Fear': The Life of Lettie Teeple 1: 1829–1850," *Michigan History* 58 (Fall 1974): 219–78, and " 'Between Hope and Fear': The Life of Lettie Teeple 2: 1850–1868," *Michigan History* 58 (Winter 1974): 291–352.

Zeilinger, Elna Rae, and Larry Schweikart, eds. " 'They Also Serve . . . ': The Diary of Benjamin Frankling Hackett, 12th Vermont Volunteers." *Vermont History* 51 (Spring 1983): 89–97.

Index